George III by Allan Ramsay

KINGS

&

Desperate Men

Life in Eighteenth-Century England

BY

LOUIS KRONENBERGER

NEW YORK

ALFRED A. KNOPF

1942

TO

LILLIAN HELLMAN

As fine a friend as she is a playwright

. . . Fate, Chance, kings, and desperate men.

— DONNE

NOTE

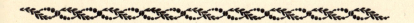

THE CHIEF AIM of this book is to provide a *picture* of eighteenth-century England until the time of the French Revolution. The whole thing lies much closer to a social chronicle than an orthodox history-book, and is more concerned with manners and tastes than with treaties and wars. All the same, I have certainly not sought to restrict the book to the merely decorative or picturesque: it attempts a big canvas, deals seriously with human ideas and emotions, and seeks to portray human beings as truthfully as possible. Perhaps the book's character can be best summed up as concrete rather than abstract, descriptive rather than analytical.

Certain things the book is not meant to be. It makes no claims to scholarship: its sources are simply the general literature relating to the period. It is principally concerned with life in London, and only a little with life outside it; and it has nothing to say of Scotland, Ireland, or the rapidly expanding British Empire. It offers no analysis of economic forces and no survey of philosophic thought. It ignores movements like the Agrarian and Industrial Revolutions — even in their social aspects — because though they were born before 1789, they flourished after. It treats the arts largely in social terms, and much less in æsthetic ones. It deals with certain important men and women, not to provide much in the way of factual biography, but to express their feelings and ideas, their values and tastes. It omits many things it might well have included; yet, for the sake of emphasis, it mentions certain other things several times. Its main purpose is descriptive, but there is also this to be added: I am given to liking facts for the sake of drawing conclusions, so that in many places the social historian has had to make room for the critic.

My thanks are due to *The Saturday Review of Literature* for permission to reprint parts of an essay on Defoe, and to *The American Spectator* for permission to reprint essays on Addison and Lady Mary Montagu. I have borrowed three or four sentences from my introduction to *An Eighteenth Century Miscellany.* I am much indebted to the trustees of the British Museum for granting me access to the Reading Room, and to Elizabeth Ames and the directors of Yaddo for visits there, during which parts of this book were written. My debt to my wife for her constant help and encouragement is very great indeed.

CONTENTS

[CONTENTS]

ILLUSTRATIONS

CHRONOLOGY

ANNE [reigned 1702–14]

1702 — War of the Spanish Succession begins
1702 — first London daily newspaper
1704 — battle of Blenheim
1707 — Union of England and Scotland
1709 — battle of Malplaquet
1710 — Tories take power
1711 — Marlborough dismissed
1713 — Treaty of Utrecht

GEORGE I [reigned 1714–27]

1715 — Jacobite rebellion
1719 — *Robinson Crusoe*
1720 — South Sea Bubble
1721 — beginning of the Walpole administration
1722 — Wood's Halfpence
1727 — *Gulliver's Travels*

GEORGE II [reigned 1727–60]

1728 — *The Beggar's Opera*
1732 — *The Harlot's Progress*
1737 — death of Queen Caroline
1740 — *Pamela*
1741 — Garrick's London debut

1742 — fall of Walpole
1745 — second Jacobite rebellion
1749 — *Tom Jones*
1755 — Johnson's *Dictionary*
1756 — Seven Years' War begins
1759 — fall of Quebec

GEORGE III [reigned 1760–1820]

1763 — Wilkes arrested
1768 — Royal Academy founded
1774 — Burke's *Speech on Conciliation*
1777 — *The School for Scandal*
1782 — Peace with America
1783 — Fox-North Coalition
1783 — procession to Tyburn abolished
1784 — Pitt becomes Prime Minister
1784 — death of Johnson
1788 — George III goes mad
1788 — trial of Warren Hastings opens
1790 — *Reflexions on the Revolution in France*

PART I

The Capital of England

CHAPTER I

THE LAST STUART

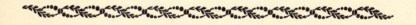

1

THE SEVENTEENTH CENTURY in England had been many things by turns — lusty, cramped, licentious. It could claim a blood-stained Rebellion, a light-hearted Restoration, and a peaceful Revolution. It beheaded one monarch and drove another into exile. It fretted under outmoded, almost mediæval ideas; and when it balked, it resorted to immoderate, almost mediæval tactics. But the blows it delivered were decisive. The Revolution of 1688 said that the choice of a sovereign rested with Parliament and not with God, and that the complexion of the Church took its colour in England and not in Rome. But not everybody at once fell in with what the Revolution said. If 1688 condemned the old idea of kingship, it was not until 1714 that the sentence was clearly carried out. The interval between, particularly the second half of it, was a far from tranquil one. During those last dozen years England — not knowing on whom to gamble, never certain of whom to trust — was to be rife with conspiracy and faction. Into those years, moreover — they sound very placid when we call them the age of Anne — were thrust not only an incredible energy, but a cold wit, a malicious tongue, and an utter want of heart.

This book is not primarily concerned with politics, but in

[3

treating the age of Anne not the most frivolous of writers could disengage himself from political issues. It was an era when politics could not be combed out of people's lives; every trifle became a badge of party, defiantly worn. You could tell Whigs from Tories by where they sat in the playhouse. You could tell a Whig from a Tory lady by how she wore her beauty patch. The writers of Anne's reign vaulted free of politics least of all: they were violently partisan, wrote on political subjects, lived by political alliances, and frequently held political office. Should they happen to write without bias, bias was inferred. In 1713 Addison's *Cato* was the occasion for the wildest excitement in the theatre, people reading into the lines whatever meanings they fancied, and hissing or applauding accordingly. It is hardly too much to say that some of the men of the times chose their wives on the basis of their politics, and that some of the wives chose their lovers with the same highmindedness.

Though politics divided the nation at every turn, they loom largest under Anne in the two great conflicts of her reign: in the long War of the Spanish Succession led by Marlborough abroad, and in what might as fairly be called the War of the Hanoverian Succession, conducted by conspirators at home. In the first, Whigs and Tories were clashing because of their opposed sources of wealth; in the second, because of their different conceptions of monarchy. These struggles, moreover, were not merely between two hostile parties; they were also between the future and the past.

The War of the Spanish Succession, which began in 1702, the year Anne came to the throne, resulted from ambitions of Louis XIV that threatened the balance of power in Europe. The throne of Spain having fallen vacant, Louis sought to confer it upon his grandson, Philip of Anjou. By blood Philip was eligible; by the terms of the late King's will he was nominated; but under an existing European agreement he was outlawed — since with France and Spain united, French sovereignty in Europe would be too dangerous. Not, however, for France — wherefore Louis supported Philip's claim, while England, Holland, and Austria banded together to oppose it at any cost. And at just such a moment, Louis promised James II, who was dying in exile at Saint-Germains, to recognize his son as " James III." This, to England, was a threat as well as an insult; and along with her allies and some auxiliary supporters, she declared war on France.

The war plainly began as a defensive war against French ambitions; but as victories piled up for England and the struggle still dragged on, it became clear that it was also something else. The Whigs need not be considered any the less patriotic because they had a stake in the war, but there can be no question that they had one. The Whigs represented the moneyed interests of their time — the bankers, the foreign traders, the City men: all those who stood to lose from a union of France's merchant fleet with Spain's. But beyond this, Whig jobbers and bankers were equipping the army at an excellent profit and lending the Government money at excellent interest. The Whigs were therefore the promoters of the war, and in the sentiment of the time it grew into a Whig campaign.

The Tories, on the other hand, were the nation's landowners and freeholders; and the war, far from enriching them through trade, impoverished them with taxes. Once England got the upper hand over France, the hard-bled Tories clamoured for peace. Out of this clash of interests there developed between the parties at home a conflict more unbridled than that between the armies abroad. It came to include every species of backbiting and double-dealing; it made and unmade reputations, it sealed and severed political alliances, and began to create, what yet far from fully existed, the modern system of governing by party.

When Anne came to the throne in 1702, the Tories were

[5

in office, with a majority in the Commons. It was they who declared war, and it was with them that Marlborough, as head of the army, threw in his lot. But it was the Whigs — already formidable through their majority in the Lords — who possessed the enthusiasm for prosecuting the war; they soon had the mass of middle-class voters behind them; and they slowly edged their way into the Cabinet, which was not yet a strictly party machine. They backed Marlborough with zeal where the Tories backed him with apprehension; and as time passed, both Marlborough and his ally at the Treasury, Godolphin, realized where their real support lay and abandoned the Tory camp. By 1708 the Whigs were *actually* in control, with their famous Junto, as the Tories had nominally been in 1702.

The progress of the war in the field belongs among the most resplendent pages of English history. Marlborough was a supremely great general. From the start he was victorious against the French in Flanders; then, when Louis's armies were about to invade Austria and besiege Vienna, Marlborough made a feint of moving against France from the Rhine, only to wheel secretly across Germany and meet the enemy at Blenheim. Blenheim crushed Louis's pretensions in Europe. Had Marlborough, in the years that followed, not been slowed down by his Dutch and Austrian brother-commanders, he would certainly have invaded France and marched on Paris. As it was, he had to content himself with expelling the French from Flanders and conquering their border fortresses: hardly less celebrated than Blenheim, the victories of Ramillies and Oudenarde were hardly less brilliant.

For a while Marlborough was acclaimed a hero: Parliament voted him its thanks, the nation lighted its bonfires, the Queen bestowed on him the manor of Woodstock, where, after many delays, was erected — " at the publick expense " — Blenheim Palace. But financial crises and the increasingly aggressive nature of the war caused dissatisfaction in England to mount. The Tories, out of power and out of pocket, were in no mood to find personal solace in national *réclame*. They began to mutter that the Whigs were continuing the war for their own advantage, and that Marlborough was directing it for his. Such charges may have been unjust, but they could not be called unreasonable: France, whipped and bleeding, was not being finical about terms for peace. But every English parley began by stipulating that Louis's troops must help drive Louis's grandson off the Spanish throne, which, even on the verge of ruin, Louis balked at.

So the war went on. But now three events, very disastrous to the Whigs, followed fast on one another. The first was the battle of Malplaquet. Marlborough never lost an engagement, but he won Malplaquet at such a terrible cost in blood that Parliament did not thank him for it. And at such a moment, with his credit lowered, Marlborough made a rash request which proved a second disaster for the Whigs: he asked the Queen to make him commander-in-chief for life. Whether he was guided by personal ambition or patriotic feeling does not matter; the point was that he exposed himself — at a time when the memory of Cromwell was still alarmingly vivid — to the imputation of a military dictatorship. It was a shocking blunder.

The third event, involving religion, carried matters to a conclusion. Religion made up the second great difference between the two parties. The Whigs, as Broad-Churchmen, were tolerant of Dissenters and opposed to any union of Church and State. The Tories, for the most part, were High-Church people, very fervent, very bigoted, and equally ready to howl down popery and dissent. When one of their number, a high-flying fanatic named Dr Sacheverell, preached a sermon at St Paul's implying that the Revolution of 1688 (which the Whigs looked upon as *their* Revolution) was illegal, he was striking at the very heart of the administration. And when he made oblique attacks on the

[7

Whig chiefs, particularly Godolphin, he was embossing treason with slander. The Whigs, with the stung Godolphin in
the lead, felt the necessity of taking action and, by impeaching Sacheverell, of proving their strength. All they proved
was their weakness.

Queen and country were for the defendant; and he converted his trifling punishment into an effective martyrdom.
The Whig glass was surely falling. The burden of the war;
the injury to Marlborough's prestige; the Queen's fierce
hostility to Marlborough's Duchess, once her favourite; the
Queen's secret alliance — through her new favourite, Mrs
Masham — with so powerful a Tory as Robert Harley; above
everything, the Queen's power to appoint and dismiss ministers — all these combined to shatter the Whig strength.
One by one their leaders were deprived of office. Soon only
Marlborough was left, and he at pasture with about six
inches of rope. The Tories, under Harley and his lieutenant
Bolingbroke,[1] came back into power.

Their object was peace. Marlborough himself was now
brought to book: the Queen dismissed him from all his employments, and Parliament impeached him for malpractice
in accepting perquisites. His defence was a waste of breath
and he went into exile. Meanwhile Harley and Bolingbroke
ran through a spectacular administration which we must
temporarily neglect. So far as the war was concerned, it
ended by means of negotiating secretly *with* France and
against England's allies, at the Peace of Utrecht (1713).
By it England swam up to the first place in European affairs.
She came off with Newfoundland and Nova Scotia, Minorca
and Gibraltar, with the rights to the African slave trade, and
with great commercial advantages. For all that, France,
which might a few years earlier have been well-nigh demolished, escaped with her whole skin. She was merely

---

[1] Harley later became Earl of Oxford, and the future Viscount Bolingbroke was at this time still plain Henry St John, but for convenience' sake
I am referring to them throughout by the names they occupy in history.

stripped, in other words, of her European ambitions; and her dream of obliterating the Pyrenees came mildly enough to an end.

2

FOR all its secret windings, the war was among the most straightforward activities of Anne's reign. It had at least an official character and definite, however disputed, aims. Far more devious and complex were the other plots and counterplots, with their slanders and self-seeking, that were hatched for other reasons.

" Great men are almost always bad men ": the age of Anne, which abounded in great men, is not one to refute Acton's famous words. Men lived then, as scarcely before or since, by party; but with the predominant motive of wanting to rise by party, or rule by party. Fortunes were at stake rather than principles, and even in the burning heat of faction clever politicians had to be thinking of a graceful way of suddenly eating their words. There was so much that threatened to drive party men asunder: it was because so little held them together that they had to be fanatical about what did. The Whigs, on the whole, stood for war, dissent, and the House of Hanover; [2] the Tories for peace, orthodoxy, and, in some quarters, the Pretender: beyond that one cannot safely distinguish them. But within that orbit enmity seethed and spat; and vast though it was, the war became at times almost a screen for men's thoughts about that other, that even more ticklish affair — England's next sovereign. It was really the War of the *Hanoverian* Succession that most engrossed the nation. To the average Englishman of 1710, the throne of Spain meant much less than the throne of England; and when he remembered that written covenants had not prevented Philip from seizing a Spanish crown, he might suspect that Acts of Parliament need not prevent the

---

[2] The House of Hanover meant, of course, constitutionalism.

Pretender from seizing a British one. Nor was it entirely a question of seizing it: many people in Great Britain sought to bestow it on him.

It is around this half-brother of Anne's, this " James III of England " with his toy court in France, that the long drama that agitated the seventeenth century plays itself out. On the score of blood, the Pretender — as the legitimate son of James II — should have possessed the throne. Even there, however, his claim was contested, since in Anne's time there was current a foolish fiction that James II's son was *not* his son, but something brought to Mary of Modena's childbed in a warming-pan. That story caused damage; Louis XIV's hateful recognition of the Pretender's claims caused more damage; but the true hinge of the matter lay elsewhere — in the vital question of whether the British sovereign ruled by divine right or reigned by grace of Parliament.

" Divine right " beheaded Charles I. " Divine right " drove James II across the Channel. And the Revolution which drove him there decreed that his daughter Mary, and later his daughter Anne, succeeded him not by right of royal blood, but by consent of the people. They were constitutional monarchs.

But they were also Stuarts, they also bore the name that signified royalty to the nation; and so long as they were there, the nation felt no desire to dispute their claims in favour of their brother's. But when in 1700 the last of Anne's six children died, there was no direct heir to the throne. James II's son was growing up, a Catholic, in France; and his religion was even more of a taint than his surroundings. Parliament, after scrutinizing family trees, at length passed an act bestowing the crown, at Anne's death, on a granddaughter of James I, the Electress Sophia of Hanover. This made sure of a Protestant succession.

And because it did, the Hanoverians came safe to the throne. But for a long time no one could be sure they would.

Men who had not been ready to exchange one Stuart for another, to depose Anne to bring in James, found the prospect of being ruled over by strangers from Germany a very different matter. One had no sense of tradition with the Guelphs, they possessed the same lack of aura as impostors. Twice during the past century England had got rid of Stuart kings — and yet it had a curious feeling that a monarch who was not a Stuart was not a monarch, and its eye travelled over the water to Saint-Germains. Besides, there were many people in England — Tory bishops and Tory squires prominently among them — who, when it came to divine right, were as royalist as James. They had believed, at the time of the Revolution, in non-resistance, and they still believed that the changes the Revolution enacted were illegal, that James should never have lost his crown, and that, though lost, his son should regain it. Such people knew better than to say all this in doubtful company, but among themselves they hatched an astonishing number of fireside plots.

Thus, owing in some cases to the pull of the Stuart name, and in others to political principle, there was a scattered sentiment throughout the country for bringing in the Pretender. Being outside the law, it worked in the dark and by way of the emotions and among those who, when a banner is raised or a march struck up, will spring into action. It had a formidable, however furtive, look, and even the best-informed men in the country, the politicians, could not be sure what would happen at the Queen's death. Nor can *we* be sure what would have happened had one obstacle been removed. That obstacle was the Pretender's religion. England, be she never so Stuart-minded, would not stomach popery. The Pretender was told this, along with being told that if Paris had been worth a mass to his great-grandfather, London should be worth a sermon to him. But James stuck by his faith and far from changing would not even dissemble it.

Many people, however, supposed that he would; and on that supposition enough plotting went on between England and Saint-Germains to pack a dozen melodramas. Even true Hanoverians like Marlborough conspired for a while. And as time went on, the conspiring became more meaningful. Until the Whigs' downfall the Hanoverian succession had been relatively safe, first because the Whigs supported it, and again because, the Queen being in no grave danger of dying, the counter-sentiment was still sketchy and diffused. But after the Tories took power in 1710, the situation changed. The Queen, racked by gout and dropsy, was coming on her last legs, and the question of her successor became urgent. Then, too, the Pretender's adherents were almost all Tories, and with their party in office they could take greater liberties. But it was the administration itself, in which Harley and Bolingbroke worked for a while in concert and much longer in conflict, that gave the Jacobite cause its real purchase.

As for the two men, Harley, who held the higher office, was all politician and no statesman, a man whose one idea was to conciliate and avoid extremes. If he had almost no principles, he had almost no prejudices, and simply looked on the Government as a business that should be made to pay. Bolingbroke, officially Harley's subordinate, chose from the first to become his rival. Brilliant, eloquent, headlong, devious, he had vast ambitions from which Harley was not only to be excluded but to which, indeed, he was a stumbling-block. Hence Bolingbroke began plotting to supersede him. He set forth, as Harley had done earlier, to bribe the Queen's favourite as a way of obtaining the Queen's favour. In some degree he succeeded; he might well have succeeded altogether had not his licentious habits aroused the rather prudish Queen's distrust. In any case he began acting independently of his chief, even to entering into secret negotiations with France to end the war by private treaty. This, the Treaty of Utrecht, Bolingbroke — though using doubtful

methods and agreeing to treacherous terms [3] — carried to
a magnificent conclusion. But by this time his high-handed-
ness had won him Harley's bitter enmity — though Bolingbroke contrived to see himself as the injured party. When
a French spy stabbed Harley and so made a popular martyr
of him, Bolingbroke was furious that it was not he who had
been stabbed; and when Harley was created an earl and
Bolingbroke only a viscount, the sense of injury deepened.
Now more than ever the Viscount was determined to work
by himself. That meant, of course, having a policy all his
own — and a policy that was better than his rival's.

It was not a moment when such a policy could be found
at any convenient crossroads. Bolingbroke's first move was
to angle for an alliance with the Whigs, whose fortunes
were rising again; but they freezingly repulsed him. The
moderate Tories, he knew, supported Harley; and Whigs
and moderate Tories alike supported Hanover. And with
all these people loyal to Hanover just when nothing was in
men's minds but the problem of the Queen's successor, it
was clear that Bolingbroke could have no spirited policy —
could have no policy at all — unless it was support of the
Pretender. In the past, Bolingbroke and Harley had both
exchanged compliments and assurances with James. But
the more moderate Harley, though still vaguely treating
with him, was now playing the safer game of Hanover. In
his desperation, however, Bolingbroke could not play so
safe. For that matter, the risk was just the sort that his con-
spiratorial temperament enjoyed. So once again, as in the
months before Utrecht, he was meeting French agents by
candlelight, this time as the tacit spokesman for England's
high-flying clergy, her crackpot aristocrats, her grandsons
of Caroline cavaliers, her sentimentalists who preferred a
known lineage, however spotted, to an unknown one, however pure. All this was not precisely a routine job, even for
a politician, and Bolingbroke did not know whom he had

---

[3] Some of England's allies were ditched by the transaction.

behind him, whether the Queen, or many of his country-
men, or but few of them. Certainly Anne — who hated the
Hanoverians [4] and would not let any of them even set foot
in England — was unofficially " interested," but not if James
remained a Catholic. And James, despite all Bolingbroke's
frantic entreaties, continued to remain one. That was the
hard, damning, inescapable fact. Oxford dons and Oxford
students might glory in their Jacobitism, and Tory squires
be ready to mount their horses for the Pretender, as already
in the October Club they were noisily drinking his health.
And it was true enough that up in Scotland many men were
waiting to raise his standard. But all these made rather a
brave show than a strong army at one's back. Bolingbroke
was working in the dark, and knew he was.

At this point, however, he saw what might be his chance.
He began pushing through Parliament an unjust law against
Dissenters, which he hoped would rouse the Whigs to riot-
ing if not rebellion; if so, he might send for a French army
to put the insurrection down and, by the same stroke, neatly
bring in the Pretender. But the Whigs were much too canny
to fall into the trap. The chance of ousting Harley was different. Harley was becoming ever more obnoxious to the
Queen, ever laxer at his job, hence easier to remove and so
supplant. Time pressed painfully, for the Queen was dying.
Yet time was needed, for Bolingbroke had no mature plans
or respectable allies, no sure way of keeping afloat in Harley's place, let alone of making the stubbornly Catholic
Pretender king. It was all a matter, at bottom, of hoping,
gambling, bluffing, a sort of profane *Credo quia impossibile:*
as though, at the Queen's death, some Jacobite should call
out " Long live King James! " and the multitude, swayed by
emotion, conveniently take up the cry.

In the last week of July 1714 the half-dead Queen, goaded

---

[4] For no better reason, apparently, than that they reminded her that
she must die. There is another tale, however, that long ago one of them
had come to England to court her, and returned to Hanover without doing so.

by Bolingbroke and Mrs Masham, dismissed Harley. A shocking public scene between the two rivals followed, and Bolingbroke was left as nominal head of the Government. But he was wholly at sea. He dined the Whig chiefs, but again they refused to coalesce with him. His Jacobite scheme was much too abortive. His influence was over only a part of the Tory faction; and to get anywhere he needed, at the very least, the whole of it. His Queen, finally, would not give him the white staff of office she had snatched from Harley. Like a hounded man eluding captors, wherever he looked he saw Whigs in pursuit. His backing shaky, his plans un-crystallized, he was forced to assent that the Lord Treasurer's staff should go to the quasi-Whig Duke of Shrewsbury. " Use it," said the Queen to the Duke, " for the good of my people." The next morning she expired. The fateful moment which men had deprecated, schemed for, counted on, de-bated about, had now arrived. . . . And without a trace of excitement or a particle of opposition, as though it was the most natural and obvious thing in the world, George I [5] was proclaimed King at St James's.

The Whigs were everywhere in power, and Bolingbroke was nowhere. " The Earl of Oxford," he wrote to Swift in words no historian ever omits, " was removed on Tuesday, the Queen died on Sunday. What a world is this, and how does fortune banter us! " For a few days, with handcuffs on his wrists, he had achieved his dream of heading the Government. Now nothing was left for him, and little for the Pretender. A year later, it is true, the Pretender sought to gain the throne through a Scottish insurrection that was easily put down. And the two frustrated men came to-gether for a time when Bolingbroke in exile joined the Pre-tender's court. But not long afterwards the man he had hoped to make king of England brusquely got rid of him.

---

[5] The Electress Sophia, George's mother, had died two months before.

CHAPTER II

DETAILS OF THE PLOT

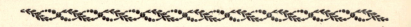

QUEEN ANNE WAS as much a "political" monarch as Charles II was a social one. But where Charles had a genius for enjoying himself, Anne was a plain little busybody in a crooked age; and having no personality, she did what she could with her prejudices and her rank. Her court was a political court: not a trace of social splendour ever inhabited it. We do not read of brilliant formal entertainments, or of jolly, titles-be-damned picnics and parties, or of witty people providing the court with the glitter of the salon. Instead we encounter a stuffy hostess who for the most part was never troubled with guests. Anne lacked the *mondain* temperament; her enjoyments were lower middle-class — card games, Newmarket, drink. She was pleasure-loving but humourless, gossipy but unsociable. And the man she married was even less impressive than she, the sort of fellow who, even married to her, was merely "the Queen's husband."

And yet the court was the focal point of Anne's reign. The Queen never forgot who she was; duty forbade her. It was almost a virtue in her father and uncle to have set so bad an example that Anne could not possibly follow it. The course that *she* must follow was plain. She must consult for her people. She must stand above faction. She must uphold the Established Church. She set herself out to help, to judge, if necessary to punish; and what the court lacked in tone it made up for in conscience.

All this would have made a figurehead only seem meddlesome and laughable. But when Anne came to the throne the English sovereign was not a figurehead, which explains why her watchful eyes were feared and her odd little ways were humoured. For better or worse, every politician knew that she was the most important person in the kingdom. The Stuarts, like the Bourbons, had excellent memories, and an ambitious man who offended the Queen might discover, long afterwards, that he stood in high disfavour for something he had ages ago forgotten he had done. Harley, to give one example, was once so misguided as to affirm a Hanoverian's right to come to England and take his seat — as the Duke of Cumberland — in the House of Lords; it was a not inconsiderable cause of Harley's later being flung out of office.

Hence such lords and ladies as were merely pleasure-loving might give the court as wide a berth as they chose; but scheming Whigs and Tories, ambitious peers and would-be peers, knew better. They must dance attendance on the Queen. Yet even there it was no simple matter of directly seeking an audience. The household habits of Kensington Palace and Windsor Castle worked differently. You were not admitted by a lackey at the front door; you sneaked up the back steps. You did not boast of your visits to the Queen; you concealed them. Nor was Anne hedged about by a numerous guard of honour; one person alone blocked the way to her, and that a woman, a confidante, a favourite. The Queen was a curious person: stubborn yet indecisive; one moment quivering with kindliness, the next callous and sullen; obsessed by the thought of duty, but reaching decisions out of personal motives; and consulting for the Church almost more than she did for the throne.

[1 7

Yet, by a kind of hare-and-tortoise logic, this jumble of un-queenly qualities somehow contrived to carry off a notable reign. Her dogged unreasoning sincerity served as a kind of faint corrective force — and there was no stronger one — in the ambition-haunted, unscrupulous, nervously brilliant England of her time. Whatever her reasons, she came to more good decisions than bad ones.

In her obstinacy Anne was bold enough, but in her re-laxed moments, in her daily life, she required, she had al-ways required, an arm to lean on. Support in the family circle had never been possible. Differing with her father over religion, she had deserted him in '88 and never seen him again. Her sister Mary, as Queen, had snubbed and bullied her and died her enemy. Her brother-in-law Wil-liam, as King, had never treated her well and too often treated her badly. Her husband was kind and loving enough, but Anne had to support *him.* Add to this the fact that all her children died in infancy except one who died in child-hood, and you have a woman who needed not support alone, but affection also. She looked to her oldest and clos-est friend, Sarah Jennings Churchill, later the Duchess of Marlborough, for both. Sarah had been of Anne's retinue since girlhood, and as the mistress rose in power, so did the servant. No favourite was ever granted a warmer friendship or a wider province. For Sarah, Anne tore off all her stately habiliments, and the two women talked together, and wrote to each other, with complete frankness, as " Mrs Morley " and " Mrs Freeman." The Queen must have subscribed her-self " Your poor, unfortunate, faithful Morley " almost as often as she subscribed herself " Anna R." And in the great years of the Duke of Marlborough's victories, his Duchess was heaped with honours and made formidable with powers and perquisites. In return for this, the Queen was plied with more advice than she would ever need, and offered, peremptorily, the strongest female arm in the kingdom to lean on.

But the faltering, lonely, childless, and, as time went on, widowed Anne wanted something besides an arm: she wanted a heart. She wanted — nor was it the Queen in her who asked for it — a little affection and gratitude. Sarah had wit, had brawn, had spirit; Sarah had a manner that could nonplus the bold and silence the proud; but except toward the man she married, Sarah had no heart. Slowly the Queen perceived the fact: the "frankness" Sarah had once been invited to show grew with time into officiousness, insolence, abuse. Sarah knew that the Duke was indispensable to Anne in the field, and she believed that she was indispensable at home. Certainly she could not have been easily replaced when it came to riding down the Queen or hacking away at those who sought the Queen's interest — whether accredited statesmen, or aspiring politicians, or necessitous gentlewomen.

"Poor, unfortunate, faithful" Morley grew less and less faithful as it occurred to her that in her choice of a favourite she was becoming more and more unfortunate. For old times' sake she tolerated much in Sarah; for holding the Duke to his job she tolerated more. But there are limits to a queen's patience and, as was becoming clearer, to a duke's usefulness; and other candidates are not wanting for a sovereign's affection. Long ago Sarah had brought to court an indigent cousin named Abigail Hill, and made her one of Anne's bedchamber women. As seemly as the Duchess was rude, as obsequious as the Duchess was airy, as considerate as the Duchess was selfish, Abigail slowly worked her way into the Queen's heart. Even in Sarah's heyday Abigail and Anne were closely allied, and they drew closer as Anne and the Duchess drew farther apart. Too late the Duchess saw, in consternation and dismay, what had happened. Once Sarah became as politically useless as she was personally unbearable, the Queen flung her brutally aside. The final audience, in which that majestic stolidness known as the grand manner was indulged to the hilt, is still good theatre.

[19

Sarah had besought Anne to receive her so that she might defend herself against "slanders," stipulating that Anne should only listen and need not reply. When the Queen at last received her, Sarah implored forgiveness. "You desired no answer," said the Queen, "and you shall have none." Sarah stormed, wept, cajoled. "You desired no answer," the Queen repeated, "and you shall have none." Sarah ascended to raving, plucked at the Queen's gown, tugged at her sleeve. Again came the stony words, with final impact; and shaking herself free, Anne marched scornfully out of the room. The two women never saw each other again.

Sarah's had been a long régime, and as a fervent Whig — far more so, indeed, than her husband — she had served her party militantly, though rather ill than well. If she had helped the Duke to rise, even more she had helped him to fall. Her itch to rule was aggravated by an itch to punish; she thrashed about, and those whom she favoured must have felt very little less browbeaten than those whom she disliked. Fearing her tongue and admitting her influence, all parties had kotowed while they must; but only between her and Godolphin had there ever been real amity, and the two of them tumbled simultaneously from power. For the rest, she had antagonized the Whigs; and simply by becoming a Whig she had antagonized the Queen. For between the Whigs and Anne there was sharp disagreement about that object of Anne's soul, the Church. Her predilections, her confidence, went to the Tories. Long before Sarah was driven forth, even before Godolphin could be sacked or Marlborough disregarded, the new favourite Abigail [1] was leading the new counsellor Harley cautiously up the back stairs.

By way of Abigail, Harley reached the Queen and cemented himself in her good opinion. By way of Abigail, Bolingbroke penetrated to Anne and superseded Harley.

---

[1] Now Mrs Masham.

Abigail knew how to make herself indispensable: whatever her ambitions, she did not disdain the menial aspect of her job, and she stayed in Anne's good graces by performing the duties of a paid companion while amassing a fortune off the Tory chiefs. She was self-effacing enough to make a good intriguante, to bide her time, to dissemble her dislikes. With Sarah she played the innocent well enough not to be found out prematurely. Self-seeking she must have been, and largely unprincipled, but she appears to have been altogether ladylike at the game. Whatever she was, she managed — without birth, looks, or intellect — to acquire genuine power in an age when power was everyone's first consideration.

Fair play went by the boards in Anne's reign, but never so much as during its last years, when Abigail was keeper of the gate, when faction boiled over, and even the chiefs of the ruling party were at daggers drawn. There was never an age of filthier politics. Nor were the slanders and personal venom the worst aspect, nor even the hired ruffianly press that boasted a Swift and a Defoe. These things were relatively out in the open and could be returned in kind. These things smacked of exaggeration even to a credulous, or a partisan, public. The basest aspect was the unrelieved treachery, the constant double-dealing. The very men who wrote letters of extravagant praise to Marlborough were plotting his overthrow; the very men who drank together stopped just short of poisoning one another's wine. An instinct to play safe — unless it was an incorrigible instinct to plot — led the self-seeking to swear fealty to Hanover while they connived with Saint-Germains. Men had hardly formed one political alliance before they were negotiating another. They must have drunk well in those days, to drink so much and not betray their secrets.

Not everybody, of course, was treacherous: there were plenty of men who were merely fanatical. The fanatics were the true party men, who could not be bought or sold and for the Whigs' sweet sake, or the Tories', would abandon all decency and pelt their opponents with abuse. No statesman in public life could have a shred of honour left in hostile eyes: at the least he was a knave or an intriguer, at the worst he sold information or betrayed his country. Where conversation ceased, nimble and not infrequently distinguished pens took up the work. As soon as the guns had slaughtered one's public reputation, they opened fire on one's private character. Scarcely anyone was not a profligate or a slut. A screed called *The New Atlantis* denuded all the respectable and pilloried all the suspect: Sarah, for example, was charged with being Godolphin's mistress — with Marlborough's full consent.

The vicious thing was not that a yellow press existed side by side with a clean one, but that it devoured the clean one. With nothing at stake, Swift abused the author of *The New Atlantis,* but as soon as he needed her " evidence," he praised her. He spat on Marlborough as only he could spit; he lived to denigrate Steele, an honest if a rash and reckless man. During Anne's reign the party machine included a press unsurpassed for utter want not only of charity but of justice. Friendships lost their sweetness, enmities their dignity.

Behind it all there lay, of course, the unrelieved swindling of a corrupt age. There were honest men, there were a few good ones — men bred to affairs in that monarchical tradition where faction plays the lesser part, men who in modern parlance did not vote straight tickets, but went with this group or that, as they saw their duty. This pivotal section had then acted as a safeguard against the rapacity of parties, but under the stress of self-preservation it slowly fell away, and by the end of the reign almost everybody was some kind of party man, however queer a one. The Whigs were running far ahead of the Tories: they had more principles and program; in Somers, Cowper, Godolphin, Walpole they had sounder statesmen; and they adjusted themselves to the future while the Tories reached vainly back toward the past. But while making the country " constitutional," while giving it a " modern impetus," while fighting for English political and religious liberty, they made England hideously oligarchic and philistine. The war, which to the Tories and the nation at large was a defensive war, was for the more knowing of the Whigs a great profiteering expedition. The capitalist egg, laid in Tudor times, was hatched in England under Anne. And it was vilely hatched, by men who stooped low to advance themselves, and who saw in the coming-of-age of Parliament the clue to indirect government by wealth.

But if the scheming was modern enough, the tactics still wore the familiar antique colours. The country at large lagged a generation behind the half-patrician, half-bourgeois minority who saw what opportunities lay in the changing form of government. The old religious heat still gave political animus its backbone; and the Schism Act, the Occasional Conformity Act, the Qualification Acts wherewith the Tories tried to check the oncoming Whig battalions reflected the dying vigour of those who saw in the union of Church and State nothing more outrageous than the union of bank and State, or State and stock exchange. But bigotry antiquates itself long before venality, and by its own momentarily successful heat the Church party burned itself out. The Tories were needed to make the peace, for their country's sake. But the Whigs' profiteering policy had penetrated so deep that the most devious courses were required to bring the peace about. And after it had been clandestinely negotiated with France, it had still to be ratified at home. The vote looked to be so close in the House of Lords that Harley and the Queen had to club together and go the length of creating eleven new Tory peers so as to make certain of a majority. The victory was to the Tories, but in the end — during the next age — the spoils went to the Whigs.

[2 3

Thus Anne's reign marks not only the end of the seventeenth-century struggle between prince and Parliament, but the beginning of two centuries of struggle between men who go through the motions and men who pull the strings. Inside a dozen years the party system had been worked out. Inside a dozen years the aristocratic formula had been absorbed into the oligarchical. They were a dozen years, both abroad and at home, during which old issues expired in a gorgeous flare, and fresh ones came into being. It was not by chance that so much was accomplished in so short a time. For men's abilities were as large as their ambitions: Marlborough, Godolphin, Bolingbroke, Harley, Cowper, Stanhope, Somers, Halifax, the rising Walpole — not one of them was inconsiderable. And with Addison, Steele, Swift, Prior, and Defoe pressing home their pens, politics were advertised as trenchantly as they were pursued. Politics was not an employment, but *the* employment, of those years; and if happy nations have no history, what cannot we deduce from a reign where history dropped every morning out of the gazette and bounced up and down on the breakfast-table?

CHAPTER III

TWO OR
THREE CHARACTERS

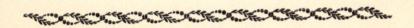

Bolingbroke

AS A YOUNG MAN Henry St John, the future Viscount Bolingbroke, chose as his models Alcibiades and Petronius. If
there was reckless vanity in such a choice, there was some
self-knowledge as well. In a way, Bolingbroke never again
admitted so honestly the kind of man he was or wished to
be; though had his exemplars seemed less lustrous, we may
feel sure he would not so openly have acknowledged them.
But he certainly never aimed at meeting their fate; nor,
when in part he met it, could he show a like dignity in misfortune. He behaved badly, and Time has behaved badly
toward him. He early won renown and early lost it, and even
obloquy has wearied of dogging his footsteps. For most
people Bolingbroke is today no more than a name.

On the surface it is strange indeed that he has suffered
above all else from neglect. It would be hard to imagine a
more suitable hero for one of those tales of dazzling wickedness which can be read for the sake of the story, or the
sake of the moral, or both. Bolingbroke has a dozen claims
to romantic interest. He was, to begin with, eminently a
grand seigneur. His lineage boasted the most ancient Nor-
man and Saxon blood; his looks and breeding enabled him

[25

to cut a dash, not merely in Augustan London, but at the most polished court of modern times — the Versailles of Louis XIV. He was an equally eminent profligate. His mistresses included some of the most beautiful, aristocratic, and expensive women in London; his capacity for drink was staggering; and his pranks ran to such things as dashing naked through the park. When he became Secretary of State, a town madam exclaimed: " Five thousand a year, my girls, and all for us! " Nor was he less eminent as a conspirator. He intrigued with the Queen of England, with the King of France, with the Pretender; he intrigued against those he was intriguing with; and his plots were no ordinary political manœuvres, but often the dark treason that ends on the scaffold.

But Bolingbroke was above everything else a genius. He had the capacities of statesmanship in an age of politics — a fertile brain, a commanding style, a will to lead; and he was the most resplendent orator, and one of the most resplendent writers, of his era. At the head of all vanished things he wished could be recovered, Mr Pitt put a speech by Bolingbroke. So late and severe a critic of prose as Matthew Arnold judged Bolingbroke a master. Swift considered him the coming man of his age; Pope called him " the greatest man in the world ";[1] Voltaire saluted him extravagantly and owed much to his influence; and Disraeli bestowed upon him the same honour that *he* had bestowed upon Alcibiades.

And yet he has kept as little of posterity's imagination as he has kept of her respect. That he deserves no better of her respect is beyond doubt (though doubt is sometimes raised), for his career offers strong evidence of misused genius and ignoble character. Perhaps the worst thing that can be said about it is that where, owing to the scurrilities of the age, we are sometimes uncertain as to the true motives of its other actors, we need never be uncertain about Bolingbroke's. If he was often defamed in his lifetime out of

[1] In the *Essay on Man* Pope merely versified Bolingbroke's ideas.

party rancour rather than honest judgment, and afterwards out of prudishness and party bias, we need only discount the motives. The verdict can stand.

Bolingbroke entered Parliament young, and at once by his oratory made his presence felt there. He seems to have joined the Tories chiefly out of admiration for Harley, for by family tradition he should more logically have been a Whig; and on principle — since he was the laxest of deists — he had little in common with a party that was violently High-Church. What he did have in common with the Tory outlook was a fierce and old-fashioned patrician instinct. With his early idol Harley he had nothing in common at all; and " the characters of these two men were in no sense complementary, which might have made for union; they were utterly opposed." Harley desired success in a simple remunerative form; he was not romantic egoist enough to insist also on power and prestige. He was no more high-minded than Bolingbroke, but he made fewer pretences of being. And he was certainly less unscrupulous: he indulged, if only from caution, in no sharper or shadier practice than situations called for. Bolingbroke, on the other hand, had unbounded ambitions and no temperament for achieving them slowly. He consequently stooped to any weapon that would help him rise. Simply to cramp the Whig power, the deist Bolingbroke was forever framing and supporting bills of the grossest religious intolerance — on the pretext that the Church must be stoutly upheld in the interest of good government. It was he who, all through Anne's reign, most loudly supported the Occasional Conformity Act and who pressed home the flagitious Schism Act at the end of it. In the same way, aggravating the practice of the age, Boling-broke never scrupled to trump up charges against his political enemies, such as Walpole, in order to ruin them. And during his days of power he employed Swift to discredit anyone who stood in his light; and at the same time sup-

[27

pressed counterblows upon himself and his party by throwing hacks and printers into jail and having men like Steele
expelled the House of Commons.

But Bolingbroke was not only ruthless with his enemies;
he was treacherous toward his friends. Professing admiration and loyalty for Marlborough, offering – though they
shared different attitudes toward the war – his co-operation,
Bolingbroke, when the time came to strike, so far from being
merciful, was unjust. Long before he openly showed hostility toward Harley, he whispered against him and attempted
his downfall. And when at last he achieved it, it was not by
fair words alone: twenty thousand pounds disappeared
from the Treasury into Mrs Masham's pockets. There are
good grounds for believing that Treasury money went into
Bolingbroke's pockets also.

It is not by such methods that a statesman arrives at principles; and the historically important fact about Bolingbroke is that he had no principles. His aim was power; and
for all his gifts of leadership, he led the Tories nowhere
because he had nowhere to lead them. So long as the war
was on, he could shout for peace; and making peace was
the one constructive act of his career. He made it in his own
way, circuitously; and though it involved treachery toward
the Catalans who were holding out against Philip of Anjou;
even though it involved desertion of England's allies; even
though it involved concessions to the vanquished that the
victorious seldom grant, far from seeming to me the great
blot on Bolingbroke's name that it is often judged to be,
the Peace of Utrecht stands out as the only useful work of
his career.

But when the peace had been made, Bolingbroke had
no sound policy to offer his party. He weakened their future
as well as his own by not having them stand for something
important to the country; and when at last he conspired with
the Pretender, it was in sheer desperation. Bolingbroke, as
others have noted, had not even the old Cavalier sentiment

Morning by William Hogarth

toward James III to impel him; he had nothing but naked self-interest. And while he temporized and plotted, the Queen died and the vigilant, consolidated Whigs moved forward, and he was undone. Losing his head at the thought of losing his neck, he fled to France and became a self-accused, an attainted, a ruined man. The rest of his life consisted in efforts to redeem and reassert himself; when he was finally allowed back in England, he joined hands with whatever opposition forces there were, implacably hostile to Walpole. He ceased to be a Tory at all, becoming a sort of liberal Whig and calling himself a man above party, a "patriot." [2] But he was in such bad odour that he hurt rather than helped the opposition's chances and was presently requested to withdraw from their ranks. But even this crowning blow did not crush his aspirations. He manœuvred to the end. He had sought to be prime minister under Anne; he had sought again under George I and George II; and now he had designs of captivating the Prince of Wales, son of George II — who, as it happened, died before his father did. Bolingbroke's brain was never quiet, nor his pen idle. The masterly rhetorician whose style so many have praised wrote on and on, justifying himself, adorning his motives, inventing benign, philosophical theories of government. Once or twice he stopped to tell the truth:

"I am afraid that we [the Tories under Anne] came to court in the same disposition as all parties have done; that the principal spring of our actions was to have the government of the state in our hands; that our principal views were the preservation of this power, great employment to ourselves, and great opportunity of rewarding those who had helped to raise us, and of hurting those who stood in opposition to us."

Yet even here, it seems to me, Bolingbroke is rather ar-

---

[2] It was of this special brand of patriotism, rather than the usual kind, that Dr Johnson made his famous but misunderstood remark.

ticulating the political spirit of the age than admitting the
baser tactics to which he stooped himself. Harley, as the
man of mediocre gifts, and Marlborough, as the man of
genius, are proper instances of types who were no better
than their age. But Bolingbroke was worse, for with superior
perceptions he fell into lower practices. He had great talents, great intellect, great position, every incentive for understanding the responsibilities of statesmanship. He had
absorbed all the lessons of philosophy, and wrote prettily
of himself as one who had. He was conscious of the artist's
sensibilities, the patrician's high aloofness. Yet as a man who
boasted of being enlightened, who knew what to be enlightened meant, who could detect unenlightenment in
others — as such a man he himself, throughout an entire
lifetime, was intolerant, deceitful, rancorous, cunning, and
abusive. Only two motives fed his actions: an itch for power
and a thirst for glory. As to his customary truthfulness, a
famous example so cheeky as to be almost disarming, will
give some indication. In his *Letter to Sir William Windham*
he insists that at the end of Anne's reign there was no movement afoot to bring in the Pretender, because " if there had
been, *I should have heard about it.*"

In Bolingbroke, the man who might have redeemed his
age, we have the tragedy of one who further debased it.
" He lacked solidity, conviction, character, all the elements
which make a public man great instead of brilliant." He
lacked, indeed, what his times lacked, and shared in what
they might choose to boast of. At bottom, however, he was
more specious. He glittered, like his prose, like his manners, and he sank all his gifts to bring off that glitter, which
has notwithstanding faded. There are latter-day romantic
Tories who, cherishing the patrician ideal at any cost, regard Bolingbroke as a misrepresented man. They see in
him all the lustre of what might have been, and because he
was pre-eminent in gifts among his generation, assume that

he pre-eminently employed them. They are still gulled by his exalting (after the grapes turned sour) the pleasures of the hermit philosopher; and still unduly fascinated by his prodigies of debauch. But such sentimentalists aside, Bolingbroke attracts very little notice today. On the surface the neglect of him may, as I said earlier, seem strange; at bottom there is a reason for it. He is like a book one reads once and never cares to read again. The glitter palls, and the man reveals himself too soon and too completely. He is not inscrutable, but obvious, and complex in nothing save his scheming. Those who seek to vindicate him must face not only a mountain of crushing evidence, but endless posing and protesting that provide the clinch. He had neither moral stamina nor intellectual honesty nor emotional benevolence; and as he was in his heart, so was he in his dealings with men. In short, he was a scoundrel.

The Duke and Duchess of Marlborough

As one of the greatest names in English history, the Duke of Marlborough not surprisingly dominated his age. He is its prime and its pivotal figure. By his exploits he altered the destiny of Europe — as vast a phrase as one can use of any man. But he is important even beyond his exploits, as someone round whom politics revolved, someone in the forefront of a disputed policy, and as a nation's hero and a nation's scapegoat. If England proved ungrateful for what he did, it is because England felt uncertain of what he was. Her lack of confidence in Marlborough arose from many causes, all reasonable, yet all confusing and, taken all together, extremely weighty. There was the Duke's past record to arouse suspicion; there was his wife's influence over the Queen, the bitterly divided attitude toward the war, the stress of party faction, the Duke's own shift in party loyalties; not least

[3 1

there were the jealous ambitions of other men. We must dwell a little upon Marlborough's career before we can attempt to weigh his character.

His early progress, as plain John Churchill, owed less to his military service than to his having been the brother of a mistress of the Duke of York, and the seducer of a mistress of the King. Through his sister's liaison he obtained preferment; through his own he obtained money. At the Revolution, though a favourite with James, he abandoned him for William; in doing which he had honest religious motives, possible patriotic motives, and obvious selfish motives. But afterwards, while serving William, he parleyed again with James and even passed on to him treasonable information. For this (though on a charge in itself false) he was stripped of influence and imprisoned in the Tower; but by the time of William's death he had not only regained his former standing, but surpassed it. Before the War of the Spanish Succession ever began, Marlborough was known to be England's greatest soldier, and his being chosen captain-general by Anne was due as much to reputation as to friendship.

From the very outbreak of the war those same tactics which attest Marlborough's genius and promoted his success antagonized Tory England. His belief in bold, aggressive campaigns as opposed to the defensive fabian warfare of his day; his large daring conceptions which, should they fail, meant not merely defeat, but annihilation; his desire to prostrate the enemy, invade France, besiege Paris, and blow up the country like a mine; his refusal to communicate his plans beforehand (for fear they should leak out and miscarry) to either his fellow-officers or the home Government — all such policies laid him open to every sort of attack. He was carrying England, said his opponents, beyond her commitments; he was threatening her with ruin, involving her in hideous expense, acting in defiance of the very Government he was pledged to serve. And had he once failed, had he answered those charges with anything less than Blenheim, Ramillies, Oudenarde, the resentment smouldering in England would have instantly blazed up. As it was, his own triumphs and the Whig power at his back gave him security until graver charges could be levied. When they were, he and the Whigs were indicted together: he and the Whigs were accused of wilfully, selfishly prolonging the war and obstructing the peace. Then, at Malplaquet, the Duke gave his enemies a wedge; next, by asking to be made captain-general for life, he gave them the arsenal. The end was coming. The last Whig to fall, Marlborough really fell with the first of them — Tory aims and Tory rancour alike encompassed his ruin. He fell, moreover, not from power to obscurity, but from power to disgrace. He was charged with embezzlement and extortion: with deducting a percentage from the pay of foreign soldiers, and accepting large perquisites from bread contractors. By the standards of his time, his defence was sound: to take such money had long been considered a commander-in-chief's prerogative; and to spend it, as he had done, to build up the intelligence service, was to spend it legitimately. But his defence was a waste of breath, and soon after he went into exile. There he played a double game with Hanover and the Pretender until, at the accession of George I, he returned to England to end his life in luxury at Blenheim.

Though in principle Marlborough was never more than a lukewarm adherent of the Whigs, and never wholly trusted by them, actually his fortunes strictly coincided with theirs. But whether or not he belonged with them, he led them. He was not merely their general, but their prime minister and their ambassador. When he was not plunging into battle, he was in England advising Parliament, in Holland conciliating the Dutch, in Sweden winning over the King, in Vienna conferring with the Emperor. Pressed by duties, harried by time, threatened by enemies, retarded by reactionaries, he yet succeeded as well in his embassies as

[33

in his campaigns. For all the dispute over his character, there is none concerning his personality. He was thoughtful, persuasive, captivating, supremely diplomatic; he seems really to have had something of that Augustan grace — including its coldness — which has chiefly been a myth. In almost all respects Marlborough's generalship was absolute while it lasted; and where he did not rule, he passed on the sceptre to the staunchest of allies, Godolphin.

Marlborough's military genius was of the very grandest type. It was neither fitful nor erratic, but both prescient and omniscient; bold, it was never rash; large, it was never flatulent; seeking scope, it never grew hasty in details. The Duke's coolness is proverbial, and was perhaps the cement for all his other gifts; and if he could be brilliant in relaxed moments, he could be inspired in a crisis. That he never lost a battle means less than that he won what battles he did; and though his later exploits were not allowed to count, and so have a smaller place in history, in certainty and skill they almost surpassed his earlier ones.

Marlborough's character, unlike that of other famous men — unlike that of his famous contemporaries Bolingbroke and Swift — never discommoded his capacities. His military genius moved unflaggingly forward to make history; his character unmade nothing more than his own reputation. But the character of the Duke of Marlborough has a claim to study beyond its psychological interest, since it calls into question that always likely cleavage between the genius and the great man. Marlborough, in spite of many champions, has not come off well. Ever since Swift called him " proud as Hell, and covetous as the Prince of it," Marlborough's image has been ruthlessly defaced by a long line of critics. The charges have been grave, and they have seemed to darken the more as Marlborough's motives have remained elusive and mysterious. And just because he had so cool a mind, so unruffled a demeanour, so absolute a self-control, no palliation can be urged of any guilt that *can* be ascertained: a man who was never rash could not have committed rash misdeeds.

That the Duke failed to act by principle alone is evident. He *may* have been honest in deserting James for William; he could not have been in betraying William to James. Again, flirting with the Pretender while pledged to Hanover argues, if anything, lack of courage as well as lack of principle: the Duke was simply trying to even up his bets. But one may still act by principle without acting by principle alone. The important thing to discover is whether Marlborough had any principles, however he enforced them. Was he a man of really high patriotism, of vision and morality, or was he a self-seeker on the grand scale who sought to carve out a career and line his pockets? The answer, to my mind, is that he was not quite either: he was a man who had a genius for his profession and who gave value received in a sense neither villainous nor lofty. He did not wilfully create opportunities for advancement, but he never shunned any that came his way. What he had to gain from his sister's liaison with James II, or his own intrigue with Barbara Villiers, or his wife's connexion with Queen Anne, he went and took. And with the utmost ease if not quite the utmost logic he could believe that his own good and his country's coincided: that the Whig objectives in the war were sound and just, that no one but him could achieve them, and that if he was superior to everybody else in ability, he deserved to be so in power. Marlborough, as it happened, loved money even more than he loved power; and a man who loves both is not apt to be morally well counselled by even the coolest of brains. There is little reason to suppose that his attitude toward the war was insincere, but none at all to suppose that it was disinterested. His talk, year after year, of throwing up his job comes at length to ring altogether hollow. Why *didn't* he throw it up, since he was weary of it, since he was hampered in it, since he was thanked so badly for it — or why, rather, in the end did he ask for it for life? Partly, I think, because he was patriotic; partly, I think, from that instinct in men who do not care to see a job botched which they can do well; but mostly because he wanted wealth and power. There is some logic, after all, for a military man to believe that those who conquer by the sword shall perish by putting up the sword.

Marlborough is an excellent example of the folly, among historians, of taking sides. He was neither hero nor villain, saint nor sinner. He loved power, but beyond wishing to hold on to it, did not abuse it. He neither sacrificed, nor exploited, nor ill-used his soldiers; and was the more strictly courteous and humane to them in that he was not warm-hearted. He loved money, yet he gave large sums of it away. He was fiercely hated without ever hating back. He was gallingly goaded without ever losing his dignity. Chesterfield said that he " possessed the graces in the highest degree." He had perhaps the best manners, the best breeding, of his generation.

But a great man as differentiated from a genius Marlborough was not. In military manœuvre he may have been a century ahead of his time, but elsewhere he was entirely the creature of his age. He dominated it, he embellished it, but he did not exalt it and he did not rise above it. He was a paragon for courts to emulate, not citizens. He schooled himself to meet the world; he did not humble himself to resist it. In an age that — despite a contrary reputation — showed little dignity, Marlborough was really dignified. We give him his exact rating if we say that he could not take that step beyond dignity to nobility.

As to his being a man of shadowy, inexplicable motives, that is mostly a fiction of people who find human nature difficult because it is not all of one piece. A legend that grew up originally because in the Augustan age everybody lied about everybody else and made truth hard to come by was abetted by the Victorians who judged men chiefly by their behaviour in sex, politics, and religion. Actually Marlborough's motives seem rather clear. Men who love money will sometimes, without ceasing to love it, spend it or give it away. Men who know the meaning of loyalty will sometimes prove disloyal. Marlborough was anything but a traitor, yet now and then he was certainly treacherous. As, finally, for men of the highest gifts failing to reveal the highest virtues, such a commonplace would not merit pointing out did it not seem, for two centuries, to have built up a mystery in Marlborough's case where none existed. Marlborough, who was not a prig, never pretended to be a saint. He was, in the most decisive sense possible, a worldling.

The courtliest man of his generation had married its most abusive virago. He had married for love, and he died still a lover. His worst enemies could never so much as hint that he was unfaithful; instead, in seeking to defame him, they had to call him uxorious. And certainly all his ambitions had at the back of them the desire to place fortune and renown at the feet of his wife. She was an inconvenient and disturbing consort, but not altogether an unequal one. Without finding much to admire in her, one persists in paying her a sort of undutiful admiration, for if she had few virtues, at least her faults were bolder than those of the people she lived among.

For one thing, the Duchess of Marlborough never held herself cheap. Half coyly, half proudly, she had made John Churchill's courtship extremely rough going before she gave in. In the very act of loving him and foreseeing his vast future, she had to make it plain that she would marry him only as an equal. Nor was this bravado. It was really a concession: Sarah looked upon everyone else as her inferior.

She served Anne for thirty years and there passed before her eyes the whole spectacle of court life, its intrigue, its cupidity, its ingratitude, its thirst for gain. She came to know everybody, to punish where she could, to reward as she chose, but always if possible to dominate. Had she not felt so secure, one might think of her as an adventuress, but in actual practice Sarah thought of herself as seated too high to fall and almost too high to rise. One can understand her contempt for a Queen who constantly besought her kindness, implored her advice, sued for her companionship: Anne had given the Duchess every advantage. But the Duchess was not shrewd enough to perceive that a Queen can give everything away and then quite effortlessly take everything back. Anne had become a habit with Sarah, and hence a bore. Violating etiquette, friendship, sense of duty, Sarah would pack up and desert her mistress for weeks and months on end. She believed she had the Queen in fee beyond possibility of challenge. Was she not Groom of the Stole and Mistress of the Robes and Ranger of the Great Park? Was she not charged with the privy purse? Was she not the Duke of Marlborough's wife and the most brilliant woman of her time?

She indulged herself to the hilt. There was no one too great to snub, too powerful to defy; with the contempt of the arrived she slashed at every wary, puffing climber; with the logic of a despot she denounced all others who wanted to rule. Her temper was violent, her tongue uncontrollable, her pride satanic. And her vanity — which she denied having at all — was insatiable, the point being that she had to be flattered *en connaisseur*, bearing out La Rochefoucauld's saying that it is never flattery we dislike, but only the manner of flattering. As to flattering others, her bluntness is legendary. She practised no wiles, she paid no compliments. In this she stood almost alone in her day, and knew it, and handsomely prided herself on it.

But there was nothing very creditable about a bluntness so dripping with ill nature. Nobody ever opened the door wider on trouble than Lady Marlborough. She had not only wreaked her fury on a whole high society, but had arrogated to herself every privilege, every office, every emolument she could put hand to. Her avarice was much greater than the Duke's, and much more offensive. For one example, she hectored and browbeat Vanbrugh while he was building Blenheim, beating him down, intimating he had cheated her, putting contemptible obstacles in his path. Even now the humour of it does not redeem the vulgarity.

It could not last forever, Abigail or no Abigail; but when the hour of expulsion came, Sarah humbled herself for the only time in her life and even shed tears. But it was much too late, and her official career was over. Rudely dismissed, she meanly sought thousands of pounds of back pay from the Queen, and was given them. She departed under a cloud, falsely accused of having mismanaged the privy purse. "Everyone knows," said Anne, "that cheating is not the Duchess of Marlborough's crime."

After a few years in exile with the Duke, she returned to England to employ her talents and direct her hate in fresh performances. Walpole, the master of the next age, became her principal quarry. But if she grew even more ungovernable and shrill, she could be set down now as a slanderer. She had been fingerprinted; she was known. So she passed into old age trying to create an uproar from the sidelines, and doubly blessed: she could hate in the present and revive her hatreds from the past. She excoriated the dead and the living alike, and, still unsurfeited, the indomitable old widow quarrelled incessantly with most of her family. One example of her family affection survives. She hung in her drawing-room a portrait of her granddaughter, Lady Bateman, with the face blackened over and these words inscribed on the frame: "She is much blacker within."

There is no reason to be romantic about her. She lacked the true touch of magnificence with which others have played much the same part. Her fist closed too rapaciously over money, there was something petty in her spite, and something really ill-bred as well as cyclonic in her manner. She was at times a splendid barbarian, but too often merely a wilful, selfish, shrewish woman of the world. And yet, as an explosive force in an age that sought above everything else to act expediently, she is at least refreshing. She disdained the rapier and banged about with a tomahawk. For all her abusiveness and rancour, the Duchess, by her own ridiculous lights, was honest. The few principles she had she stuck to. She whooped up the Whigs in Anne's Tory face, and shrugged at the Church when Anne knelt down to pray. She feared nobody. She shied away from nothing. And she knew how to swallow her medicine. Where other people's conduct was concerned, there was a crazy strain of the moralist about her which lost all its meaning by never being levied against herself. She had an energy so boundless it must have appalled even her indefatigable husband; and despite her utter lack of restraint and her full quiver of prejudices, she had a penetrating and critical mind. She took the measure of the men and women around her, and she was not for the most part wrong. And merit she could sometimes applaud, even in someone she hated: her enmity toward Swift did not prevent her from going into raptures over *Gulliver*. She is not a woman one would have enjoyed coming to for a favour, but I can think of nobody I would rather have watched, for an hour, in the household at Windsor.

The conjunction of the Duchess with the Duke was no mere routine of marriage. Sarah strongly influenced Marlborough's career. As the Queen's favourite, as the Whigs' unofficial adviser, as the recorder of the pulse of England when the Duke was fighting abroad, she had great political importance. They were a strong pair, welded by love and greed and ambition and a just sense of each other's superiority. He must often have found her intolerable, yet that sublime patience which won him battles smoothed out all their difficulties. Two anecdotes will convey something of what each felt toward the other. Of all Sarah's charms, the

Duke loved most her beautiful fair hair. One day, when he had offended her, she cut it off to annoy him and laid the shorn locks where he was sure to see them. Concerning her act, however, nothing was ever said by either the Duke or the Duchess. But after his death she found her hair carefully preserved in a cabinet where he kept what he held most precious; " and at this point of the story she regularly fell a-crying."

As for Sarah, when a son of the Duchess of Buckingham died, his mother requested the loan of the funeral chariot which had borne the Duke of Marlborough to rest. Sarah replied curtly that the car had carried the body of My Lord of Marlborough and should certainly carry no other. There is much more of My Lord of Marlborough's wife in that remark than the degree of her esteem for him.

CHAPTER IV

WALPOLE AND
THE HOUSE OF HANOVER

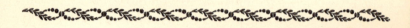

1

THE ACCESSION OF the House of Hanover to the throne of Britain marks the commencement of a visibly modern England. Anne's hotly charged short reign had been like the crisis of a slow-gathering fever in the nation's blood, with a dozen doctors — many of them quacks — hovering in a fever of their own about the sickbed. Then the crisis passed and, more from its own recuperative powers than the doctors' remedies, the patient rallied.

The fever itself did not at once totally subside. There were to be recurrences in the next age, which, though one of prosperity and peace, was far from tranquil. But the old madness and the superstitions it fed upon could be held in check; and Englishmen were satisfied to replace venom with mere pepperiness, and to launch forth in the open where they had once conspired in secret. Politics ranged themselves, in some rough sense, along the modern lines of a government and an opposition; the religious uproar ceased to shake the national foundations; while Jacobitism, though it still patiently schemed and twice fomented unsuccessful uprisings, was rather a dying cause to be guarded against than a living contestant for power. After 1715 the Jacobites were much like the royalist party in an increasingly sturdy republic. They flared up for the last time when they raised the standard of Prince Charlie in the '45, " marching with a feudal army into a bourgeois society "; and the notorious Lord Lovat, who was to forfeit the head that Hogarth has so superbly pencilled, was their last important martyr.

The complete power which the Whigs commanded at the Queen's death was not to pass out of their hands for upwards of forty years. Harley and Bolingbroke had ruined the Tory interest by the same tactics with which they ruined themselves; but something beyond Tory defection—namely, the resolute loyalty which the Whigs had shown to George I before he was crowned — now enabled them to grasp all the places of government and to win and maintain the confidence of the King. Their strength was indeed so great that they became, as one party, both government and opposition; survived no end of squabbling and disaffection inside their own ranks; and triumphantly overrode some delicate and even explosive moments in English history.

The Whig régime under the first Georges constituted more than ever before the maintenance of power by the moneyed interests; it was to sink, indeed, to the level of a despotic oligarchy, the " Venetian oligarchy " of Disraeli's famous if inaccurate phrase. The Whigs had been the war party under Anne; they now became the peace party under her successors. The fruits of Marlborough's victories and Bolingbroke's treaty-making existed for the Whigs to grow fat on in prosperous trade, canny money-lending, and unlimited political spoils. Under Anne, England had regained a footing in the affairs of Europe: now she could stand on equal terms with France, usurp much of Spain's colonial commerce, multiply her manufacturing. She could brim over with renascent zest and press forward with understandable covetousness, slowly disregarding the half-mediæval privileges of caste for the direct, measurable, bourgeois rewards of money. As a nation she had demanded

[43

political liberty and, by being implacable, had achieved it. Now that it was won, the modern class system could go to work in earnest; the English people, as Burke was to phrase it later, should be " entitled to equal rights, but to equal rights to unequal things."

The long Whig reign is dominated by one figure — Robert Walpole. This burly Norfolk squire who established the practice of long parliamentary week-ends in order to have his fill of foxhunting, inhabits a different world from that of the grandee Marlboroughs and glittering Bolingbrokes among whom he first fought his way to power. He was a man, above everything else, of sense. He associated, as one of Bolingbroke's stripe never did, rule with management, and success with foresight. He first planned to enter the Church, and we can approve his statement that had he not become Prime Minister he would have been Archbishop of Canterbury. In Walpole we encounter no hint of men who fight for dimly apprehended causes or from loving the heat of battle or preening themselves on their lanceman-ship. Walpole fought — fought leoninely — but for a purpose. He was determined to keep England at peace. No prospects of colonial enrichment, no finicking ideas of national honour, no gambles on the dynastic fluctuations of the Continent, should tempt him so long as he saw that peace at home meant prosperity at home. There were men who disagreed with him, there were men who resented his power, there were men who coveted his power — all of them ranged against him in an almost comic sequence of oppositions; but when the hounds barked, Walpole cracked his whip and rudely silenced them. In time their barking mounted to an uproar, and he could silence them no longer; but by then twenty years had passed during which he had had his way and England her reward. When, following the excitement of Jenkins's Ear, the country so clamoured for war with Spain that Walpole had either to sacrifice his opinions or resign, he chose to remain. He gave in to the voice of an entire nation which included, besides his enemies, the King who had shielded him from them, and his own adherents. But the voice of an entire nation was roused as much against Walpole as for the war, and in 1742 — after the longest ascendancy of any first minister since Burleigh — he fell.

He had preserved not only peace, but the Hanoverian succession. George I had come to England a stranger, with gross ways, ugly mistresses, complete ignorance of the language, no grasp of English problems, and no interest in English life. The country had nothing to give him (except money), nor he the country. Anne's was a dull court that hatched violent plots, and George's a dull court that hatched vulgar scandals. The King had long ago taken his wife in adultery and locked her up in a fortress; and he despised and openly quarrelled with his son, the future George II. There was neither an aura of majesty nor a solid picture of good works to imbue the English with love of their sovereign; and if, in those first years, violence was rare, tongues still wagged busily concerning the Pretender, and all appetites save those of the great Whigs went still unsatisfied. At length in 1720 the collapse of the South Sea Company, in which everybody who could command any cash had been speculating, blew London up like a mine. It was a moment of suspense and danger. But Walpole, whose ascendancy dates from that disaster, kept in future so even a keel that not any or all of these disadvantages put the House of Hanover in further peril; and he there won for it the security that has made it outlast all the other first-water dynasties of Europe.

Beyond all doubt the years of the Walpole régime were years of increasing venality and corruption. The great Whig oligarchy commandeered office, perquisites, and party spoils in high buccaneering fashion. Rather than acting in concert with the court, or being receivers of court favour, they set themselves above it, as far wealthier and more powerful. The uses of privilege were shifting. Most of the great Whigs — notably the Dukes of Portland, Newcastle, Richmond, Grafton, Bedford, and Devonshire — were great aristocrats, temporarily preserving power as well as position to a small class. But here and there jutted up a parvenu, and inside a generation there would be other parvenus grasping power through wealth or ability.[1] Moreover, in early Hanoverian England the political interests that the great Whigs represented were those of the prospering commercial classes. The oligarchy were a kind of pivot, socially identified with the land, politically with the town, and dominating both. As the century advanced, the old practice of court sinecures, rising among the most fortunate to truly lucrative and exploitative court offices, became negligible compared with the newer practice of party and parliamentary sinecures. From the dipping in the privy purse or the tapping of Treasury coffers, we pass on to that array of jobs and joblets whereby sons and brothers and nephews, and usually children, and sometimes infants, got into the government employ, only to have subordinates, who drew perhaps a tenth of their pay, do the whole of their work.[2] It was only thus that the Horace Walpoles and the George Selwyns could maintain their standing in the world. When, during Robert Walpole's ministry, the Commons, in protest against these tendencies, passed bills to diminish corruption, at once the ruling Whigs blocked them in the Lords. In Walpole's own family, it is worth noting, his relatives held some very odd offices indeed. And hand in hand with this wholesale nepotism went corruption on straight political lines, all the way from direct bribery up (I suppose one says) to pocket boroughs. Such abuses were to grow and grow until

---

[1] Cf. Lecky: *A History of England during the Eighteenth Century*, I, 229. Somers, Montague, Churchill (i.e., Marlborough), Addison, and Walpole himself were all men who advanced themselves to the level at which the great Whigs operated.

[2] A baroness, for example, was made "Sweeper of the Mall in the Park"; others had jobs connected with wharfs and cranes.

under George III they reached appalling magnitude; but in the Walpolean era they unquestionably went many leagues forward.

With such corruption Walpole's name has long been associated. His accusers have seen in him the cynical and predatory man of power, running the country for the interested few, and establishing a tradition of misgovernment by clique that later generations were still more flagrantly to pursue. As to concrete instances, it is certain that Walpole enriched every last member of his tribe, that he manipulated the secret-service money, that on occasion he bribed members of Parliament to obtain their votes, and that, by way of Parliament, he bribed George II and Queen Caroline with large personal incomes. Walpole was certainly as often a politician as he was a statesman. But the evidence, for all that, still favours the assertion that he used discreditable political means to achieve creditable statesmanlike ends, and that his private ambitions, in any large sense, were not in conflict with the public interest, but in treaty with it. As certainly as he thirsted after power, he sought conscientiously not to abuse it. Where he stooped, it was not through out-and-out rapacity, but through purpose. He was lastingly in opposition to men who called themselves by every kind of high-sounding name but who had, many of them, not only less ability than he, but less decency and on the whole less principle. The very best of them were morally superior to him as individuals, but morally of a piece with him as administrators, and mentally not within hailing distance. Whenever they touched power, or the semblance of it, either during momentary interregnums in Walpole's career or after his fall, they either blundered by ignoring his advice or only succeeded by seeking it. And some of them were monsters of incompetence. Sir Spencer Compton, whom George II chose as minister until Queen Caroline speedily got rid of him, could not even draft the King's accession speech; he had to ask Walpole to do it. The finely-

[47

spoken Carteret, who on his deathbed quoted Homer in the original, had such trouble holding an administration together that a wit averred it was unsafe to walk the streets for fear of being pressed into service as a cabinet minister. The Duke of Newcastle's *gaffes* are classic: " Oh — yes — yes — to be sure — Annapolis must be defended — troops must be sent to Annapolis — Pray where *is* Annapolis? " And again: " Cape Breton an island! wonderful! — show it me in the map. So it is, sure enough. My dear sir, you always bring us good news. I must go and tell the King that Cape Breton is an island." [3] Beside such men Walpole had an unassailable value. As someone put it, the best eulogy of Walpole's administration was supplied by the ten blundering years that came after it.

His value, it is true, lay not in anything he created or enriched but in what he preserved and prevented. It was a value in every sense material. He did nothing to strengthen England's moral fibre, to fortify her intellectual endowments, or even to improve her social tone. But he did seek to keep her well fed and well disposed and to save her from war and from internal disruption. Judged by his opportunities and the standards of his time, Walpole's malpractices are moderate rather than glaring, and less grave than the malpractices of all but a few other men with comparable opportunities. It was only when his power was threatened that his statesmanship really faltered; the Spanish war was inevitable, but since he opposed it he need not have participated in it: he could and should have resigned. It is certain that he hung on chiefly because he would not part with office. It is tenable, however, that he also hung on because he felt that no successor could possibly cope with the job. It seems to me, who have no admiration for the Walpole type, that he was honestly influenced by this added consideration. The whole thing raises a moral problem (not fully relevant here, since self-interest played the major role) of

---

[3] See *Humphrey Clinker.*

some niceness, as to whether on a specific occasion it is better to stand by principle and see great harm brought about
by others, or to abandon principle in an effort to mitigate the
harm. It must also be said for Walpole that he long urged
peace at the sure risk of acquiring unpopularity and en-
countering royal disfavour — which is not the usual pro-
cedure of the opportunist.

As to his policy in general, it is as untrue to say that Walpole directly fostered corruption as that he did anything
to check it. He countenanced it. Like Marlborough, he represents his age. He was bluff where Marlborough was
courtly, and as vigorous a careerist of peace as was Marlborough of war. But the two men were alike in their so brilliantly serving the State while they uninterruptedly served
themselves. They both had useful intentions but not mag-
nanimous ones; they both had a boundless love of power
but a capacity to use it well; they both lacked any real concern for the people; they both were administrative saviours
of their nation without being in any sense its moral benefactors; they both executed large jobs and exacted large
remuneration. Walpole's cynicism, however, is his own,
and the product of an eminently modern temperament. He
was under no illusions whatever concerning the kings he
served,[4] the Parliaments he controlled, the oppositions he
flouted, the country he safeguarded; nor, one would hazard,
concerning himself. He ascertained that men are vain, self-
interested, and stupid, and proceeded to act on the information; no doubt he was grievously limited in not thinking
that men could be anything else. But his cynicism can only
have deepened when proposals he had most reason to be
proud of, such as his Excise Bill, convulsed the nation with
rage, whereas measures of which he had most reason to feel

---

[4] It is worth noting that George II referred to Walpole, *before* he became King and perceived his minister's usefulness, as a "rogue" and a
"rascal," while saying of him afterwards: "He is a brave fellow; he has
more spirit than anybody I ever knew." Similarly Walpole, prior to their
entente, had called Queen Caroline a "fat bitch."

[49

ashamed went unchallenged. And his ego can only have
swelled from observing the costly mistakes of others. The
famous observation ascribed to him, that every man has his
price, is something he never said; of specific men on a specific occasion he remarked: " All these men have their price."
But I see no reason to suppose that he would have gagged
at the more sweeping condemnation. As Lecky says, he accepted the maxim that government must be carried on by
corruption or by force, and deliberately chose corruption.
And we have the truer key to his cynicism and to its justifi-
cation in Walpole's saying that he " was obliged to bribe
Members not to vote against, but *for* their conscience."

Most of Walpole's peccadilloes can be excused as based on
sound political expediency. Where he must be gravely and
lastingly charged is for leaving political morality where he
found it, and political malpractice worse than he found it.
He, again like Marlborough, was not anything of a great
man. He is rather a great spoke in the philistine wheel and
a heavy stone in the capitalist edifice. That, historically
speaking, is as important with regard to Walpole as his unrivalled parliamentary efficiency, his establishment of government by party, his creation of collectively responsible
unipartite ministries. For hand in hand with the phlegm
and grossness of his Hanoverian masters went Walpole's
coarse materialism. It was, as conduct goes, a vast improvement over the hole-and-corner stealth of the Harleys and
the Bolingbrokes. Walpole, to his credit, moved in a direction away from the vicious impeachments, the festering ran-
cours, the intemperate revenges, the whispering cabals of
Stuart governments. He did so for two commendable reasons: because he was modern-minded and because he was
not vindictive. Simply as a human being he is likable, where
his grandiose predecessors are not. We are all familiar with
his joviality, his obligingness, his lack of pique, his filthy
talk, his belly-laughs, his zest in riding to hounds, his falling
asleep so soon as his head touched the pillow. If not great-

Horace Walpole by J. G. Eccardt

NATIONAL PORTRAIT GALLERY, LONDON

Robert Walpole by J. B. Vanloo

NATIONAL PORTRAIT GALLERY, LONDON

hearted, he was stout-hearted, open-handed, healthy; and he leads us out of stuffy royal closets into the open air.

Nevertheless, if his conduct is a great improvement over the venomous shams of the preceding age, his policy, when sounded to its depths, represents nothing more admirable. He foreshadows the national future, politically, morally, culturally. Far from checking, he sped on an oligarchical spirit that was to devour modern life, that was to brush aside whatever may have been good in the aristocratic tradition with its devotion to the land, its paternalistic conception of the landlord, its " inner check " of hereditary honour, its arrived rather than *arriviste* character; a spirit that, as in Walpole's day it was gobbling up trade, was soon to exploit the vaster resources of the Industrial Revolution. Walpole's merit is that he made England prosper; his vice, that he made England value prosperity too much. And culturally this man who, when out of power and in declining health, confessed he could get no pleasure from reading; who patronized none of the arts (except to buy pictures as a financial speculation) and failed to befriend or assist the creative minds of his day — culturally he incarnates all that is most arid and philistine in English life.

To indict Walpole personally for tendencies far vaster than himself is, in one sense, beside the point. The full rise of the moneyed classes to power, the shabby moral delinquency of several generations, the soulless impulses of a complacent nation of shopkeepers, Walpole could never, whatever his influence or ideals, have seriously deflected. But by so egregiously representing all these things, Walpole is the clear exemplar of his age; and if not altogether sound, it is at least convenient to chalk up a score against him as a symbol and a protagonist.

2

IT was Walpole's good fortune, it was indeed his necessity, to have at his back, while so many powerful men opposed him, the influence of the court. If Walpole preserved the House of Hanover, it is equally true that the House of Hanover preserved Walpole. Each rendered the other an indispensable service, and each recognized — though Walpole cynically — the other's usefulness. The determined minister entertained of his royal masters no high opinion, and though he depended upon their support and manœuvred for their goodwill, he only let them think they had their way. But this, on most occasions, was enough. They had no great desire to meddle. What principally interested them was Hanover and money and their mistresses; they were not precisely frivolous kings, but they were not precisely *English* ones either. They were temperamentally pliant, as no Stuart ever was, to the doctrine of constitutional monarchy. It has often been weighed just how important for England was the fact that George I could speak no English. In consequence he did not preside, as Anne had done, over Cabinet meetings, or attend Parliament, or send dispatches to ministers. He got through the day's work by talking dog-Latin to Walpole. Thus the royal isolation, however much on the cards, was accelerated from the throne. With George I the old royal veto on Acts of Parliament ceased: Anne might write threateningly: "*La reine s'avisera*," but since her day English monarchs have gone no farther than: "*Le roi le veult*." George I, though he could make himself personally offensive to his subjects, failed to make himself politically dangerous to the country. In his own way he was a man of sense. Though a tyrant in Hanover, in England he could practise moderation because he felt no ties with her. She was nowhere in his blood and not often in his thoughts; he must always have regarded his coming to her as a lucky draw in a lottery. His being's heart and home was Hanover, whither he hastened as soon as it was decent and sometimes when it was not. London was never more for him than a business address.

A grosser, more phlegmatic, more insensitive man, with a heavier *echt Deutsch* taste in everything from food to women, it would be hard to imagine. In Hanover, when young, he had married his witty, lively cousin Sophia Dorothea. She early loathed him and involved herself passionately with a Danish count. Her indiscretion proved her undoing: one of George's old mistresses spied upon his wife's young lover. The lover was waylaid and assassinated; Sophia Dorothea was locked up for life; and George consorted happily with two hacks, Madame Schulenburg and Madame Kielmansegge. Both came with him to England, where Schulenburg acquired the title of Duchess of Kendal and the nickname of The Maypole, and Kielmansegge the title of Countess of Darlington and the nickname of The Elephant. They came and went as he did, and like him were happier in Hanover, but better compensated in England. Both the King and his favourites were formidable; both must needs be propitiated; and both could only be propitiated by money. Bribes and perquisites were common. It was the Duchess of Kendal who was meant to profit by the monopoly of Wood's Halfpence, which precipitated an uproar in Ireland and drew forth Swift's impassioned *Drapier's Letters*. Again, it was through paying twelve thousand pounds to the Duchess's niece that Bolingbroke conspired to get back to England. They were a greedy group — greedy to spend, but greedier still to hoard. Schulenburg's first words on English soil were unintentionally prophetic. The King, after Anne's death, arrived belatedly from Hanover with his spectrally thin and monstrously fat consorts in tow. Their appearance provoked hoots, whereupon Schulenburg leaned out of the coach and cried: " Good pipple, what for you abuse us? we come for all your goots." " Yes, and our chattels too," someone called back from the crowd. Twelve years later, when George I expired, his Duchess packed off to Hanover loaded with plunder.

The court, it may be surmised, left something to be desired. It was in his social capacity that the King was most unpopular. He did not like the English, he did not understand them, he was unable to talk with them. He was elderly and awkward, and as unimpressed as he was unimpressive. And he was the first of the Hanoverians, though by no means the last, to raise commotion through family quarrels. There had never been any love lost between himself and the Prince of Wales: George II is said to have hated his father for so mercilessly punishing his mother, for tearing up his mother's will drawn in favour of her son, for being unwilling to designate him regent while the father was at Hanover, for trying to make a will of his own disinheriting the son from the Hanoverian throne. George I hated back fiercely. One over-obliging courtier even went so far as to suggest kidnapping the Prince of Wales and taking him to America. A final breach had arisen between the two over a christening, when George I chose one godfather for a child who died in infancy, and George II another. The Prince, as a result, was banished the court and took up hostile residence with his wife in Leicester Fields. There migrated all the politically disaffected as well as most of the youth and wit of London society; and there the future King became the centre of a predatory opposition which resisted all that the King espoused. It was no wonder that when the father died in 1727, the Walpole who had enjoyed the old King's favour should have expected the new King's ill will. He counted on extermination no less than his enemies did. But matters righted themselves almost at once. The new King, for all his soldierly, royal, and German airs, was not his own master. He was managed, and with perfect diplomacy, by the Queen. The Queen knew Walpole's value, and Walpole remained.

George II conceived of himself as an Englishman and

though, like his father, he much preferred Hanover to London, he desired to make his presence in London felt. The two strategists who reduced him to almost a political cipher let him bellow and blow to his heart's content; no man was ever more happily deceived. "Charles I," he once told a large roomful of courtiers, "was governed by his wife, Charles II by his mistresses, James II by his priests, William by his ministers, Anne by her women: who do they say," he demanded, under the delusion that he was asking a rhetorical question, "governs now?"

The Queen, who governed George then and always, played a strange role and led a strange existence. The daughter of a Margrave of Ansbach, Caroline was educated under the guidance of the intellectual Sophia Charlotte, her future aunt and the grandmother of Frederick the Great. The pupil absorbed a certain culture, was introduced to certain eminent men, and continued long afterwards, as in the case of Leibniz, to maintain a correspondence with them. Offered marriage by the future Emperor of Austria, she refused so brilliant a match because she refused to turn Catholic. But her Protestantism foundered at the same juncture, for by comparing the two religions she lost faith in both. Her reward was to become in time the Queen of England.

Her irascible, impatient husband — of marked courage on the battlefield, of marked petulance in the palace — richly esteemed her. He said at her death that no other woman was worthy of buckling her shoe. He proceeded during her lifetime to browbeat and unnerve her at every opportunity, to lose his temper when she kept him waiting, to grumble if she became ill, to taunt her for being too feminine, to sneer at her for being too wise, to inflict on her the duties of a nursemaid, and to harangue her in the capacity of a whipping-boy. In all this she had not only the wit to pacify, but even the patience to endure him. Nor was the end yet, since his esteem for her went farther: he made her his confidante in the matter of his mistresses. Whenever the fascinations of Henrietta Howard, inside the palace, palled, Caroline seconded the King's desire for the tonic companionship of Madame Walmoden at Hanover. Unembittered, however disillusioned and exhausted by the wry part she played, she clung to the King because for one thing, it is said, she loved him; because, in whatever mattered, she had power over him; because she knew, beneath a surface irony, that his esteem for her was genuine; and she humoured him because, for reasons more obscure, she had honestly at heart the nation's good. Nothing reveals their relationship so well as that amazing scene at Caroline's deathbed when the King, after pooh-poohing the fatal illness that the Queen had tried to conceal, at length was faced with the truth. A love that had never included devotion now convulsed him with tears. The Queen urged him to remarry. " No, no," George answered in French, sobbing at every word, " no, I shall have mistresses "; and Caroline: " Ah, *mon Dieu, that* needn't prevent you from marrying! "

The court had considerably more tone than its predecessor. George II, unlike his father, enjoyed pomp and display. At his coronation the Queen " had on her head and shoulders all the pearls she could borrow of the ladies of quality at one end of the town, and on her petticoat all the diamonds she could hire of the Jews and jewellers at the other." In the days before George II became King, they had gathered round them, at Leicester House and at Richmond, some appearance of wit and lustre — charming maids of honour, clever noblemen like Chesterfield and Hervey, and such writers as Pope and Gay. The young women seem to have been exceptionally bright facets of the court life; such unkindly critics as Pope, Hervey, and Chesterfield unite in praising them, and one of them, Mary Lepel, Hervey married. Two others, Mary Bellenden and Henrietta Howard, were alluring to the future King. Bellenden presumably had " the scandal of being the Prince's mistress without the pleasure, and the confinement without the profit." She appears to have withdrawn unscathed in favour of Howard. Howard, it is thought, succumbed. Her amiability and grace won her a group of distinguished hangers-on; but unlike the Kendals and Darlingtons, who would do your business for a bribe, the future Lady Suffolk — as Bolingbroke, Gay, and others were sadly to learn — was without influence. The petulant stingy King held her, in the small affairs he could dominate, on short leash; and the Queen, with her unwavering support of Walpole, rendered her helpless in affairs of state.

George II, though without social decency, was not without character. He pigged it, and played the bully and braggart; he was inclined to be vindictive; he had his father's greed for money and less than his father's willingness to part with it; and his petty selfishness, puerile in any man, was ridiculous in a king. But, by not resisting his slovenly day-to-day appetites, he could the better resist the more serious temptations to which the kingly Charles I and the courtly Charles II had succumbed. In so far as he was allowed to rule at all, he chose to behave — or was brought round by the Queen to behave — with moderation. A nonentity, he was also for his day the pattern of a constitutional monarch. Warlike, and at his best in the field, he deferred better than the rest of the country to Walpole's policy of peace. He was presumably truthful, for on someone's saying that the King did not lie, his highly cynical minister was content to say: " Not often." Most graceless of boors, he had the sharp, shrewd mettle that sometimes goes with boorishness. Both George I and George II, who had no sense of style, no turn for elegance,[5] were undeceived by the blandishments of such things. When Walpole wisely urged the first George to receive the repatriated Bolingbroke and listen to his highfalutin diatribes against the Government, George reported on them to his minister as " baga-

---

[5] " I hate all Boets and Bainters," said George I, and he was said to get really angry at the sight of a book.

telles." Similarly George II somewhat injudiciously called Chesterfield a " tea-table scoundrel."

George II, who had hated and quarrelled with his father, also hated and quarrelled with his son. In the case of Frederick Prince of Wales, history repeated itself in several particulars. The final rupture, like that between the two Georges, came about through the birth of a child. When his wife's labour for George III began, Frederick defiantly bundled her out of Hampton Court and up to London, with Caroline following after. For such a misdeed Frederick, like his father, was banished the royal presence and like his father became the centre for the opposition. The hatred on both sides, and it engrossed the Queen, was furious. Caroline cursed the day Frederick was born and wished he would drop dead of apoplexy. There were the old efforts to depose the heir from the throne of Hanover. The same law was laid down that whoever visited the Prince was *persona non grata* with the King. The schism produced all the old social nonsense that had been practised, in Anne's reign, by Whigs and Tories. Frederick espoused the light operettas of Lincoln's Inn Fields; the King sat freezing over Handel at the empty Haymarket. (So few others froze with him that Chesterfield remarked he would not go to the Haymarket for fear of intruding on the King's privacy.) A reconciliation between George and Frederick was at one stage effected, but without noticeable results. The breach was widened by disputes and grievances over money. Perhaps the best quality the Stuarts ever had was that of loyalty between fathers and sons: what stands out among their eighteenth-century successors is a lack of it. The four Georges were forever quarrelling with one another.

But George I and George II, in their passive, oddly obedient way, left behind them a very different England from that which the Stuarts bequeathed. Meagre and untidy as were their courts, they yet mark the early stages of a court life gaining in social, while losing in political, importance.

There could be brilliant courts in England for the future, socially resplendent courts or socially stiff or socially tame or socially crude ones; but never, except for a while under George III, a court politically powerful. Parliament had superseded kings. Hervey, in George II's own time, wholly scoffs at the doctrine of divine right, and says " it became the interest even of the princes on the throne for three successive reigns to expel it," and that " the clergy, who had been paid for preaching it up, were now paid for preaching it down." There was still to be some clash between kings and ministers; there was still a minister's need of his king's support; there would be stubborn rulers, complaisant statesmen; there would be confederacies and oppositions. But no longer could the throne put forth inflexible commands, nor could plots originate in the royal closet beyond the power of others to compass or hold in check.

CHAPTER V

ARISTOCRATS,
WITH A PORTRAIT OF
ONE OF THEM

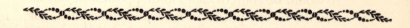

Aristocrats

NEVER MORE, perhaps, than at the beginning of the eighteenth century was London the capital of England. It was already a great city rebuilt on the ruins of a great fire, and nowhere in the whole island did any other city even faintly rival it. Bristol, the second city in England, was just one fifteenth its size. London ranked with Amsterdam as one of the world's two greatest trading centres; with Paris as one of its two proudest centres of intellect. It was the seat of government, the home of royalty, the heart of business; there fashion was set, praise bestowed, scorn discharged; and the rest of England had no choice but to acquiesce or be in the wrong. The rest of England, to be sure, was different in its character, divided in its pursuits, and sometimes opposed in its opinions; and where politics and religion entered in, these opinions might have to be deferred to. But of what was written, acted, or sung; of what was danced and displayed, hawked about or allowed to lapse; of everything by which we greet life and are prone to remember it, London was the final if not the only judge.

The City itself was virtually independent of the nation's laws. It was almost haughtily self-governing, and Westminster — which in those days lay outside the city limits — knew it must keep its distance. One recalls how even in the time of Charles I, when the King sought to impeach Hampden and five others for high treason, they escaped into the City and remained there safe and inviolable. Always Parliament looked to London for encouragement and support; and if London seemed displeased, Parliament grew concerned. On more than one occasion the City threatened to cause trouble, either by forcing Parliament's hand or by paralysing it. At Anne's accession, we must remember, all the wealthy burghers and half the persons of quality lived close to the City gates, with mansions around Covent Garden or in the Strand, or with comfortable quarters over their shops and offices. The movement was only then afoot to spread fashionably westward. In the course of half a century villas were to spring up along the river, all the way from Chelsea to Richmond, and parklike squares were to be laid out in Bloomsbury and Soho, or in Mayfair and Belgravia.

But in retrospect Westminster seems inseparable from London, as even then geography and charters alone divided those who lived equally at court and in coffee-houses, or who legislated on week-days at St Stephen's and worshipped on Sunday at St Paul's. Social life engrossed all the avenues of the city: the river lay at one's door to carry one down to Hampton Court or up to Greenwich; men ran footraces in the Mall and rode horseback in Hyde Park; coaches lumbered out to Kensington and sedan chairs carried ladies abroad for their shopping. And this is only the London of the elegant faded engravings; there was a plainer London as well, very prosaic and unpicturesque; and a foul, miserable London kept for the most part out of sight, but which Hogarth and others were to preserve for us.

The polite world, hoarse though it was with cries of Whig and Tory and in quarrelling first over war and then over peace, was undergoing a gradual change in manners. England under Queen Anne, desiring to be correct and seemly, looked hesitantly into the glass of form. For more than half a century she had been running to extremes, and neither at one extreme nor the other was her behaviour commendable. When the austere Puritan world that produced a Milton ended, it gave violent birth to a debauched Restoration which produced Rochesters and Buckinghams. This was perfectly natural, for, as Macaulay said, the profligacy that leads to an age of strict morals is never so great as the profligacy that follows one. Too little liberty under Cromwell led to too much licence under Charles. The Restoration, moreover, was as cynical as it was pleasure-loving, and far from practising virtue, did not pretend to any. We recognize its character from the theatre, in which it found its best outlet of expression, and which ran largely to plays about fops, seducers, adulteresses, and cuckolds. Infidelity was taken for granted; the interest lay merely in the twists and ruses by which it was carried out, and the laugh lay in insolently deceiving some middle-aged dullpate of a husband. In so far as Restoration comedy has a villain — in so far, that is, as it has a stock figure to hoot at — the role is allotted to the cuckold.

This attitude could not last. It was not a matter of people becoming more virtuous. But such cynicism, one must say cynically oneself, was too much for people's normal wish to appear better than they are. Nor, for that matter, can a merely heartless laughter keep on renewing itself. Decorum and correctness were bound to reappear, if only as theoretical rules for playing the game; they represented social qualities which put no pressure on a man's morals, but a considerable premium on his deportment. It was by such reasoning that the celebrated Augustan age, which enjoys a reputation it far from merits, came into existence. It was Augustan rather in what it professed to be than in what it was, for only in the very best of its art did it succeed in realizing its ideal. On the whole, society under Queen Anne was simply hypocritical, and not very gracefully so. There was too great a gulf between the stiff punctilios of form, the gross degrading flattery, the sleek homage paraded on the one side; and the shiftiness, the squabbling, the immoderacy, and the back-stabbing displayed on the other. It was a makeshift age lying as it did between one that had callously shrugged its shoulders and another that would deftly raise its eyebrows. In the next and greater era of English society, life is almost altogether artificial and hypocrisy has become a graceful habit; the clothes, as it were, fit the man. But early in the century society is only a bad compromise between the indulgence of natural instincts and the practice of empty forms.

The patrician world was narrow, but perhaps not so narrow as one might suppose. The middle classes, as much through their inability to speak its language as through any overt snobbery from above, were, it is true, excluded from it. But the well-born could mingle with the high-born. Country squires' sons coming up to London could maintain their footing with the sons of lords; and country squires' daughters might marry them. Nor were distinguished names all ancient ones. A century of shifting political fortunes had raised part of the gentry to the nobility. Within " natural " bounds there existed a free and easy intercourse to which, in addition, men of talent were almost always admitted. Congreve, Addison, Steele, Swift, Pope, Gay, Prior, Vanbrugh, Kneller, Newton, Bentley not only advanced their careers through patronage but became the friends and even the intimates of their patrons.

The amalgam of Caroline profligacy, Gallic tone, hotheaded politics, and the first pencillings of modern thought produced a race of aristocrats who resemble, more than anything else, quick-change artists. The variety of their interests and amusements is staggering. There were not simply bookish lords, at home in one another's libraries; or rakish lords who stole one another's mistresses and exchanged tales of conquest over a fourth bottle; or horsy lords stamping about their stables and scrutinizing next month's card at Newmarket; or political-minded lords who devoted their lives to safeguarding the future of England. Nor was it that one man of brilliant parts drank too much, and another whored too much, and another gambled too much. Without giving sleep a thought, any of a dozen men might go round the clock, transacting business over breakfast, galloping for two hours of a morning in the park, waiting on a great lady in her boudoir, translating a satire of Juvenal before afternoon dinner, drinking two bottles of port before he rose from table, exchanging impromptu verses at Button's or White's, holding Parliament spellbound for an hour and a half, and, when the House rose at midnight, managing a hoax or brawl before banging at some courtesan's door to stay with her till dawn. To call these men rakes is to forget that they were scholars, statesmen, wits, polished social figures also: if they trifled and fooled as wantonly as the debauchees at the court of Charles II, they worked as hard and as well as the most spotless of the Victorians.

Considering their feats, there were an amazing number of them; but of the actual society of their time they made up only the minutest part. Though its members as a class had an uncommon quickness, few had any real brains or stamina. The dissipated moral tone of the day tended to make society depart widely from its self-chosen classical norm, and to reveal, whatever its talent for veneer, no inner balance. In whatever direction it went, it went too far. Its worldlings tended to be, on the one hand, not manly but brutal; and on the other, not sensitive but effeminate. Almost all the *habits* men formed were bad ones. They ate and drank far too much: gout is overwhelmingly the upper-class disease of the eighteenth century. Their pranks were heartless and their jests insulting: callousness is perhaps the chief upper-class failing of the eighteenth century. At their worst these boorish aristocrats, so keen to detect a fancied insolence in their inferiors, were themselves as insolent as any high-born stage villain. But the beery fathers got themselves sons who could beat them at the game. The "bloods" under Anne and the first Georges chose to assert themselves by bedevilling the public. Their high spirits form a part of that roast beef and Old England which those who sigh for it might not have relished. The most famous doings were carried on in the reign of Anne by a gang known as the Mohocks or Town Rakes. They scared nocturnal London out of its wits, assaulting women, rolling people down hills in barrels or trussing them up for the night and sometimes, in their drunkenness, even gouging out eyes.[1] It is not to be supposed that these Indians were so numerous or savage as they are sometimes made out to be; but in an age long on highwaymen and short on lamp-posts, the mental havoc they caused was widespread. They terrified Swift and unnerved Sir Roger de Coverley.

Set against the boors and bullies were an equal number of fops who minced along the London streets like so many Bunthornes. Here the desire of the age for delicate manners found expression in the form of caricature. Young lords led practically the life of young ladies. They woke up languidly to sip their early-morning chocolate and at last, after several hours' grooming, went forth for a sight of the town, wearing velvet and satin and lace, and quite likely carrying a muff "to keep their hands at an even temperature." They haunted the boudoirs and drawing-rooms of women of fashion, paying highflown compliments, inventing double-entendres, spreading gossip, and elaborating on scandal. They courted the reigning belles, whom, like Sir Willoughby, they would willingly die for but could not possibly arrange to meet at eleven the next morning. They seem to

---

[1] Four of them were once arrested, but when it was discovered they belonged to aristocratic families, they were fined 3*s*. 4*d*. apiece and turned loose.

have lingered on into a pasty middle age when, in fops'
language, they ogled and simpered and leered, preserving
their faces with paint, their figures with stays, and solacing
themselves for the loss of youth by becoming inveterate
card-players. Yet not all of them were utterly frivolous: in
an age of ready expression half the fops were wits, and
some of them writers and successful courtiers. Lord Hervey,
a pillar of George II's court and its most vivid historian,
had genuine acumen; and as he is perhaps the least worthless of the whole group, has surely been the most vilified.
He and Lady Mary Montagu used to exchange witticisms
with Pope and got enough the better of him to win his un-
dying hatred. Hervey, in the character of Sporus — " that
mere white curd of Ass's milk " — lives on as hero of the most
violent piece of abuse ever written by the greatest master of
it. But Pope's insults are the wrong note for both Hervey and
the fops; the right one was struck by Hervey himself when
asked if he would have some beef. " Beef? Faugh, don't you
know I never eat beef, nor *horse*, nor any of those things? " [2]
And the whole race of macaronies have been characterized
as too dainty to walk and too precious to commit their
frames to horseback.

The fops provide a kind of weak link between the men
and the women in high society, since for the most part the
two sexes followed separate pleasures, or the same pleasures
separately. The want of a lustrous court life was one reason;
the constant pressure of politics another; the state of English
manners, unripe for the amenities of the salon, a third. Except for the fops, men went mostly their own way. We hear
of no great hostesses or distinguished dinner-parties, but of
lavish hosts and stag suppers. And whatever men's purpose
in coming together, drink would keep them there. Never,
before or since, has upper-class England drunk so hard. It

---

[2] This notable sensibility reminds one of the make-up of a worthier
soul, the poet Gray, who, when asked if a certain dog was his, answered:
" Do you suppose that I would keep an animal by which I might possibly
lose my life? "

was almost obligatory to be a two- or three-bottle man at any single session. The inconspicuous Methuen Treaty with Portugal in 1703 began an era in English history which has yet to end: it signified " Circulate the port " on a giant scale. Under Anne, port put claret and burgundy in the shade. It became the great Whig wine and the grandfather of gout. Owing to the war with France, claret and burgundy were considered unpatriotic; though the Tories, who opposed the war, drank claret as a party defiance. In any case Whigs and Tories drank themselves into loquacity and on, at times, into stupors. Englishmen, then as now, appear to have needed liquor in order to shed their reticence: Addison, perhaps the greatest talker of the age, sober was no talker at all. Indeed, it was on wine and brandy that much of the nation's charm was exerted, its wit turned loose, its politics transacted, and its business performed.

Yet the real centre of London social life, even among the high-born, lay elsewhere; and where it lay explains perhaps best of all why men and women consorted so little together. As it is the most familiar, so the coffee-house is the most important feature of Augustan society. Fifty years before Anne came to the throne, there were not half a dozen coffee-houses in London; before she died, there were three thousand of them. In the course of her reign they mounted to their peak of popularity, then slowly began to die out, or to be transformed into the very different English institution of clubs. The coffee-house professed and achieved a function, very much that of the Continental sidewalk café of today, which it utterly failed to perpetuate. Englishmen might or might not have liked its inherent democracy; they could not live up to its free-flowing social spirit.

But coffee-houses, while they lasted, flourished inordinately. Existing at all levels, they catered to all tastes. They were open to everybody. Ever since Restoration days, when Dryden kinged it at Will's, they had offered the obscure a chance of seeing the great, the dull a chance of listening to the brilliant, the poor a chance of rubbing shoulders with the rich. " You have a good Fire," wrote a contemporary, " which you may sit by as long as you please; You have a Dish of Coffee, you meet your Friends for the Transaction of Business, and all for a Penny, if you don't Care to spend more." There too the newspapers were available, and the latest gossip; there one spent one's leisure at one's ease; and when one had nobody to talk with, one could always sit quietly and eavesdrop. The policy of first come, first served provided a basis on which all classes could mingle. Noblemen engaged writers in talk; merchants clutched at crumbs of news from politicians. Any conceivable topic might become the theme of a Socratic dialogue, whatever it might lack of Socratic calm and lucidity. Only one subject was taboo — religion.

In an age of pronounced convictions, men of similar feelings very soon fell into the habit of frequenting the same coffee-houses: one knew that one would encounter scholars at the Grecian,[3] or musicians at the Smyrna, or wits and writers at Button's or Will's, or businessmen at Lloyd's. Lloyd's, where ship news was then first brought and wine and merchandise were auctioned off " by the candle,"[4] grew, from its coffee-house origin, into the great organization of today. One knew, too, that at Button's, for example, where Addison held his " little senate," politics were exclusively Whig, or at the Cocoa Tree exclusively Tory.

The coffee-houses possessed a character not at all like that of the taverns; they were places rather of convenience than pleasure, and they aimed at decorum. Fines were imposed for swearing or quarrelling; cards and dice were banned; and though liquor was served along with coffee — and pretty barmaids were shrewdly hired to dispense it —

---

[3] Where a fatal duel once arose over a Greek accent.

[4] The custom of auctioning " by the candle " was then widespread, and retains an interest: When the bidding started, an inch (usually) of candle was lighted, and the last man to bid before the wick went out was declared the buyer.

men seem to have gone elsewhere to get drunk. In truth the coffee-houses offered a change of air, an opportunity to vary and broaden one's existence; kings were as disposed to go to them to look at cats as cats at kings.

There grew out of the coffee-houses, already in the age of Anne, the first adumbrations of London's famous eighteenth-century clubs. The better-born wished for a comfortable place in which they might dine and drink together and were soon commanding private rooms — and then the whole house — on particular evenings. It was in one such place that the most celebrated of all dinner clubs before the age of Johnson, the Whig Kit-Cat Club, used regularly to meet. Its narrow roster claimed three dukes, twice as many states-men in power, and such men of letters as Congreve and Ad-dison. Politics inspired the first toast; wit, the second; and last and longest, gallantry. Each member had to compose an epigram to a Whig beauty, which was engraved on his glass. The Duke of Kingston having chosen his eight-year-old daughter, it was demanded that she be produced; and to the Kit-Cat came the future Lady Mary Montagu to prove her beauty and reveal her cleverness. So notable a Whig club soon had its counterpart, in brilliance if not in fame, among the Tories. The Scriblerus, with Harley in his most attrac-tive role of literary patron, with Bolingbroke, with Arbuth-not, with Atterbury and Swift, threw formality to the winds, went satiric and (when Swift was out of earshot) bawdy, tried its hand at hoaxes, burned off the nation's flesh with its acid comments, and toyed communally with the first vague outlines of what afterwards, under one hand, became *Gulliver's Travels.*

But it was rather in fashionable St James's Street that the club life of the future, with its special associations, got its start. In a London honeycombed with coffee-houses there were, with a cachet of their own, a few chocolate-houses; and the best-known of them was to grow into the best-known of all the clubs. At White's, from the very first, assembled the young bloods and men about town. At White's the greatest " vice " of eighteenth-century high life — greater even than the prodigious drinking — fast got under way, so that inside a generation the casual chocolate-drinkers had bowed themselves out and the gamblers had walled themselves in. But already in Anne's day men went there to drink and gamble. It is true that Bolingbroke's contemporaries did not play so high or sit so long or lose so much as Selwyn's and Fox's, and were drinkers first and gamblers afterwards; but play was frequent and steep, and in a slightly different sense never at any time was mere card-playing more the rage. Dozens of games, now completely forgotten, had their brief innings; basset, ombre, bezique, spadrille, and whist had a steady run; while, as we shall soon see, women outdid men in both enthusiasm and endurance.

But it was at the races, where the English patrician could indulge his twin loves of horseflesh and betting, that the Augustan world found itself happiest. It was at the races that the Queen herself came most to life. Anne bred her own horses, raced them under her own name, gave gold cups, and was an habituée of Newmarket. Godolphin was as much addicted to racing as was Walpole to riding to hounds; and it was equally a passion with men like the Dukes of Devonshire and Bedford. Purses ran as high as three thousand pounds, while individual bets might go higher. On the other hand, the *spectacle* of the racecourse was quite unknown: there were no brightly dressed jockeys, no grandstands or refreshment stands, and there was seldom more than a thin line of spectators.

As apart from their country sports, men of fashion were not without athletic amusement in town. The riffraff loved and the bloods excelled at sword-play. It was an age of duels,[5] when every man wore a sword; and as it was an age supremely quarrelsome as well, men did not take their prowess lightly. The most celebrated duel of Anne's time —

---

[5] Duelling was illegal, but the law was almost never invoked.

Noon by William Hogarth

most celebrated, perhaps, because it is vividly described in *Esmond* — was that between the Duke of Hamilton, on the eve of his setting out for France as Bolingbroke's ambassador, and Lord Mohun, in which both men were killed. But there were many others. And when lives were not at stake, men played for wagers with buttoned foils, craving excitement even while they displayed finesse. Tennis was fashionable, cricket just beginning to be noticed, and ice-skating, which appears to have had no country vogue at all, was a diversion of the town. On occasions when the Thames froze over, if we can judge by old engravings, the whole city seems to have gone skating in holiday style. Men took exercise indoors also. Addison, we know, swung Indian clubs and dumb-bells; and at home and at some of the more thriving coffee-houses " the gentile, cleanly and most ingenious game of billiards " was a common pastime.

In terms of sex, the profligacy of Restoration times, when the King himself was almost the leading rake in England, was somewhat less indulged and much less advertised; but high life still meant high living, and society was notoriously licentious. Marlborough was not admired, but ridiculed, for being a faithful husband. Far from becoming a model, Addison's supposed virtuousness was long a target. Pope, very pathetically, sought to make himself out a roué. Bolingbroke, the greatest statesman under Anne, frankly sought to out-Rochester the greatest debauchee under Charles II; and Walpole, the greatest statesman under the first two Georges, lived openly in sin. The brilliant young Duke of Wharton, rakish heir of a brilliant rakish father,[6] burned out his life when he was hardly thirty. Cowper, perhaps the finest type of public man in the reign of Anne, was indicted for bigamy. There was hardly a man in public life whom the stress of political malice did not succeed in embarrassing by scandal; and as all the great men in society were accused

---

[6] The author of *Lillibullero,* which to Purcell's music had " whistled " James II off his throne.

of having mistresses, nearly all their wives were accused of taking lovers. As has been said, intrigues did not distress the morality of the age; but they paid a certain tribute to decorum. It was not yet required, perhaps, that you dissemble your sinfulness, but you no longer chose to flaunt it.

A curious distorting mirror of the life of lords is found in the life of their servants. Every fine household had, besides its cooks and sweeps and scullery maids, besides its coachmen and pages, a quota of footmen; and the footmen were their masters' apes. Though not tricked out so gorgeously as they would be later in the century, they wore pretentious livery; the best wore, not wigs, but their own hair, which they powdered; and their snobbishness must have outdone that of their employers. They moved in their own sets, and took rank according as they served it. Among themselves, indeed, they often assumed their masters' titles, and it was common to hear them milord one another, or refer to the Duke of Y or the Marquis Z. While waiting for their lords to emerge from Parliament, they would gather outside and hold mock sessions which exceeded the real ones in pomp and gravity. Their privileges were sometimes extensive. It was the custom for gentlemen to send their footmen ahead of them to the playhouse, to claim and hold their seats till they themselves should arrive; and the servants, on being turned out of their places, straightway mounted to the gallery, where they sat free, by prescriptive right, for the rest of the performance. The footmen, as a matter of fact, could make or break a play: if they liked it, they clapped and cheered vigorously, causing others to fall in line; if they disliked it, they hooted and booed and stamped their feet more vigorously still, and either by their ability to turn the tide or more probably by their determination to stop the show, ruined its chances. Often their masters down below had to hiss them into silence; sometimes they even had to be whipped. Theatre proprietors were furious at the power wielded from the gallery, but were impotent to curb it.

The position of footmen was most formidable in the matter of tips or, as they were then called, vails. Visiting a great house for even an hour meant facing a squad of men in livery who complacently expected to be tipped. There at the dining-room door they stood, perhaps ten or a dozen of them, and you parted with two or three guineas with whatever grace you could muster. A poor country clergyman dining with his bishop might have to give up the best part of a week's income; a poor poet dining with his patron might have to give up all he had in his purse. To pay a visit of some duration at one of the really great establishments involved a truly large outlay of money. It is told that whenever the Duke of Ormonde invited a certain impoverished nobleman, he sent tipping money along with the invitation. Steele, oftener broke than in funds, once had to run the gantlet of footmen without a shilling in his pocket, and only saved the day by his ingenuity: he invited them to come and see one of his plays. One good thing must be said, however, in defence of this embarrassing exploitation: the footmen received extremely low wages — perhaps six pounds a year — and needed more money than they earned. And as time went on, and the practice of vails grew more and more irksome, masters had to give in by raising their servants' pay.

Other servants in upper-class households seem to have fared less well. We hear less about them, but we know that they too were underpaid. In one sense they were not overworked: every large house had rather more people in service than it needed. Two types of domestic deserve a moment's comment. It was no longer usual, but not yet entirely obsolete, for great ladies in the age of Queen Anne to employ male valets who tripped about the room with a mirror in their hand, or spent a whole morning combing their ladies' hair. And the black page boy who stares out at us from Beardsley's drawings for *The Rape of the Lock* added a touch, at once exotic and chic, cultivated by every grand establishment. But these Negroes, who often, like dogs,

wore silver collars around their necks, were not servants;
they were slaves. If sometimes they achieved the standing
of household pets, more often they must have been given
ignominious jobs to do. A few were lackeys, but the most
were drudges. Certainly the better part of them were always running away, only to be apprehended and brought
back. But the majesty of the law was shortly to assert itself
and abolish slavery in England forever.

The first decades of the eighteenth century were the great
age of dukes. They represent the coming of the peerage to
its second full growth, the first, which was feudal, having
been cut down by the slaughter of the Wars of the Roses.
It is interesting to trace the progress of the great new Renais-
sance families — such as the Russells or the Cavendishes —
as they mount from baronies through earldoms and marquis-
ates to the final lustre of the strawberry leaves. The special
traffic in dukedoms began to flourish during the Restoration
when Charles II made dukes of his bastards. At the accession of George I the peerage had been much extended, and
there were many more dukes in England than there are
today.

The English aristocracy, though often taking itself just as
seriously, yet has never held itself quite so high as the
French: it has freely consorted and intermarried with the
gentry, patronized the more presentable type of artist, and
even legalized its dalliance with the stage.[7] And if at the
beginning of the eighteenth century its world was narrow
and intensely selfish, it was by no means omnipotent.
Strachey has pointed out how Voltaire, in France, giving
no great provocation, met severe punishment at patrician
hands; whereas in England Pope mercilessly abused the
great and came off scot-free. Voltaire, indeed, was much
impressed by the state of English manners and the degree of
English liberty. But Voltaire's enthusiasm must be guardedly

---

[7] For example, Lavinia Fenton, the original Polly Peachum of *The Beggar's Opera*, married the Duke of Bolton.

received, coming as he did from a place that had injured him, and meeting as he did men who esteemed him highly. It is inconceivable that an age racked by indecent political feuds and zealotic religious upheavals should have been truly libertarian. The Whigs, it is true, pleaded for tolerance, but it was only the thriving middle class they wanted tolerated. Walpole, among men who counted, was the most forward-looking man of his day; and the best really that can be said for him is that he preferred peace profiteering to war, and government by bribe to that by arms. Sunderland, we know, styled himself a republican and professed a desire to see monarchy abolished; but Sunderland was never in favour with Queen Anne, and talked rather to startle than convince. Aristocratic sentiment, on the whole, lay in the other direction, so much so that at times it was comical. When Bolingbroke was negotiating the Peace of Utrecht with France, the Duke of Shrewsbury refused to be co-ambassador with Prior because it was degrading to associate on equal terms with a mere writer and commoner. And no one can forget the stories about Somerset, "the Proud Duke," whom even his contemporaries looked upon as ridiculous. He *never* spoke to servants, but communicated with them by signs; he never travelled without having the roads cleared of bystanders; he never permitted his own children to sit down in his presence, and when (while he was dozing) one of them did, she forfeited twenty thousand pounds of her inheritance as a result. His second wife was of high but not the highest rank, and happening one day to tap the Duke playfully with her fan, he turned on her in anger, saying: "My first wife was a *Percy*, and she never dared to take such a liberty." We may rejoice that when Somerset was seeking a third wife the widowed Sarah Marlborough turned him down.

Sarah stands perhaps at the top of female high society of those days, or perhaps altogether outside it. Her position, penetrating into a world of men and politics, was as little typical as her personality. Indeed, if we except the three women (Sarah, Lady Masham, and the Duchess of Somerset) who were Anne's confidantes, the two women who were George I's bedfellows, and the one woman who suffered marriage with George II, we may almost dismiss their sex from the realm of public affairs; and — where sexual intrigue does not enter in — two thirds dismiss it from the realm of men's pleasures. Women somehow led a life — by no means restricted, by no means Oriental — of their own. It is true that times were changing, and that during the very years we are considering the role of women was becoming ampler. There was, for one thing, a great improvement in their education. The Lady Marys of the beginning of the century, acquiring, as they did, some grounding in the classics and some familiarity with French and English literature, were very much a minority, and learned things chiefly by teaching themselves. Moreover, they were far from being Lady Jane Greys. The run of young gentlewomen learned little if anything — " the Needle, Dancing and the French tongue; a little Music, on the Harpsichord or Spinet; to read, write and cast accounts in a small way " — nothing else. Such an education, plainly, could only qualify them to speak as vapidly in French as they did in English. At a time when France could display its brilliant *salonnières,* and when the greatest Frenchmen sharpened their minds by conversing with adroit Frenchwomen, there was nothing in London that resembled a Parisian drawing-room. A little later emerges Elizabeth Montagu, the first of the eighteenth-century bluestockings; already there is a bit of give-and-take at the future George II's opposition court; an age, too, of clever hostesses is preparing. But on the score of personality, no high-born women come down to us from the first quarter of the century except Sarah, Lady Mary, and perhaps Gay's Duchess of Queensberry. Swift, to be sure, was always paying calls on London women of fashion and writing well of them to Stella; but Swift, for all his captiousness, was too much flattered by their attentions to be a fair judge of their talk. The real Swift, from whom I shall soon quote, knew how they generally passed their lives. And further and almost final testimony is provided by Bolingbroke's French wife, who in her boredom repeated the stupid female chatter of English drawing-rooms.

For the most part, ladies were pleasure-loving merely. Ill-educated, light-minded, irresponsible, born too early to dispense fashionable charity, they recognized but a single adversary — ennui. They might wake late in the morning (or be wakened by their restless lap-dogs) to find callers already in their bedroom, since it was the practice for them to receive in bed. But if possible they sought time to make their toilets first, arranging their hair in becoming disorder, touching up their cheeks with studied carelessness, throwing their nightgowns enticingly off their shoulders. The fops were the first persons called in during the day to amuse them. While a lap-dog or a parakeet or a monkey or a marmoset ranged over the coverlet, the young men drawled and tittered, while their hostess nodded or laughed, until it was time for them to take their leave. Then she made a second toilet and rose for the day. She might go out in a coach or a sedan chair to shop; she might just chance to ride horseback; she might step out somewhere from her coach and greet other women on promenade. She gave a good deal of attention to the fashions. Her dresses and mantles were made from a vast variety of materials; her hats were of every shape and weight and colour. She tripped about on incredibly high heels; she might have a fancy to pad herself out with false hips; she might affect, now and again, extremely mannish clothes. The day was not long past when women in society wore masks; but as they were now forbidden at the playhouse, and suggested indiscretion generally, they were no longer chic. In their place, however, women, when they wished to go unobserved, wore veils. They wore muffs too and furs, and carried sunshades and umbrellas. Men wore muffs also, but considered umbrellas effeminate.

The fashionable London dinner hour was growing steadily later. It had once been set at noon, but by 1700 was more likely to be two or three o'clock, and ten years later Steele puts it, in the *Spectator,* at four. Formal dinners were long and wearisomely elaborate, but a plain one — taken *en famille* or with a guest or two — consisted of two courses only. But even this meant both meat and fowl, followed by both pastry and pudding; and one washed down one's food with a great deal of wine. Brandy and more wine followed. Men were accustomed to linger at table for hours, in racy or pretentious talk, to rise tipsily at length for the night's activities. Women, on the other hand, frequently rose with dispatch to get down to what Sarah Battle approved of as the chief business of life. Women were likely to sit from late afternoon till the small hours playing cards. Sometimes men played with them, but it was because men so often followed pleasures of their own that their light-minded wives clutched at this one escape from boredom. They gossiped, of course, as they played, and Swift has set down, in the poem where he imagines his own death, the substance of their conversation:

> *The Dean is dead (and what is trumps?)*
> *Then Lord have mercy on his soul.*
> *(Ladies, I'll venture for the vole.)*
> *Six deans, they say, must bear the pall.*
> *(I wish I knew what king to call.)*
> *Madam, your husband will attend*
> *The funeral of so good a friend?*
> *No, madam, 'tis a shocking sight,*
> *And he's engaged tomorrow night!*
> *My lady Club would take it ill*
> *If he should fail her at quadrille.*
> *He loved the Dean. (I led a heart.)*
> *But dearest friends, they say, must part.*

His time was come, he ran his race:
We hope he's in a better place.

Women do not appear to have read much. There was a
vogue for tattle, and they presumably looked at the news-
sheets; but the appeal of the *Spectators* and their like was
rather more among the middle classes. The period was just
beginning in which a kind of trashy and lewd romance,
hardly to be described as full-fledged fiction, was circulated; twenty years after Queen Anne's death there was a
steady flow of this sort of stuff, not disdained even by the
brilliant Lady Mary. The memoirs of important people
(whom people in society had known personally) were read
eagerly, as they are read eagerly by the social world today.
If they did not strike too close to home, they were apt to
be the most amusing reading of all. But there is no evidence that the typical great lady of the period felt any summons of culture. Among the social qualifications, book-
knowledge was barely reckoned in. On the other hand,
quickness and brightness in talk were decidedly called for.
Even a harebrained gadabout might have a true turn for
phrase; and though women in comedies of the period talked
with very short breath, and tergiversated badly, and pecked
at one topic and darted round twenty, their words were
often pointed, and their stings showed wit as well as malice.
The talk of society women, both among themselves and in
mixed company, was — as is well known — extremely free.
There is no reason, indeed, for calling it anything other
than foul-mouthed. Lady Mary, who though a coarse was
not a vulgar woman, makes no bones in her letters of writing
as she thinks; the Duchess of Marlborough could swear like
a trooper; and Queen Caroline, whose virtue was unsullied,
talked filth by the hour with Walpole. There was little, too,
that young ladies did not know. To illustrate what society
was then like and what it afterwards became, we may use
once more Sir Walter Scott's famous anecdote of his grand-

[79

aunt. She had read in girlhood, along with everyone else, the novels of Aphra Behn; happening sixty years later to pick one of them up, she felt shame in reading as an old woman what she had once heard read aloud in a London drawing-room to a group of people in the highest society.

Like the men of that age, the women were inordinately cynical.[8] They believed the worst because, from their own lives, they had reason to believe it. There was something really absurd to them about sexual virtue; there was something spurious about idealism and high-mindedness; it never entered their heads that morality should prove an inconvenience to living, that ethics meant more than a far-fetched way of supposing things. That people should be poor and overworked and overburdened, that they should live under conditions of disgraceful squalor, lose their jobs over trifles, go to prison for years for peccadillos, that character was anything you should wrestle with, that power was anything you should feel responsible about — this was the nonsense of cranks. In modern society those who command are well aware that they must hold what they have against a clamour from without; but among the typical aristocrats of Queen Anne's day, privilege was taken wholly for granted. Such people felt that their position derived from something obscure and ultimate like God. There was not the faintest need for justifying themselves, hence it is not surprising that they were quite free from cant. They had an uneasy code among themselves, fractured time and again by the political violence of the age; they deported themselves with a certain wilful elegance that had about it little of good breeding or good nature. Society, if untroubled by the masses it trod upon, had no serenity at its own level, because every patrician, of no matter how great name, had to be something of a careerist. At a levee following the accession of George II, Walpole's wife entered a room where all the

---

[8] " Caress the favourites, avoid the unfortunate, and trust nobody," counselled Lady Mary.

women present pointedly turned their backs on her; then the news leaked out that Walpole had been retained, and when his wife withdrew the ladies bowed so low before her that she could have " walked across their heads." Almost all the aristocrats with brains spent their life misusing them. There were many men who, like Bolingbroke, were nominal deists or indifferent churchgoers; yet every one of them professed strong party views on religion. There were many men who, like Bolingbroke, had enlightened ideas about politics; yet not half a dozen practised them, and fewer still held fast to them in a crisis. And Swift and Steele aside, where shall we find among men of letters who climbed into the great world anyone with the interests of humanity at heart? The exemplary Addison, for instance, was content to murmur the smug Christianity that takes flight at the first sign of trouble.

The age of the Augustans, stamped for two centuries as dignified and elegant, was in truth as noisily quarrelsome an era as history will reveal. The political animosities stand foremost, and bitter and brutal they were; but on the social side quarrelling was not less intense. The drawing-room differences were unending; and to thread one's way through high society without being embroiled for giving offence — or for refusing to take offence — must have been a hazardous business. Mary of Orange at her death was not on speaking terms with her sister Anne; Anne at her death was not on speaking terms with the Duchess of Marlborough. The first two Georges were actual enemies of their sons. Steele fell out with Addison, Bolingbroke with Harley; Lady Mary fell out with half her friends, Sarah with almost everybody she came to know, Pope even with people he did not know. The list could be much extended. We may judge the character of these people not only because they quarrelled, but by what they quarrelled over and by how they behaved in their quarrelling. It was hardly a dignified age, or even an age of moderation and good sense, when people recognized no better tone for their friends than one of unctuous flattery, or than one of unbridled vituperation for their enemies.

Lady Mary

LADY MARY MONTAGU was the most interesting English-woman of her century. Very much of a personage and some-thing of an eccentric, she revealed in both roles — as it is reasonable to expect — an independent mind. Her eccen-tricity, manifest in a few anecdotes by which she is now chiefly remembered, has been a good deal overstressed: it only arose because she had more sense than the people around her and was bored by them. Her personality, though it had its inconveniences while she lived, is exactly the sort that is welcomed in the dead. It is pungent, it is many-sided, it is never blurred; and it reaches us at first hand in those volumes of letters which Lady Mary wrote in her firm eighteenth-century English.

She began life by rebelling against the place assigned to women in the intellectual world of Augustan England. It was a despicable place,[9] and women were groomed for it by despicable educations. Englishmen never brought back from the Continent any appreciation of the European salon; they were content with the growing tradition of the coffee-houses, which was in time to become the fixed tradition of the clubs. London had its handful of clever women, and its indomitable Sarah cutting across the bias; but no true *salon-nières,* no accredited bluestockings. The more fortunate women of good birth were turned loose on the elegant trifles of the town; the less fortunate had only the horsy diversions of the country. It was in a barn of a country house, indeed, that Lady Mary — the daughter of a lord

---

[9] Lady Mary herself once said: " The one thing that reconciles me to the fact of being a woman is the reflexion that it delivers me from the neces-sity of being married to one."

who became a duke — was abandoned to grow up. She was determined, however, on an irregular but solid education of books, and later on an irregular but solid education of life. As a young woman she fell in love with Edward Wortley (the Montagu came later), who most unwillingly reciprocated her feelings. He was as amazed by her schoolgirl erudition as if " he had heard a piece of waxwork talk." But this prim, cautious Whig liberal whose infinite capacity for taking pains fell far short of genius could not be easy in his mind about the prancing, impetuous Lady Mary and adopted the tone of a moralist toward her. There could have been no worse way of losing the lady. She grew inflamed with passion that was partly pique; and when her father opposed the match because Wortley would not settle money on unborn heirs who might turn out to be dolts, Lady Mary pushed him into an elopement.

They moved among lords, statesmen, and wits. Wortley was a great friend of Addison, and his wife became as great a friend of Pope's. Montagu's star rose with the Whigs', and he was presently sent as ambassador to Constantinople, whence Lady Mary wrote the most famous though not the most engaging of her letters. On their return she earned a place among the world's benefactors by being the first Occidental to adopt and champion the Turkish custom of inoculation against smallpox, a heresy that shocked everybody until it was shown to work.[10] Then for twenty years Lady Mary divided her time between society in London and the wits of Twickenham. Her immense acquaintance was just large enough not to cramp her instincts for quarrelling; she quarrelled systematically, with gusto. Her most famous battle was, of course, with Pope. It is said that he made love to her and was laughed at; it is also said that his mother lent her some sheets which were returned unwashed. Either story is plausible, since Lady Mary was as physically dirty

[10] Smallpox proved, on the whole, the worst affliction of the eighteenth century.

[83

as she was mentally derisive. Pope's revenge was to asperse
her poetically as " Sappho "; and a description of one of
Lady Mary's friends as

" Poxed by her love and libelled by her hate "

is a fair example of his aspersions.[11] With the rival personality of her age, the Duchess of Marlborough, Lady Mary
appears to have got on very well. Doubtless each looked
the other unflinchingly in the eye, which engendered mu-
tual respect; or perhaps they got along by abusing Robert
Walpole, whom they both hated.

In middle age Lady Mary left England and remained
away for twenty-two years. She and Montagu had long
since ceased to matter to each other; now he could matter
to her a little again, as someone to write letters to; writing
letters was necessary to her, where love was not. And from
the Continent she sent, to her husband and her daughter
and her friends, a steady stream of correspondence packed
with her impressions of a constantly altering life. She moved
about from place to place, staying six weeks in one and ten
years in another; she met everybody; she heard, or over-
heard, everything; she moralized; she satirized; she ridiculed; she devoured all the good books of her day and most
of the trash; she held a sort of caravanserai court; and in
untroubled exile grew old and ill and unsightly. London's
charms vanished for her, not even producing nostalgia, and
it was by playing the great lady against a provincial back-
drop, and by sometimes ceasing to be a great lady, that she
found the world diverting. At sixty-nine she confessed she
had not looked into a mirror for eleven years. When past
seventy, she crept back to London only just in time to die.

She had lived her life in a richly personal way, using her
patrician prejudices as a kind of alpenstock while she

---

[11] For a more damaging insult of equal conciseness, we must go to
Dr Johnson with his: " Sir, your wife, under pretence of keeping a bawdy
house, is a receiver of stolen goods."

tramped up and down Europe, but never bothering to be fussy or correct, and never influenced by public judgment. She was an aristocrat in that she knew what she wanted and went and took it without apologizing; and perhaps she was also one in the narrower sense of distrusting sentimentality and defying ennui and in seeking, if only in her letters, to please. " To please " did not mean to consider people's sensibilities — she could be coarse, small-minded, cruel — but to have a care for their time and patience and convenience. How often, for example, she apologizes in her letters for talking about herself! Such shrewd courtesy is very typical of the world in which Lady Mary had been bred and of which, spite of all her oddities, she was a representative part. Its responsibilities were confined to the drawing-room; its generosities stopped with playing the patron or requiting compliments. To people like Lady Mary privilege was second nature. All her values, accordingly, are theoretical ones. Like others of her time she could notice things that were amiss — such as the cruelty and chaos of war — but when she saw a battlefield bloody with corpses, though common sense said it was ghastly, common sense also said it was unavoidable. Lady Mary had the sharp insight of her age, and the blunted moral awareness.

And to please meant for the most part to please oneself. Lady Mary had to find pleasure at the cost of conformity and the cost of tact. She hated bores, and she fled from them. She hated fools, and she quarrelled with them. She tired of London, with its shams and repetitions, and she made of Europe a kind of Protestant convent. Like Horace Walpole, she gradually reached the point of paying her most enjoyable visits by letter. And in letter-writing she found her greatest social gift. What went on before her eyes was well enough: she could mix with the people who trooped in and out of her wayside Continental habitations and divert new company with old anecdotes; fuss half-humorously over her gardens, look at scenery and ruins and churches, and taste the ceremonial parties wherewith the provinces mimic the great world. But all this was chiefly something to put in her letters; she wrote on and on, happily, indefatigably.

Pope and Horace Walpole between them, out of unequal dislike, have very plausibly condemned her. Clearly she had faults enough. She was certainly unsparing of faults in others, and sometimes meanly rancorous; she appears to have been close; she had no magnanimity, no pity, no sweetness; and if prejudiced report is true, she was repulsively unclean. There is the unforgettable story of her being told at the opera that her hands were dirty, and of her answering: " You should see my feet." [12] She was limited too in ways that the age was not conscious of and that Pope and Walpole had no notion of rebuking her for. She exploited her position, she was cynical, she was sometimes highhanded. And where the moral and mental attitude of her age coalesce, in *hardness,* she is no exception to it: she is hard as nails. No mother ever saw through a weak and worthless son more shatteringly than she did hers; or wrote to his father about him with less emotion; or handled him more like an inquisitor. If Lady Mary had no temptations to be notoriously bad or ignoble, she was certainly never inclined by her moral sense, or warmth of heart, or delicacy of feeling, to be one whit better or kinder than she had to be.

Yet Pope, at least, went too far. There was nothing outrageous about either her character or her conduct; nothing of the virago or the villain; nothing, so to speak, purely gratuitous in her misdoings. She had too much good sense, too much humour, too much vestigial taste, too much inner health, too much social poise, not to draw the line, for the most part, at excess. She was not at all of the Duchess of Marlborough's kidney. She could appreciate very keenly the nuances of everything except human feeling. Her mind was

---

[12] It was not, of course, a very clean century. Pasquin was said to have " died of a cold caught by washing his face."

sharp, perceptive, stinging, alive. It was interested in a great many more things than the age itself was; it had a superb turn for piquant trifles; it was witty. It survived, quite unimpaired, the coarsening influences of her bohemian travels. Her mind alone really interested her as she grew older; her vanity was gone, her sense of propriety was going. She did not care a straw whether she was being named in all sorts of grimy liaisons because men came and went in her house, and sometimes stayed. Nobody cares now either, but it is hard to conceive of an aging slattern who did not look in her glass for eleven years being very much concerned about lovers, or much encumbered with them. She lived as she did because she cared much less about participating in life than in observing it.

Lady Mary is of that class whose character and ideas fall short of deserving extended critical analysis, yet go beyond the possibilities of competent paraphrase. Half a dozen women of her age had the rather commonplace cynical wit she sometimes descends to: "Mrs West . . . is a great prude, having but two lovers at a time: I think those are Lord Haddington and Mr Lindsay; the one for use, the other for show." Half a dozen others retailed particular description as well as she; or wrote as easily of London social life; or commented as entertainingly on people and books; or had as worldly and cosmopolitan a tone. Yet Lady Mary is far and away the superior of them all. She wrote better, she saw more, she knew more; she had certainly more vivacity and spirit. She cannot be paraphrased because she is inseparable from her letters. They are no longer much read, though it is hard to imagine why, unless it is because Lady Mary is no longer much thought of as a "writer." Yet, though not the best, they are perhaps of all eighteenth-century letters the least given to arid patches; and they are certainly, for their bulk, the most varied. They formed the only book that Dr Johnson in later life read through — simply for pleasure — to the end. It profits nothing to discuss in what particular ways they are inferior to Horace Walpole's letters, or to Gray's, or to Cowper's. The real point is that they present vivid pictures of many kinds of society in terms of a most expressive mind; and that they are the only way of knowing a woman who, lacking glamour and magnetism and charm, is yet the best platonic female company that eighteenth-century England can provide.

CHAPTER VI

SHOPKEEPERS

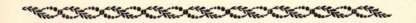

THE MIDDLE CLASSES, rapidly expanding, belonged to a different and far more restricted world. Here and there, springing from their ranks, a merchant or financier, a professional or military man, swam up to a place among the aristocrats; but to an overwhelming degree class lines still held. It was political rather than social gains that the commercial classes had chiefly made since the days of Elizabeth; politically — in London at least — they exercised great power. They voted, held office, owned property; they made up the city's backbone so that no politician could ignore, or statesman override, their interests. The Bank of England, which was a vast creditor of the nation itself, exemplified middle-class power at its strongest; but at lower levels the small tradesman and the small manufacturer were conscious of their liberties, alive to their opportunities, emancipated from feudal fears and patrician threats. Parochial these petty bourgeois might be, even in London; they knew their place and accepted it; but they were not to be imposed upon, even in their own interests.

London was perhaps then, as now, a middle-class world run on middle-class standards. The poor were shut out from most of life, and the great shut themselves in; it was those somewhere between who ensured the success of the coffee-houses, filled the theatres from the second night on, built sturdy Nonconformist churches, stayed in town winter and summer (they had no lust or experience of travel and vaguely disapproved of it), sent their sons to the plain homespun day schools, thronged Vauxhall and later Ranelagh, saved their pennies while the aristocrats squandered their pounds, and went to bed at night in comfortable rooms over their shops. They depended upon one another for their livings, and in the main had the same politics and something like the same religion. They constituted a London that has not too greatly changed, whereas the London of Bolingbroke or Chesterfield has been almost annihilated.

It was to the more prosperous class of cit, harbouring the snob and moralist in his breast, that Addison and Steele particularly addressed their *Tatlers* and *Spectators*. It is not the moderation of perfect breeding that the *Spectator* espouses, but satire at the expense of the grotesque in favour of the genteel. The middle classes had not much instinct to be silly, and Addison showed them how silly people could be. Nor had they, as did their betters, an inveterate tendency toward wickedness and cynicism; they were well satisfied to be preached at, to be shown how virtue might be profitable, or conformity remunerative. They were by no means Victorian; they were creatures of a coarse and downright age, not easily shocked; but deep down was the ghost of an idea that things in life could be shocking. It was they who modified in time the licentiousness of the playhouse; who, while lords got drunk on port, and wretches on gin, drank nothing headier than beer; who clung, for all it might hurt them, to their thriving Nonconformist faiths; but who also under guidance improved their table manners, adorned their homes, wore Sunday velvets, enjoyed being aldermen, hankered after coaches, and sought in every genteel way to rise in the world.

Still, this is not to deny that for the most part the middle class led a very unexemplary existence. Many of them were bawdy and brutal; many more were sots and gamblers. The wives of aldermen, who in Restoration comedy had always been unfaithful, were now more likely virtuous, but not so the aldermen themselves. Sluts overran the town. The tavern, a much less well-conducted place than the coffee-house, was on the whole a middle-class hangout. There men went to carouse, and might end the night in a brawl, or laid out flat in a stupor of drink. It was no uncommon sight to see someone, in the early morning, brushing his teeth at a ground-floor window. "A tavern," wrote a contemporary, " is a little Sodom where as many vices are daily practised, as ever were known in the great one." And he goes on to list the types who come there: libertines "'to drink away their brains"; aldermen " to talk treason and bewail the loss of trade "; gamesters, and sober knaves who " walk with drunken fools "; bullies and cowards, sots and beaux, fools and spendthrifts. Allowing these to be the designations of a preachy satirist, we may still suppose that they create a fairly true picture of the ungodlier give-and-take of middle-class enjoyments.

Like their betters, many of these people gambled immoderately. Though they were not Dukes of Devonshire who could lose an estate at a single game of basset, their stakes must have been correspondingly high: in one case a man gambled away his wife with her own consent. Though a few professional gamblers like Beau Fielding and Macartney moved in upper-class circles, it was the middle-class world that was most preyed upon by sharpers and swindlers. More popular with the citizen than even dice and cards were the lotteries. Perfectly legal, though perhaps not perfectly straight, they were run off in unending successions, and offered high prizes — thirty-six thousand pounds for one recorded example. It was by means of a lottery, indeed, that Queen Anne's debts were once partly paid off. An ardour for lotteries led straight — and with fatal consequences

— to an ardour for stock speculations, and soon every man
in London who had cash in his pockets was investing it
in the South Sea Company or any of the dozens of similar
projects which followed in the South Sea's wake. Swept
off their feet by vast if vague promises of gain, men literally
invested their money in anything. There were companies
for making salt water fresh, for extracting silver from lead,
for importing jackasses from Spain, for trading in human
hair, for promoting perpetual-motion machines; there was
even a company, liberally subscribed to, which merely announced "an undertaking which shall in due time be revealed." Calamity followed. The South Sea Company, by
far the greatest of these projects, roared its stock up to
over a thousand per cent of par, whereupon the promoters
sold out. At once the price of the stock began catastrophi-
cally to fall; the price of all other stocks followed suit, and
a panic resulted. Insignificant Londoners by the thousands
were ruined, the very props of Government seemed on the
verge of collapse. If the South Sea panic briefly cured London of a joy in speculation, it increased its itch for gaming.
What had been an upper-class became more and more of a
national disease.

There were other ways in which London amused itself —
the pleasure haunts of Vauxhall and Ranelagh, which are
like commemorative engravings of the period, coming first
to mind. One went, in the great age of the Thames, by boat
to Ranelagh, which, with its vast rotunda'd hall, offered refreshment and dancing, music and fireworks, and the opportunity of seeming, among so many dressed-up people,
to be in the swim. The aristocracy, which had made the
river popular, had latterly abandoned it to lesser breeds. A
society woman seen there was too likely to be mistaken for
a woman of the town. There is no doubt that at places
like Vauxhall and Ranelagh the immoral temptations were
many. These pleasure resorts maintained their respectabil-
ity, however, until late in the century; perhaps the most ac-

curate description of them is that they were oddly democratic. London amused itself, too, at freak shows and fairs.
The fairs — Bartholomew Fair, Southwark Fair, May Fair —
lasted anywhere from two to six weeks; there were booths
and sideshows of every description — tightrope walkers, ac-
robats, merry-andrews, Indian rope-dancers, and perhaps
wild animals. But the great place to see wild animals was at
the Tower of London, whose lions became the rage; we owe
to them the phrase " to lionize." Finally, there was the annual Lord Mayor's show, all parades and pageantry by day,
all boisterousness by night. Perhaps it should be pointed
out that the boisterousness was rather plebeian than middle-
class.

The life of the citizenry was not so richly coloured that
special occasions had no meaning. Baptisms and funerals
might both be elaborate events, though weddings were seldom fussed over. It rather mars our conception of the solid
burgher to realize that among middle-class young men marriage was something to avoid and oppose. To these not too
distant heirs of Restoration profligacy who revelled in their
fun, there was nothing at all welcome in the thought of
settling down. Fathers had to go to a good deal of trouble —
and expense — to marry off their girls, so that marriage set-
tlements were often the real, and young men's high spirits
only the fancied, bone of contention. Once terms were
drawn up, the weddings were quickly and quietly conducted. So-called " private " marriages had almost a clandestine touch about them, and it was not unusual for a
young couple to become parents before they were known
to be husband and wife. To the middle classes the old style
of wedding, with its lavish nuptial symbolisms, came to
seem showy and costly; and it may too have been so lively
as to turn the home of the bride's family into a shambles.
There were good reasons, certainly, for dispensing with it.

The London citizen was part of an altering, though not
yet altered, world. Much from the past still lingered on —

street-criers,[1] astrologers, pedlars with a dozen hats piled high on their heads, men with swords on their hips, Negro slaves, bull-baiting, smallpox. But much that was ubiquitous in 1700 had almost disappeared by 1750. The belief in witchcraft, for instance, steadily declined, and prosecution for witchcraft altogether ceased. Inoculation against small-pox, introduced into England by Lady Mary in 1722, though slow in winning over even the medical world and though militantly opposed by the Church, made gains, and after 1746 far greater ones. Sanitary conditions were improving: there was better sewerage and plumbing, and purer water; streets were widened, straightened, raised, more evenly paved, and by night much better illuminated. Medicine, however, had far to go. The list of complaints and diseases — many of them carrying old-fashioned names like " scour-ing and flux," " appoplex and suddenly," " soremouth and thrush " or " the rising of the lights " — was an interminable one. The infant mortality was appalling, and increasing. The treatment for most disorders was still bleeding and purging, to which were added all varieties, from the proved to the fantastic, of medicines. There were a few eminent doctors: Sir Hans Sloane, whose botanical collection be-came the basis for the British Museum; Sir Samuel Garth, a much loved man and the friend of Addison and Congreve; Radcliffe, damagingly immortalized by Prior and notorious for not turning up at Queen Anne's deathbed. But however eminent, none of them seems to have been in any sense great. They were highly successful, however, and lived in splendid luxury. The profession itself, judging by its stand-ard fee of a guinea a house visit, appears to have been well paid. There were many private hospitals, sanitariums, and madhouses; the handling of mental patients sounds suspi-ciously primitive if we are to judge by such a phrase in an

---

[1] No one needs to be reminded of the smells of eighteenth-century London, but the noisiness — from all kinds of hawkers, bell-ringers, and jostling carts — was almost as unpleasant.

advertisement as " A dumb young man broke his chain last
Wednesday night." One sign of medical progress — except
that it seems more likely a proof of Hanoverian indifference
— may be adduced: the laying on of royal hands for " the
evil," a custom originated by Edward the Confessor, died
out with Queen Anne, the lady in " diamonds and a black
hood " who " touched " the infant Samuel Johnson.

One virtue of the times was a vast improvement in communication. It is easy to see what a difference was wrought
by the birth, in 1711, of the London penny post, which not
only made letter-writing to points in or near the city cheap,
but made deliveries regular and frequent. The rise of newspapers dates from this same period. In the seventeenth century there had been a few London gazettes of sporadic
appearance and very limited contents; but it was the peri-
odical literature of Queen Anne's reign — whether political
in purpose, as with the party organs presided over by Swift,
Defoe, and others, or social, as with the *Spectator* and its
competitors — which spurred journalism on. The first daily
paper in London, the *Courant,* appeared in 1702, and by
1724 there were three daily and five weekly papers in London, besides ten which appeared three times a week. Very
soon after, the *Gentleman's Magazine* ushered in a kind of
reading-matter which before the middle of the century was
to become the fashion, and before the end of the century
the rage.

Side by side with this went a growth in middle-class education. Shopkeepers' sons, though not sent to the great public schools, had more and more at their disposal the London
day schools, where tuition was cheap, or such famous free
schools as Westminster, the Merchant Taylors, Greyfriars,
Christ's Hospital, and Paul's. There must have been thirty
or more such free institutions where all subjects then judged
important were taught. These included arithmetic and math-
ematics, English, French, Latin, Greek, and Hebrew, history, geography, and accounting. It was all very unspecial-

ized, and competent to equip students, as one prospectus announced, " for the University, Study of the Law, or other Business." Girls learned to be genteel, and among other things were taught to " make waxworks, japan, paint upon glass, to raise paste, and make sweetmeats and sauces." Two other matters attracted wide notice. One was penmanship, which the eighteenth century, like the nineteenth, held in high if not ridiculous esteem; the other was stenography. Many methods were taught, each professing to be the quickest and easiest; and whoever is interested in the minor culture — and the minor characters — of the age may find amusement in the career of John Byrom, that jack-of-all-trades who cultivated, among so much else, the science of shorthand.

The middle classes, though a heterogeneous race, unequal in wealth and prospects, in manners, morals, education, and religious feeling, had on the whole those characteristics which at once consolidated and overwhelmed a later England. Walpole's peace régime not only advanced their interests but also hardened their outlook. They were at bottom neither an imaginative nor an emotional people. They had principles rather than ideals; they believed rather in things which had been attained than in things yet attainable. They were possibly of that stock which innocently regards its own moment in history as the culmination of all progress. Thus, while struggling jealously to preserve their liberties, they struggled much less to enlarge them; while eager to exploit their opportunities, they were not forward in creating new ones. Then as now your shopkeeper could not safely be ill-used, but it was not so much that he wanted to take something on as that he refused to give anything up. Such conservatism, such literal-mindedness as it were, has been the source of preserving a stationary class under the form of a democracy. These people were rapidly becoming the backbone — and the safety-valve — of England. They welcomed a life within enclosures; as upper-class manners grew suaver, theirs grew more rigid; as upper-class morals grew more artful, theirs grew more intolerant. They even felt self-conscious with those men of similar origin who, by their adventurousness and greed, their foresight and assurance, climbed into a larger world — an " upper middle class," an oligarchic, an exploitative, an empire-building world. Uneasy as capitalists and unwilling to be workers, the great shopkeeping population of London became a hardy visionless race, with a hatred of being cockneys and a fear of being gentlemen.

THE POOR

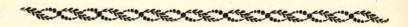

THE ANNALS of the eighteenth-century poor are short enough; no doubt to their more fortunate contemporaries they seemed simple also. Of the virtuous poor — before the great novelists of an approaching age took a hand in the matter — we have almost no reminders at all. Defoe, Swift, Pope (when he descends there purely for contrast) paint a world that is mean, sordid, deep in squalor. What good and hard-working people there were lie hidden in the blackness they inhabited; in the picture that catches the light we can almost describe poverty as crime. The second quarter of the eighteenth century would seem to represent the depths of lower-class life. All other classes were prospering; England herself was in train of becoming the first nation in Europe. Fresh and more emancipated impulses were penetrating the country's thought and manners, and into its politics was thrust a more enlightened turn. Yet so soon as we glance downward we might better be among the thieves and cutthroats and stinking hags of Villon's Paris. The later period may have been less barbarous, but it was not less depraved.

An audacious age of crime usually means a bitter season of need and discontent. There must be many hungry people, and no desire on the part of the well-fed to feed them. A London weaver's wages, in the early eighteenth century, were roughly ten shillings sixpence, a laborer's nine shillings, a week. Where the masses were not actually trampled down, they were with much the same consequence neglected. As it was a supremely cynical and predatory age, managed by unprincipled men who scoffed at principle in others, so it was an age untouched by public spirit or philanthropy. Far from attempting to relieve conditions, the Government, with Walpole at its head, never troubled to investigate them. Prisons and slums, left all that they had been, necessarily grew worse. Private charity was at its lowest ebb. Neither the pulpit nor the press was able to exert any influence over the public conscience. It was a dark age.

Queen Anne's had been a bad but better age. A nation at war is always a more united nation, for all except those who wax fat on war are ready to make sacrifices and suffer hardships. The war, too, had provided army employment for large masses of impoverished men; and the Queen, for all her shortcomings, had some sense of responsibility toward her people. With the coming of the Georges everything conspired to distress the poor. Both sovereigns were greedy men; both were indifferent to their English subjects. An era of unequalled corruption had not only its moral, but also its economic, disasters. The South Sea Bubble, temporarily wrecking middle-class security, had more lasting repercussions on the poor. Higher up, a huge and hideous debtor class arose; the debtors, thrown into prisons or on the fringes of society, became at one stroke a part of lower-class life.

It was at this time that a phenomenon swept over England which in some respects was the most ruinous of all the events of the eighteenth century. Gin-drinking became the mania and undoing of the poor. Not twenty years earlier gin-drinking was negligible, and the London masses were content with beer and ale. But once its powers became known, it swept along an entire class, became their passion, their mainstay, their sop. It incapacitated them for whatever work they might find; it ruined their health; it threatened their sanity; it lowered their morals; it broke down their respect for the law; it built up their instincts for crime. The whole story, hardly exaggerated, stares out at one from a hundred printed and painted testimonials of the age — most ineffaceably, perhaps, from Hogarth's *Gin Lane*. " Gin," wrote Fielding, " is the principal sustenance of an hundred thousand people in this metropolis." With this terrible craze for gin, every symptom of decay and degeneracy made itself at once apparent. Gin was sold in every conceivable sort of shop, in chandlers' shops, in weavers' shops. Signs outside the actual ginshops proclaimed — satirically — that you could get " drunk for a penny, dead drunk for twopence, straw provided free." Drinkers, when they could no longer stand up, were flung into straw-covered cellars until they should come to their senses. People went homeless or swarmed in unspeakable slums; people turned to violence — robbery and rape, murder and arson; people died like flies.

The craze for gin, however, cannot be set down as the merely isolated phenomenon that historians of an earlier day made it out to be. If it led to worse conditions, it arose out of bad ones. It indicated a desperate condition of life among the poor, who felt on the one hand the wildest need of escape, and on the other an inarticulate impulse toward emotional anarchy. It was at once the most pathetic and the most tragic of proletarian revolutions — an overthrow of order by the worst means, and toward the worst ends. When gin-drinking at last achieved such horrifying dimensions that even a shoulder-shrugging Parliament saw that strong measures were called for, a very heavy tax was laid on spirits in the hope of greatly reducing their consumption. But it was too late. What ensued was not moderation, but protest in the form of riots.[1] Traffic in gin momentarily wa-

---

[1] There were many riots during the century: personal in origin, as in those over gin; political, as in those incited by the Wilkes case; religious, as in the Gordon Riots; and frequently economic, as in the Spitalfields and the Wages Riots.

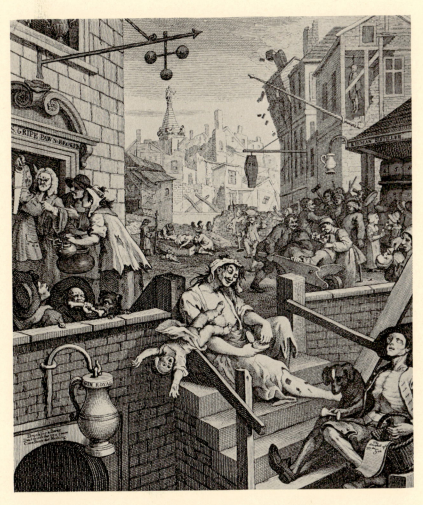

Gin Lane by William Hogarth

vered and sank; then re-arose in the form of wholesale bootlegging.[2] The bootlegging became so profitable that the Government, finding its revenue depleted, removed the preternaturally high tax on gin and substituted a preternaturally
low one. The condition of the people remained exactly the
same.

Steadily London became more lawless. The Mohock out-
breaks of a generation back, isolated and prankish, were as
nothing compared to the forays of determined ruffians, the
systematic invasions of thieves and robbers, the drunken
crimes of starving and homeless men. They wholly over-
awed the constables and the police, who slunk by them,
warrants in pocket. In any clash of arms, it was the des-
peradoes who won. More often than not, the constables
hugged the warmth of beer-houses; or, when it seemed urgent to make some arrests, arrested innocent people. The
very constabulary, indeed, were as lawless, when drunk, as
the men they were hired to hunt down; even when sober,
they indulged in petty thefts and any possible form of
blackmail. Among their quarries were some of the most romantic names in the history of English crime: the burglar
Jack Sheppard, whose two daring escapes from Newgate
made him the idol of the people, and who at last was hanged;
Jonathan Wild, hanged a year after Sheppard; the highwayman Dick Turpin, also hanged; and the highwayman
McLean, who, wearing fine clothes, sporting fine manners,
and living in fashionable St James's Street, survived these
others by many years, but came at last to the same fate.

The criminal classes were swelled out by the clergy themselves, who, in an age averse to marriage and addicted to
drink, contrived out of the general lawlessness a racket of
their own. " Fleet marriages " became a common abuse of
the times. Hard-up parsons, many of them actually in prison
for debt, ground out a livelihood by uniting helpless and

---

2 In place of neat gin, all sorts of synthetic concoctions were sold, with
names like Ladies' Delight, Cuckold's Comfort, and Bung Eye.

speechless bridegrooms to eager and spotty brides. Young men down from the universities would, in the fury of drink or passion, be hurried along to the clergymen who officiated at almost every street corner. When the fleet was in, sailors were taken in hand by prostitutes, potted with gin, and swept at the rate of two or three hundred a week into matrimony. The parsons did not merely sit waiting for trade, but had hirelings prowl the streets for customers. Viciously enough, such clandestine marriages were binding. They were performed, it is true, without a licence; but the lack of a licence did not invalidate the marriage — it merely constituted a fraud against the public revenue. To the press-gang tactics by which these marriages were brought about, there was frequently added the use of false dates and fictitious names; so that many victims who long after felt it was safe to enter into more voluntary alliances might find themselves facing charges of bigamy. Even where this did not happen, the usual outcome was either a miserable union or immediate infidelity and desertion. The marriages worked out little better even when both parties were of plebeian background. The only people for whom the system proved helpful were those who prized its secrecy or could profit by its peculiar legality; at least, among so many disastrous unions, there were also such convenient ones as the Duke of Hamilton's with Miss Gunning, the Duke of Kingston's with Elizabeth Chudleigh, and Henry Fox's with a daughter of the Duke of Richmond. And when Lord Hardwicke's famous Marriage Bill, which ended the abuse by making it illegal, was debated in the Commons, Henry Fox opposed it almost with his fists! Indeed, the bill did not become law without violent opposition. Nor did clandestine marriages at once cease; the custom was too deep-rooted, and the business in them too profitable.

If the conduct of the masses was ungovernable, if their crimes were numerous and shocking, the punishment they

met with far exceeded their wrongdoing. The backwardness of the law, the indifference of those who could have
modified it, the rapacity of those who administered it, are
no revelation to us and were nothing new in eighteenth-
century England. But the steady progress England had
been slowly achieving in so many other directions is barely
if at all reflected in her criminal system before 1740. Almost
everything that we would confidently associate with the
Middle Ages and the bloodier passages of the Reformation
was still, if on a diminished scale, part of the majesty of
the law. Reform was only in longclothes, reformers were
few and inadequate. A harsh retributive system, from which
there was almost no appeal, still prevailed. In an age when
even the great and strong, should they take the wrong political side, often found their strength and greatness futile,
what might not overtake the poor and helpless? A huge
number of offences, some of them truly venial, were punishable by death. In the reign of Anne executions were so
frequent that men made jokes about them; jokes, it must be
remembered, not about what they heard tell of, but about
what they themselves went to watch. Hanging was the
commonest but not the only form of death. Political prisoners still went to the block. Women guilty of murdering their
husbands could be burned at the stake. Men guilty of high
treason were cut down, half-dead, from the scaffold, and
disembowelled. Prisoners who refused to plead were laid
naked on their backs and slowly pressed to death under
the weight of stone or iron. It is not startling that, within
a generation, such practices would be modified; what is
astounding is that they had remained in force so long.

Prison life was often beyond description. "When first we
entered" (a contemporary is describing a prison common
room), "the mixture of scents that arose from mundungus-
tobacco, foul sweaty toes, dirty shirts, stinking breaths, and
uncleanly carcases, poisoned our nostrils far worse than a
Southwark ditch." Underfed, overcrowded, men lived in

cold and darkness, and in the most outrageous filth and want, " wearing out their life like an old shirt, the sooner the better." The drainage made them sick; vermin overran their bodies; water from the floor of their cells rose up and slowly rotted away their beds. There were instances of prisoners thrown into dungeons lying over sewers full of corpses. In such an atmosphere epidemics of jail fever [3] easily followed. All this, the natural outgrowth of the prison system, was made worse by the rapacity of the prison attendants. Debtors who could not tip them they threw into the cells of prisoners suffering from smallpox; from some of their charges they withheld food, and from others beds; they made use of irons and the thumbscrew; they neglected the sick and tortured the crippled. Small debtors, mostly poor people, were treated worse than heavy debtors, mostly dishonest ones. Men jailed on trifling counts were intentionally exposed to the companionship of the most vicious criminals. Other men, after being discharged for debt, were flung back again into their cells because they could not meet the " fees " demanded by the jailers. Even someone falsely charged and subsequently acquitted by a jury might be lugged back for failure to meet these fees.

The public was not unaware of these abuses. It caught sight, willy-nilly, of dirty spectres standing in rags behind barred windows, chanting: " Pray remember the poor debtors "; but though it sometimes tossed them a coin, it never protested their plight. Writers, to be sure, drew affecting pictures in the hope of making legislators act. But the evils were very little mended. There was almost no public pressure because, during many years, there was almost no public indignation. Almost all that was done was done by a handful of philanthropists, the notable exceptions of a thoroughly unphilanthropic age. There was Lady Elizabeth

[3] When, in 1750, judicial sessions were held at Newgate, " four out of six judges on the bench caught the infection and died, and so did forty jurymen and officials of the court."

Hastings, who lived a saintly religious life outside London and who was a liberal benefactor in educating and maintaining poor boys and girls. Berkeley, a good and humane as well as accomplished man, ignored what was directly under his nose and set about founding a Christian university in Bermuda. (Walpole promised him twenty thousand pounds, never thinking the bill would pass Parliament; when it did, Walpole reneged.) By far the most constructive work of amelioration was started by Oglethorpe, who first investigated prison life and made Parliament conduct an inquiry, and who later obtained a charter of land in the New World and founded Georgia as a refuge for debtors. This may be considered the only valuable reform project earlier than 1740, and even it applied only to certain classes of debtors. Again, only one class of debtors — those jailed for trifling sums who had served at least a six months' term — could save themselves by enlisting in the army or navy. For the rest, these men who made up such a large criminal class, and whose crime was a lack of money, were to all intents and purposes prisoners for life. We may gauge how intolerable they thought their lives, and how hopeless their futures, by the fact that many of them, clutching at straws, sold themselves into bondage on the overseas plantations. There, driven by work and manipulated into endless debt, they enjoyed the status of convicts and the freedom of slaves.

Something better, though often not much better, awaited those who, merely penniless or sick or mad, were exempted from the horrors of prison life. London had at least one workhouse where vagrants and beggars might go and, in exchange for food and lodging, do a long day's work. Here too many parish children were received, passably cared for, taught a trade, and given the rudiments of an education. " Every nurse combs her children with a small tooth comb three times a week; mends the children's clothes; makes their beds, washes their wards; and sees that the children go neat and clean and that they wash and comb themselves

[105

every day." This strikes a singularly bright note in the midst of shadows; but we are once more among the shadows when we enter the portals of Bethlehem Hospital, the Bedlam founded centuries before. There, as the hospital put it, lunatics received exemplary care; but the reports of visitors strike a very different note in which chains rattle, iron doors reverberate with thumping, and filthy-looking maniacs with bestial habits rave and yell. Among the Board of Governors — Swift was one of them — there seems to have been a humane enough instinct, but the men in charge of the patients were never members of the Board.

All the literary emphasis of the age is thrust on the most sordid elements of lower-class life — on drunkards, ruffians, beggars, lunatics, prostitutes; on the ravages of dirt and disease; on immoderate lust; on crying poverty. This, inescapably, is the master trait. It could not be otherwise when even a workman of industrious habits had to support his family on some ten shillings a week. He had to live in slums, work long hours, eat tainted food — meat and milk he almost never saw. There was always the threat of disease; there was never the chance of free medical care. There was the undermining effect of a raw, penetrating London climate — another incentive, in an age when tea was still a luxury, for soaking up on gin. Amid smells and vermin and darkness and overcrowding, the workingman could find no comfort at home, and much of his free time at night was spent on the streets or in mughouses. He had, for pleasure, the sights of London, an occasional pageant or trip to one of the great fairs; he might go to see cocks fight or bulls baited; or, like the rest of London, play cards and dice. Gambling, at his level, might well end in picked pockets and a broken head.

He had no temptations to be a moral animal. Family life exerted no pull: sons spent little time at home, daughters were driven to repeat their parents' marriages, or go into domestic service, or become women on the town. The

Church exerted little pressure: the great popular religious revivals had not yet begun; there were no influential temperance societies, no reformers to intrude with tracts and soup. The poor man lived obscurely and untended. Strength of character merely kept him clear of crime; it never spurred him on toward any such chimera as rising in the world. The English conscience, which afterwards for so long a time was to become a badge of probity and absurdity, was then not yet awake. In that age, whatever might be happening in the upper levels of society, Chaos still ruled below. The poor, in those days, simply did not believe in tomorrow.

THE ARTS

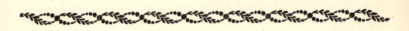

1

THE THEATRE HAD BEEN the great mouthpiece of the Restoration. It had bodied forth, with boldness and brilliance, all the lewdness and frivolity of upper-class life. But a point of view always lax and not seldom lewd was bound at length to encounter opposition; and as the seventeenth century dies, an era in the theatre dies with it. Scarcely had Congreve, the last and greatest dramatist of the period, got into the saddle when he was pulled up short by the first onslaught of the new morality. A spokesman for reaction had arrived in the person of Jeremy Collier, who in 1698, with his *Short View of the Immorality and Profaneness of the English Stage,* gave Restoration drama a furious thrashing. Thus attacked, Dryden, Wycherley, Congreve, and Vanbrugh retorted that to exhibit vice was to set a standard for virtue. It was a good retort, if an improvised one. But the victory went notwithstanding to the reformer. Congreve's next play, *The Way of the World,* was so coldly received that its author quit the theatre. The coarser pen of Wycherley had already been laid aside. And Dryden, who was as much the voice of the Restoration as Wycherley was its pulse, died with the century, in 1700.

The theatre of the next age was similar, but not the same. A more moderate tone was inevitable: people were beginning to respect appearances, and London more than ever echoed Paris. Charles II, a great francophile, had confused the taste of Paris with its immorality. But Addison and Pope, up to their necks in Boileau, took French taste more seriously. The theatre, except for bouts of sentiment contributed by Steele and of ribaldry continued by Vanbrugh, was to go erroneously classical. But correctness never got the stranglehold on the drama that it did on poetry: it simply made it ponderous. The Augustan theatre was as wavering in its impulses as the Caroline theatre was firm: far from having fixed laws, it veered with the winds of fashion; and though it has a certain value as a social document, it has almost none as art.

Indeed, all the best of it is a kind of hand-me-down from the Restoration. Vanbrugh is the playwright who has best survived, and his are the comedies most filled with the old bawdy antics. Yet if the same frivolity persists, some of the heartlessness is gone. Vanbrugh does not bait morality: he merely ignores it. He writes for an audience mindful of Collier's rebuke, an audience willing to pretend, at least, that it is shocked. Until the Queen forbade the practice, society women went masked to the playhouse when comedies like Vanbrugh's were performing. These society women were tacitly admitting that the stage was less than it ought to be — for the alderman was still cuckolded, the bewildered maiden was still debauched, and the plot still turned on an axis of adultery.[1]

The newer tradition came to life in Steele, who was somewhat the kind of dramatist that he was a man. " The comedies of Steele," wrote Hazlitt, " were the first that were written expressly with a view not to imitate the manners but to reform the morals of the age." Supremely a sentimentalist,

---

[1] As late as 1719 a nobleman's private chaplain " demonstrated " that the plays of the times offended against 1400 texts in the Bible.

Steele is the archetype of repentant sinners, forever getting into trouble through his emotions and forever trying to get out of it through his wits; spending too much money, drinking too much wine, falling too maudlinly in love, too weakly adoring his wife. Possessed of all these shortcomings, he had a conscience to match up with them, and so became, without effort, a moralist. But Steele had also what his age had not — an honest tongue and a generous heart, and he put something of both into his plays. He looks upon women, not with the old cynicism, but with something akin to chivalry; and for cuckolds shows sympathy rather than scorn. The weepyness mingled with wit which characterizes Steele's plays marks a change in the drama which is to grow and grow: as time passes, the wit disappears, to be reclaimed only by Sheridan and Goldsmith; and the sentimentalism, as specious as Restoration callousness was at any rate sincere, overwhelms the theatre until it becomes totally worthless. In Steele it is simply likable and a little uninteresting — as, to my mind, Steele was himself.

On such second-rate fare, poorly eked out with examples of frigid " classical " tragedy, Augustan London had to content itself. The theatre was not quite so popular as it once had been. Collier's attack led to others; the Queen disliked the drama on personal grounds and disapproved of it on moral ones; indeed, at one time there were fears that the playhouses would have to shut down. But on the whole these tangles must not be taken too seriously, nor must the vicissitudes that attended Congreve's, Vanbrugh's, and Steele's efforts to operate the Haymarket and the Drury Lane. The theatre was oftener up than down, and, by having an appeal for all classes, was a really democratic institution. Nearly everyone went to the play — great ladies in the first tier of boxes, merchants' wives in the second; gentlemen on benches in the pit; and in the galleries above, their footmen and the plain people. Everywhere were

women of imperfect reputation, from grandly toileted cour-
tesans in the boxes to businesslike molls under the roof.
That class of girl made famous by Nell Gwynne — the
orange wench — still hawked her fruit, engaged for rendez-
vous in whispers, and carried notes from gentlemen in the
pit, who ogled, to ladies in the boxes, who dropped their
eyes. The theatre was a spectacle and a social occasion, but
despite the blaze of flambeaus between the acts, despite
the show of dress and roll-call of names, it could scarcely
pretend to tone. Men, until they were stopped by law, used
to sneak behind the scenes while the play was performing;
the galleries seldom failed to start a commotion; young
bucks had a tendency to clown; women, to chatter. Political
feeling, too, ran very high. Most of the playwrights were
fervent Whigs and, wherever possible, injected sound Whig
sentiment into the dialogue. This, hailed with enthusiasm in
one part of the house, would be greeted with hisses in another. But sometimes the Tories, too, came into their own,
as when, near the end of the war, a topical song about
Marlborough's avarice stopped the show for a full quarter
of an hour.

The technique of stage production was still, by modern
standards, crude enough, though something of an advance
over the scenic shortcomings of the Elizabethans. There
was, indeed, a grand attempt at décor, not very ably fulfilled if we are to judge by the *Tatler's* burlesque descrip-
tions of Drury Lane: " Three bottles and a half of light-
ning "; " A sea, consisting of a dozen large waves, the tenth
bigger than ordinary, and a little damaged "; " A mustard
bowl to mix thunder with." Yet the endless failures and
bankruptcies among actor-managers and playwright-man-
agers prove that even if the age had invented better props,
it could not have paid for them. But among actors there was
more, it would seem, to be thankful for. Betterton, who survived from Restoration times, was credited with being a

genius, while Cibber — also remembered as a middling play-wright, an adapter of Shakespeare,[2] an admirable autobiog-rapher, an execrable Poet Laureate, Fielding's butt and Pope's King of the Dunces — seems to have had talent. Round the name of Mrs Bracegirdle still clings a faint bou-quet: she it was who received from a group of noblemen a purse of eight hundred guineas in recognition of her virtue, and whom Congreve addressed as Celinda:

> *Would she could make of me a saint,*
> *Or I of her a sinner.*

But until Garrick appears, there is really no name to which posterity can attach any meaning.

When we move on to the age of the Georges, two things stand out. The first is the beginning of a Shakespeare re-vival which, as time passed, was to haunt and crowd the stage like no other thing. This revival first gained impetus from the numerous editions of Shakespeare's work which, beginning with Rowe's and Pope's, followed rapidly one on another. Except as Dryden and others had rewritten him, Shakespeare had all but taken leave of the stage; now even his less famous plays were produced once more. *King John* was performed for the first time since Cromwell closed the theatres, *The Winter's Tale* for the first time in a hundred years, *All's Well* for the first time since the death of its author. A monument was erected to him in the Abbey. Shakespeare societies sprang up. Revivals became the rage. Adaptations, many of them frightful, abounded. As some-one wrote not too classically:

> *After one hundred and thirty years' nap,*
> *Enter Shakespeare with a loud clap.*

What else stands out under the first Georges is the rise of political satire in dramatic form. Under Anne, plays often bore a political symbolism and a strong odour of party; but

---

2 " Off with his head: so much for Buckingham," etc.

they almost never chose particular abuses for their theme, or particular statesmen for their target. But now the satire became personal and pointed. Among others, Fielding twice wrote political plays, one of them directed against Walpole. More and more, indeed, satire turned its guns on Walpole. In *The Beggar's Opera*, the greatest stage success of fifty years, Macheath, Lucy, and Polly Peachum were judged by common consent to stand for the Prime Minister, his wife, and his mistress Molly Skerett. These repeated stings became sharp enough to make Walpole rush a Licensing Act through Parliament [3] which gave to the Lord Chamberlain those powers over the stage which he enjoys even today. *Polly*, Gay's sequel, was thus flatly denied a production, and much else of a similar nature met a similar fate. The Lord Chamberlain was kept much busier (as was intended) freeing the stage from libel than from lewdness. But it did not lose much from his vigilance. The theatre was moribund from anæmia. Nor was it to be refortified for a generation to come.

2

The Beggar's Opera brings us at once to the world of music. If, between the end of the seventeenth century and the beginning of the eighteenth, English drama underwent a change, then inside the same period English music underwent a revolution. In that short time music, as a native art, expired. It had long flourished: there had been the splendid anthems and chorals of Tudor times, the lovely madrigals and airs and music for the lute of the Elizabethans; a little later had come the masques. In Puritan days it is true that music was robbed of an outlet in the Church and as a public entertainment, but good composing and good playing remained alive in the home. Then, following the Restoration, there arose in Purcell one last great musician to pour forth,

---

[3] Chesterfield vigorously opposed the act, as putting " a tax upon wit."

as it were, an English swan-song. His *King Arthur* (to a libretto by Dryden) and his *Dido and Æneas,* though perhaps not opera in the modern sense, are the only opera on which England may really look with pride.

England now, like the rest of Europe, turned to Italy for aid. The Italian opera ruled supreme. Faint echoes of its sway had already been felt in England a generation earlier, as we know from the diaries of Pepys and Evelyn; but it was not before Anne that any Italian opera was performed upon a London stage. At first it was very impurely rendered in a hybrid form, English composers touching up Italian scores, and the recitative performed in the adopted language while the arias were sung in the original. At first, too, it was by no means well received. There were still those who wished for a native opera and who tried to create one. There were those who, applying the more realistic standards of the theatre, found Italian opera absurd. There were even those who associated it, at a significant moment, with popery. Addison and Steele did nothing but heap ridicule on foreign music, Handel's included. All the same, within a few years the Italian opera had driven out the English. No native music flourished but the song — D'Urfey's *Pills to Purge Melancholy,* Carey's *Black-Eyed Susan* and *Sally in Our Alley,* and the beautiful work of Thomas Arne.

The overwhelming success of Italian opera, when it came, was really due, not to the music, but to the drawing power of the great Italian soloists. Taste had so far degenerated in England that the singer outweighed the song. On the one hand, there were the famous eunuchs, Nicolini, Senesino, and Farinelli, all commanding high prices; on the other hand, there were the great women singers, La Faustina and Cuzzoni, commanding even higher ones. Their effect on the musical life of the time was in almost every respect a bad one. It was bad enough that they diverted to themselves the emphasis that belonged on the music. But their exorbitant salaries ruined promoters, and their quarrels and feuds caused endless friction and dismay. Senesino's feud with Handel cost the composer years of eclipse. Faustina and Cuzzoni, appearing in London at the same time, became such bitter enemies that society split over them. Lady Burlington and her friends fiercely championed the Faustina; Lady Pembroke and her friends just as fiercely championed the Cuzzoni. Whigs and Tories, Guelphs and Ghibellines, were hardly more at daggers drawn. Walpole's wife, for a wonder, "succeeded in getting both to sing at her house; neither would sing in the presence of the other, but the hostess managed to draw first one and then the other out of the music room while her rival enchanted the guests." Perhaps better remembered is Handel's rivalry with Buononcini, which shook the town no less violently, and brought forth Byrom's immortal if unprophetic epigram ending:

> *Strange all this difference should be*
> *Twixt Tweedledum and Tweedledee.*

So great at last was the success of Italian opera that London erected a Royal Academy of Music in which to hear it sung. Then, abruptly, the vogue for it foundered and the Academy collapsed when, in 1728, *The Beggar's Opera* took London by storm. Even the great prima donnas and *castrati* lost their allure — here was something infinitely more alluring. Musically there might be no comparison. *The Beggar's Opera* was a mere arrangement of tunes, some of them well known for generations, though others had been stolen from Handel's early operas. The Italian music, if florid and artificial, was also deft and polished. But, on the other hand, here were no bloodless gods of antiquity, no extravagant heroics, no highfalutin postures; here was the pungent underworld of London, here were comedy and caricature, here was a take-off on Italian grandiloquence — and the effect was thundering. *The Beggar's Opera* swept everything else aside. It ran for sixty-three days; it was repeated the next season; it had long runs in Bristol and Bath. Ladies inscribed its songs on their fans and drawing-room screens. It was to triumph for two generations to come, and though there is nothing in the music itself that calls for comment, in the particular kind of musical entertainment which it typifies there is something very significant indeed. The huge success of *The Beggar's Opera* gave the English a permanent feeling for travesties embroidered with tunes. Hence travesties embroidered with tunes became part of the English heritage, and after a century of good, bad, and indifferent ones Gilbert and Sullivan appeared with the Savoy operas.

With the decline of the Italian opera, the one great musical force in England was able to shake off the tyranny of fashion and strike out in a bolder and more brilliant style. Handel had thus far been chiefly concerned with making a living; he had had to compete directly with other musicians, cater to prevailing tastes, sue for court favour; he had composed not only many vigorous imperfect operas, but birthday odes, coronation anthems, thanksgiving hymns, music following after royal barges on the Thames. Yet, for all his efforts to please, he had not really touched the pulse of England. Italian opera did not really express Handel's nature, or really arouse his public's. He was well known to them, but merely a well-known foreigner; sometimes he succeeded, but often he failed. It was not till late in his career that, with the opera in ruins, Handel composed much of his best organ and orchestral music and almost all his towering oratorios. With these he became the great master of English music. Though he was twenty-five when he came to London, and though he came as a German under Italian influences, by virtue of his later work he remains an Englishman. The oratorios especially — *Saul, Israel in Egypt, Judas Maccabæus, The Messiah* — are music particularly magnetic to the English people; they minister, as someone has said, to two of the Englishman's ruling passions: his reverence for the Bible and his love of choral singing. Handel himself gauged his audience in no very different way: "What the English like," he told Gluck, "is something they can beat time to."

Handel, the foreigner, best carried on the tradition of English music, which the English could not carry on for themselves. This tradition did not chime in with the eighteenth-century ideal of elegance cultivated on the Continent and imitated at home. We can draw no sound conclusions from the fact that England in the eighteenth century produced no musical geniuses; but from the fact that she produced no adequate music expressing that polished and aristocratic temper she is said to have cherished, we may judge that she never had it. She hungered after something else. And in Handel — not the operatic and Italianate Handel, not the gravely classical Handel, but the vigorous, healthy, now rollicking, now sonorous Handel — she found what she wanted. Here was nothing too sensitive or too subtle, but music for the lungs and hands and feet, music on simple themes or exalted ones. In the genius of Handel there is perhaps something which, though not philistine itself, can appeal to the philistine nature. It is all brought out into the light, strongly charged, clearly marked, firmly set. And the imposing themes of Handel's oratorios, set forth with such a wealth of religious emotion and such an absence of mystical refinement, have the same appeal to the English as the robustness of his music. Perhaps it is no more than coincidence that the oratorios began winning immense favour at the moment when religious revivalism first swept over England, but at least the two things point in the same direction. If Handel's abiding and special place in English musical history is in great part due to his genius, it is in some part due to his carrying forward a congenial tradition and working in a congenial idiom. He has meant more to England than any other composer, the reason being that more than any other he has stood for what England is.

AMONG the fine arts, the period can boast but one distinction: the blaze of Hogarth's genius, with which it ends. Hogarth aside, perhaps the best work lay in architecture; though we must not suppose that because Wren lived throughout two decades of the eighteenth century, he flourished then. But in Augustan and early Georgian London there was much creditable building and rebuilding of churches. The most notorious architect of the age is Vanbrugh, who, with no technical training, managed to rear some of the vastest piles of domestic architecture ever attempted. Nothing better reveals the grandiosity of the times than the heavy baroque massiveness of Blenheim Palace; and though Blenheim somehow gives a kind of virtue to Castle Howard, Castle Howard by comparison with anything less is itself a horror. The famous epitaph on Vanbrugh is also a final criticism:

> *Lie heavy on him, earth, for he*
> *Laid many a heavy load on thee.*

Nor was the period more than a precursor of the days which produced, in town and country houses, what we commonly describe as Georgian architecture. The Dutch influence exerted by William of Orange accounted for many trim Queen Anne houses, and a few delightful ones; and in the next generation the feeling for pleasant homes was to produce some early Georgian examples in an impressive style; but prior to 1740 there is little to compare with what came after it. There still persisted too much respect for the stiff, the ponderous, the showy; there was too much bogus, ill-reasoned Palladio and " classicism " or too much Frenchifying or too much display of mere wealth. The simple elegance which represents a mature taste could not be attained in an era *straining* to be elegant, an era when despotic rules frightened parvenus out of all spontaneous appreciation.

The true state of affairs becomes plain when we turn to painting. Before Hogarth, there are no good painters at all; to mention Jervas or Thornhill is only to prove our point. The English were still the losers in that " struggle against foreign invasion " which had been going on for hundreds of years. All England's favourite painters came from abroad. But her taste in foreigners did nothing to mitigate the stigma of having no good painters of her own. In times past she had imported such men as Holbein, Van Dyck, Rubens, and Lely; now she paid homage to Vanloo, who is scarcely better than third rate, and to Kneller, who is scarcely so good.[4] Only in one sense did these men carry on the work of their predecessors: they, too, functioned as portrait-painters. Portrait-painters were the only ones in whom England had any interest. Her vanity was aroused, not her passion for art. To sit to the right man, to hang the finished portrait near the oils of one's ancestors, to see oneself going down to posterity in a flattering light — this was all that mattered. It is significant that while face-painters like Kneller and Vanloo made fortunes in England, far greater foreigners like Canaletto and Watteau found no patronage at all.

On the surface it may seem that the English of those years were much absorbed in painting. " Art " was one of the notable reasons for setting out on the Grand Tour, and Englishmen forever haunted the picture galleries of Italy. Moreover, they would return with canvases acquired on their travels, and ornament their town houses and country places with the spoils. England became in that way the repository of many celebrated and beautiful pictures — and the storeroom for an incredible amount of rubbish. There were, to be just, a handful of connoisseurs with taste and judgment who vaguely led the way and enriched England with valuable art. But there were many others, self-styled lovers of the beautiful, who had nothing better to rely on than the

---

[4] Yet as late as 1752 a court painter could pontificate: " Shakespeare in poetry, and Kneller in painting, damme! "

word of Continental dealers and the depth of their purses. And there were still others who, like Sir Robert Walpole, bought pictures merely as a speculation. It was an excellent moment for speculators, if only they knew what to buy. But most often they were duped; and the auction rooms sold off the work of hacks signed with the names of masters, or the work of masters who today are regarded as hacks. Not that prices were necessarily high: Swift speaks of buying a Titian for two pounds five.

Art, in a double sense, was the handmaiden of wealth. The paintings themselves reflected upper-class sitters, upper-class graces, upper-class artifice. Broad humanity was as much lacking as artistic greatness; there was no effort made to express anything vital in English life. And if the general public had no share in the canvases, they had little more share in appreciating them. There were no exhibitions before 1760; there were virtually no galleries. Not even very much of the best painting was in London. Most of it lay salted away in the great manor houses of England, masterpieces and rubbish equally treasured or equally ignored; and was to moulder there through several foxhunting generations.

Then Hogarth, a man of the people, with as strong an interest in people of every kind as any painter has ever displayed, burst upon London. He looked around with a piercing eye, and reordered what he saw into vivid and imaginative designs. Life did not embarrass or intimidate or unbalance him; flaring, swarming, roaring, it fed and nourished him and drove him on. He could emerge unscathed from fire and unpolluted from filth, and his passion to seize life had the guarantees of robust health, large humour, and resolute intention. Hardly anyone else in eighteenth-century England is so central as Hogarth, and no one else (unless it be Fielding or Defoe) is so English. He surveyed the dense life around him from a wholly congenial perch, with no prejudices against his age or race, with no need to

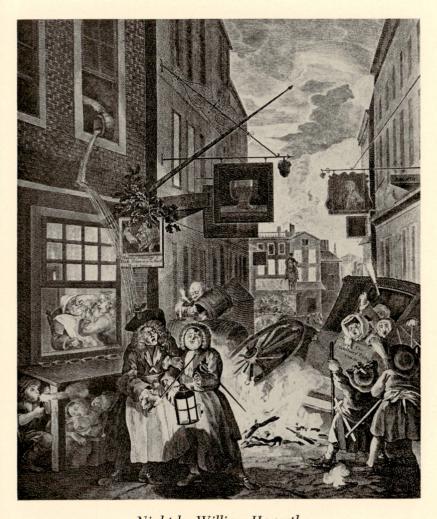

Night by William Hogarth

put on a French coat, an Italian blouse, or the antique toga. Whenever he put them on, indeed, he was lost. He drove straight toward the core — with a drive that no realistic satirist has ever excelled. In the real sense of the phrase, he struck home.

The art of Hogarth offers a picture of eighteenth-century London and a scorching criticism of it. It signifies an hour of history caught and fixed, and a permanent commentary on the folly, the cupidity, the degradation of human life. If but one picture and one commentary of the age are to survive, let them be Hogarth's. He has the most range, the most cut, the most sanity. Hogarth, having entered into all that he portrays, himself remains uncontaminated. This is not quite the truth about Swift or Smollett or Defoe.

To be sure, Hogarth spread the paint on thick: his pictures often wilfully exaggerate and are sometimes grotesques. But the final effect of a great artist in any form, no matter how profoundly he has studied the world, will be something a little outside, and a little bigger than, life. And the final effect in Hogarth is the satirist's effect, not the realist's. If sordidness bulks overlarge in the painter's choice of material, the balance is restored by the health and freedom of Hogarth's approach to it. Hogarth curiously cleanses his degraded scene by discharging from it all cant, all artifice, all wishful thinking, by releasing the dammed-up current of an age into the river of endless life. His pictures show, not only a fidelity to truth, not only a satiric surcharge, but rebellion. He is running away from all fashionable schools of painting and all fraudulent theories of life!

Hogarth was a satirist like Swift and Pope and Fielding and Smollett and Defoe, so that like all of them he was a moralist also. Anyone who studies the scenes of *A Harlot's Progress* or *A Rake's Progress* may draw conclusions as to the wages of sin. So too may he conclude from *Marriage-à-la-Mode* that society life corrupts, or from *Gin Lane* that intemperate drinking crazes and kills. And he may read in all of them a burning protest on the painter's part against what money does, or the lack of money, or the desire for money. But didactic (and harmfully didactic in terms of his art) though Hogarth was, his mind was too tough for him to have any faith in lame sanctimonious appeals to the good life; and his mind was too broad for him, while castigating excess, to disparage pleasure. Instead he disparaged cruelty, and while revealing folly and vice, fiercely attacked the way in which they were punished. He set out to expose human nature, he exposed human nature, and his morality is never at real variance with truth. The ministers who used his pictures for sermons, and all such men ever since, have made of him a narrower moralist than he was. For Hogarth is on a higher plane than they; he is on a different plane. It is not that he has diminished vice; it is that he has diminished fraud.

Hogarth's pictures came as a blast of cold air. They were not only much more truthful art than anything which coexisted with them, but they were an art to which all of London could respond. They swept the city as *The Beggar's Opera* had done. Moll Hackabout, the heroine of *A Harlot's Progress*, became the reality of the hour, was put into pantomime, into opera, into street ballads, and painted — though not by Hogarth — on fans and screens and china. The reason may not have been the best possible; sin, not the wages of sin, was what caught the popular interest. And the result was not lasting. But another result has accrued with time, and Hogarth has become a great social historian. " Other pictures we see; Hogarth's we read." As for the painter — it is no doubt true that *The Shrimp Girl* is worth all his didactic paintings; it is perhaps regrettable that Hogarth put into his work too much " story," too much moralizing, and that on that account he fails, as he might otherwise have succeeded, in reaching the level of the Dutch masters of genre. But whatever his exact importance as a painter, there can be no question of his importance as a force.

WHERE the drama of the age has honour only in Vanbrugh, painting only in Hogarth, music only in Handel, it is for literature that the England of those years is truly distinguished, and most worthy to be called Augustan. We are at once confronted by the great names of Swift, Pope, Defoe; we are at once reminded of a literary scene swarming with movement, quivering with emotion, and blazing with wit. There are almost as many masterpieces as there are quarrels. On the higher levels statesmen and great ladies move arm-in-arm with writers and poets, and the whole scene acquires a retrospective glow. The mind dwells with pleasure on an age so notable for intellect that Wren, Bentley, and Newton were members of the same evening club, and that Pope gave informal dinners for Bolingbroke, Swift, Arbuthnot, and Gay.

It is the social aspect, perhaps, that has most vividly survived. And the social aspect counts: if you had won your spurs in literature, you were almost certain of a footing in great men's houses and of conversance with affairs of state. Prior became an ambassador, Steele a member of the House of Commons, Addison a Secretary of State and the husband of a countess; Pope visited half the peerage, and Swift bullied it; Congreve brings to mind Henrietta Duchess of Marlborough, and Gay the Duchess of Queensberry. Nor were these men merely given their peep of high life: it was half by reason of them that a truly polite world existed. They came in the end to be the real arbiters of taste; society acknowledged their importance as much as they acknowledged society's. If Pope at his Twickenham villa cherished an invitation to Hampton Court, visitors at court delighted equally in going to Twickenham.

The result, for literary men, was both good and bad. It is easy to see that writers, by entering a society having traditions, worldliness, and address, might exchange a provincial for a cosmopolitan manner. They might quicken their innate sensibilities through a knowledge of external good breeding. They might sharpen their wits against men who, having none of their genius, sometimes had more than their cleverness. It was indeed through becoming the pupils of these men that they at length became their masters. But it is plain that such writers entered too long and too acquiescently a world not truly theirs. They lighted up its values, but abandoned their own. The shapely walls at length closed in on them, obliterating the world outside, making their eyesight remarkably keen but remarkably myopic. Addison turned into a social climber and Pope into a snob. Congreve, as everyone knows, told Voltaire he wished to be thought of as a gentleman and not as a writer. Swift, though he saw through the great world, was never too much disgusted not to insist upon a place in it.

What grew out of such a situation was, then, a better art but a poorer stimulus for art. The dance of life narrowed down to a faultless execution of the minuet. With no real depth of purpose Addison wrote much impeccable prose, Pope much impeccable verse. In them we find the grace and sense of fitness that society pretended to. In them, while being deprived of the best in art, we may come to know the best in commonplace. And even before naming what Augustan literature lacked, we may say this of what it had — that to make a god of Taste is almost certainly to fall, before long, merely into tastefulness. All the second-rate writers of the age fell into it and were drowned.

Historically, however, Augustan literature amounts to much more than exquisite decoration. The Augustan writers, being participants rather than mere observers of high society, have painted it with a frightening accuracy. And far from being its eulogists (however much they were its slaves), they criticized it, they moralized over it, they exposed it with a blistering bill of particulars. What emerges are folly and mischief and vice hardly redeemed by a single grand or generous impulse; and what unwittingly transpires is one long confession on the part of the writers that they are hugging a life unworthy of them. Their exposé is the severest of self-indictments. For most of them expose with much more vigour than they protest; and fall back — Addison unctuously, Pope mechanically — on much easy Christian sentiment, and such precepts of virtue as time out of mind have made virtuousness seem a little . . . well, improbable. They are quite without real vision; it never seems to occur to them that there may be a larger, wiser, better world than their own. They *had* to be gentlemen; obviously, then, they could not be pioneers. Even the virtue they preached must be hall-marked by tradition.

The temperament of such writers is thus too restricted to convey more than a conventionalized picture. Writing out of cynicism or malice or complacency, they reveal the same defects as the life they write about. Human action, human emotion, human suffering in the large sense are things they can scarcely understand, let alone try to express. Sir Roger de Coverley with his good impulses at the mercy of his class feeling, is as near as these men can come to a broader view of humanity; and even so, Addison and Steele had to take the precaution of making Sir Roger something of a character. The only intensity the Augustans display is produced by jealousy or hatred or bitterness. The few times they peer beyond their walls, they turn away amused or disgusted.

Not quite all of them remained walled in. One man escaped, to become the most terrifying voice in English literature. Swift, though he wanted power with the great and had contempt for the vulgar, could not remain immured. He saw in the outer darkness such forms and shapes as proved themselves not worthy to be called, or ready to become, human beings. He could not draw close to them, but he could hate the selfishness and vice of those who stamped them down; and he could retort upon savage cruelty with savage denunciation. If he no more than his contemporaries could believe in a larger, wiser, better world, he would not tamely sit down in this one. That is why his, the sharpest pen of all, was dipped in the most lasting ink.

The advantages that these men enjoyed were seldom owing to their purely literary excellences. Their rise was in most instances exactly in proportion to their usefulness. Their rise was the fruit of patronage, for a writer without a patron was almost a writer without a chance. And the patrons were politicians who, for all they might appreciate the turn of a phrase, valued writers most for the service they could render in party conflicts. Not Addison, or Steele, or Swift, or Prior, or a dozen now half-forgotten men, could ever have become social lions or masters of taste had they not first been Whig or Tory pamphleteers. The offices they held, the pay they took, were in recognition not of their literary but of their political importance. Only Congreve and Rowe received outright rewards for their services to literature and even they, if they did not write in the Whigs' behalf, were Whigs by affiliation. Pope himself was patronized, first as a means of cozening Swift at a time when Swift was invaluable to the Tories, and second as a means of tempting Pope into the Tory camp.

And in the final reckoning, these men who rose by the politics of Queen Anne's reign were *in* the great world, yet never of it. It was perhaps less their origins that mattered than their purses. Always, on no matter how sumptuous a scale, they were dependants. They had to thread their way with care, to flatter, to kotow, to placate, to sing for their suppers. Swift, it is true, bulldozed at times, and Pope boasted, but not until they had arrived. Masters of ceremony all of them might be, and were, but masters of circumstance never. They might be treated with a deference becoming to their achievements, but in that lay only a willing condescension, and where the bread and butter of life obtruded, it was they who must defer. All the glitter of the

scene thus was tarnished for them by uncertainty, and is tarnished by obsequiousness for us. And the game of keeping
up appearances threw these gentlemen authors into perpetual debt and panic. The few who could count their pennies, like Swift and Pope, have come down to posterity with
the reputation of being close. But it was rather that they saw,
in an age of hirelings and endless ups and downs, where
today's peer-foolish writer might find himself tomorrow.

We must save our sympathy, however, for a class of writers with whom the gentlemen authors had no sympathy at
all. While Pope and Addison sat gracefully on the top of
the heap, the whole race of Grub Street swarmed round the
bottom. While Steele and Gay were running into debt
through high living, a tribe of nameless hacks were running
into debt for want of food. Between the two groups of hirelings stretched an uninhabited gulf: those of the great lords
had nothing but harsh disdain for those of the booksellers
and newspaper-owners. " Sons of a day," Pope called these
desperate scribblers, and perhaps referred as much to their
bodily as to their literary life. " These are — ah, no! these
were — the gazetteers "; what Pope intended for a gibe at
the hacks, Time has turned into a shaft at Pope. Exploited
by rascals, or launching out hopelessly on their own, these
drudges earned enough to sleep three in a bed, or not to
sleep in a bed at all, but on a bulk; and lacking the clothes
to go out, worked at home shivering in filthy blankets. It
has been easy for critics to censure such men for their " dissolute habits." Doubtless they drank too much; but they ate
too little. Doubtless, lacking the means to marry, they co-
habited with the only kind of women who would have them.
They were slovenly and unwashed, and had table manners
no better than their food. But it would be hard to produce
a race of more justly embittered, more blightingly frustrated
men, destined not only to be sweated but also, when they
gave offence, to be broken. Defoe in the pillory is famous,
though possibly not famous enough. Johnson's early strug-

gles in London are a chronicle of bad jobs, bad pay, bad food, bad lodgings. And Johnson and Defoe were anything but dissolute men.

The great days of patronage hardly outlasted Queen Anne, and with the coming of the Georges the hacks notably increased and the gentlemen authors notably declined. Statesmen like Walpole and the later Bolingbroke did much political writing themselves, while the men they hired to do the rest were underlings they did not consort with. Though journalism had grown tremendously in scope, it had decreased tremendously in opportunities. Employers were supplanting patrons; protégés necessarily became wage-earners. A few men, by striking out professionally, were able to build up independent positions for themselves: Pope rose above patronage to end up with a handsome profit from the booksellers. But the Popes were the exceptions, and for the most part the record consists of long and hard struggles, not merely to win the favour of the public, but also to out-bargain the publishers and newspaper-owners.

But the growth of journalism, however badly paid, does indicate the presence of a much larger reading public. Before the eighteenth century reading was almost as much an upper-class pursuit as travelling. Most middle-class people were indifferently educated, most books were expensive, most writing was serious, special, unpopularized. Frivolous writing belonged to the stage. The modern novel was not yet born, and in place of it was nothing better than the lumbering old-fashioned romance. The change, when it came, came suddenly; and if journalism attracted a larger reading public, it also helped to create it. One cannot overestimate the revolutionary character of the *Tatler* and *Spectator* papers. They appeared on every breakfast-table from the Queen's to the greengrocer's. At one stroke they brought into existence a kind of literature — gossipy, personal, humorous, and preachy all at once — for which masses of people were ready, and hungry. These people can be called the eternal magazine-reading public, who, besides wanting nothing heavy or deep, want nothing long or expensive. As the creatures of their own time, it is true that for a while they were satisfied with essays and sermons rather than stories. Even so, *The Spectator*, at the very moment it perfected a genre that had long to live, saw the possibilities in a genre that would live forever; and in Sir Roger we find, superimposed on the essay pattern, a purely fictional technique. But straight fiction itself was stirring; one generation more and it would come into its own. While the hacks starve, Fielding (himself a hack) and Richardson are getting into harness. Already, indeed, while other writers are cabined inside the patrician scene, England's first great novelist is painting, with bold realism, the life below. *Moll Flanders* and *The Fortunate Mistress* are, if one be necessary, the corrective to *The Rape of the Lock*. Defoe saw London, saw England, with a width matched by no other writer of his day. He alone was really in the midst of life, and if Swift's dark pages are the greatest art, Defoe's are the greatest document of the age. Both men would seem to have their reward. Between them they have written two of the three most popular fictions in the English language. No novel written since, and only one before, has been so widely read as *Gulliver* or *Crusoe*. Only most of the readers have been children.

The early eighteenth century has had an extensive literary reach. Not only did it produce books which in themselves are works of art; it produced many things which became the models, and some things which became the germ, of the art of the future. Few other ages have been better adorned by literature, better revealed, or more harshly castigated. To create the modern essay and the modern novel and — in the very business of creating them — produce masterpieces in their kind; to achieve masterpieces of letter-writing as well; to perfect a style of poetry that for upwards of three generations would not only flourish but almost enslave — to

[129

do so much is to leave behind a burning, inextinguishable mark. All this was not, however, the practice of empty forms, though some was the practice of narrow ones. The literary mastery of Pope encompassed a whole aristocratic world; the literary mastery of Addison encompassed a whole bourgeois point of view; the literary mastery of Defoe encompassed a whole lower-class existence; while Swift, with the widest mastery of all, touches now one of these preserves and now another. If at no level we are inspired, at each level we are fascinated and relentlessly informed.

THE ARTISTS

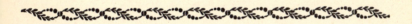

Addison

NEVER IN ENGLISH HISTORY, we have just seen, has the world of writers so interpenetrated itself with that of lords and statesmen as in the first decades of the eighteenth century. Literature then had unnumbered patrons to fawn upon and boast about and conspire against. Three men in particular rose, by the power of words, to commanding heights, freely participating in what went on, and permanently recording it. And if they mirrored, they also moulded at times the high life of their era; and, one of them mildly, one of them maliciously, one of them brutally, they have impaled it for good and all. Addison exposes and chides, Pope exposes and sneers, Swift exposes and tears to tatters.

It is interesting that these three men who lighted up the society they moved among should in themselves remain shadowy and still be quarrelled over. About none of them has posterity reached a decisive verdict: the social whirlpool near where they spent their lives sucked them in after it. We may read about them between the lines, but with less confidence than we should like. We suspect, however, that these men have shown up sharpers and time-servers, zealots and hypocrites, too well to have relied for their facts on observation alone.

[131

Addison is in most respects the least interesting of the three. On the face of things, and in the opinion of numerous biographers, he emerges as a Christian gentleman, an agreeable party man, and a writer packed with graces. Thackeray and Professor Courthope approved of him, and Macaulay eulogized him without stint. Leslie Stephen limped along with them. Dr Johnson hemmed and hawed, but did not dissent. Two other commentators, however — the earliest and the most recent — have taken a different view of the matter. Pope's characterization ranks among the most uncomplimentary, as among the most famous, judgments in the language:

> *Damn with faint praise, assent with civil leer* . . .
> *Willing to wound, and yet afraid to strike* . . .
> *And so obliging that he ne'er obliged* . . .

and all the rest of it. Its insinuations will keep Addison's name alive long after even Sir Roger de Coverley has vanished. And recently Mr Bonamy Dobrée, rather allying himself with Pope, has applied to Addison an epithet that Pope, could he have comprehended it, would have relished. Addison, says Mr Dobrée, was the first Victorian.

After being at Charterhouse and Oxford with Richard Steele, Addison came as an obscure young man to London with some idea of entering the Church. By his early writings, however, he won praise from Dryden, and soon after caught the eye of Montague, a powerful Whig statesman who saw talent in Addison which he felt the Whigs could use. He therefore sent the young man, with all expenses paid, on a tour of the Continent; and Addison sequestered himself in a small French town, to learn the language, before going to Paris to practise it. From Paris he turned toward Italy, where he seems to have gazed on all the right objects and to have greeted them with all the right quotations.

On his return to London, unemployed and penniless, he joined the Whigs, who, to whet his appetite and test his steel, gave him a slender sinecure. Then, almost it would seem for Addison's sake, Marlborough triumphed at Blenheim; at any rate Blenheim was the occasion for so many bad poems that Addison was sought out to compose a good one. It was not good, but it made Addison's fortune. From then on, his rise was assured: he became a Whig scribe, a commissioner in the excise, a chief secretary in Ireland; in time he entered Parliament, and before he died was a Cabinet minister. Nor did his literary career lag behind his political one: the *Tatlers* and *Spectators* he wrote had wide popularity, and his *Cato* ran for thirty-five nights, a very long run considering the age, not to speak of the play. He made distinguished friends and, in middle age, a distinguished marriage with the dowager Countess of Warwick. Their life together is supposed to have been discordant; Addison's own was fast approaching its end. He died, in 1719, at the age of forty-seven.

His political success is the more remarkable in that he was never in any real sense a politician. It is true that in Addison's day good writers sometimes became party leaders because parties led chiefly by the pen; but even then so official a career as Addison's must have grown out of something more than clever journalism. The truth would seem to be that Addison was a shrewd bargainer. He had tact, and saw no reason why it should remain a merely social asset. He could write, and saw no reason why he should be paid by the line. The coin he was paid in was happily at the Whigs' disposal and, even more happily for them, did not come out of their own pockets. As a party man, Addison proved loyal and honourable and should be remembered for attacking corruption, though he might not have fared so well had his age, or even his party, been less corrupt.

His writing, as opposed to his political career, has consequence; and of the broad, as it were the bourgeois, life of his time it is the brightest mirror. If the *Tatler* and *Spectator* papers have been overrated as art, they cannot be dispensed with as memoirs: they provide an intimate and, for all their moralizing, a disinterested picture of London under Queen Anne. We may discount Addison himself as the fashionable Fifth Avenue preacher of his day, but we cannot dismiss his talents. He has the scepticism of his age, but, unlike his age, does not make a vice of it; he has its wit — though not, like Swift, the wit to impeach such wit; and he has the useful gift of keeping his temper. For his time, his values are high, though hardly high enough for a generous nature or a virile man of thought. In the ideal they would produce an urbane Christian, but in practice they offer nothing better than a genteel rector.

It is when we come to the man himself that we rub up against a psychological tangle that is quite lacking in his career. For two hundred years the world has been divided over whether Addison was a paragon, a hypocrite, or a prig. There has always been Pope's annihilating thumbnail sketch to reckon with; it is plainly scurrilous, but it cannot be called implausible. And though we know that Pope never required much to build on, he must have required *something;* and the truth does not lose all its fangs by being twisted.

Addison was a careerist. He wanted to get ahead, but was vain enough to want to get ahead gracefully, as if it were none of his doing; and he wanted to get farther ahead than any of his friends. This last weakness was deep-rooted in him; generosity he could only show in the form of condescension. There can be no doubt that he sought, sought very carefully, to keep up appearances. He never lost his temper; there could have been no better way for making other people lose theirs. He never quarrelled; but Swift, Steele, and Pope all contrived to have grievances against him. He almost never made mistakes; but that, while an asset, is not necessarily a virtue. He cultivated, in other words, the arts that a careerist requires. He mastered himself, he ingratiated himself. He had a cool brain for doing these things, and for the best of reasons — because he had a cold nature.

Whether or not he was a " good " man depends on one's definition of morality. But what one can conclude, with some show of reason, is that to get as far in life as Addison did, in the age he himself has so vividly described, he must often have been politic and disingenuous and knowing. He must have been very worldly, for in those days naïveté was fatal. It is the next step, however, that really seems to damn Addison: as his manœuvring never turned him into the least bit of a cynic, it is fair to assume that he must have been to a large extent a hypocrite. He must even, to avoid being found out a self-seeker, have risked being accounted a prig.

But Pope's " Atticus," who was also a Secretary of State and the husband of a countess and a renowned writer, played his cards well. He learned wisdom and applied it — applied it so skilfully that it passed for virtue also. It may be that he deserves the good name he so long has borne; perhaps men in history, like characters in fiction, fail to be convincing if they are more than reasonably virtuous. No amount of research, at any rate, reveals anything worse of Addison than that he was vain, secretive, smug, covetous and calculating. He may well have been " enough of an idealist to be blind to the things he did not wish to see." Perhaps lynx-eyed posterity has provided him with punishment enough: the Addisonian mould of form is now thought a trifle stilted, and Addison is coming in for a share of what made him writhe the most — ridicule.

Pope

I_F Addison has come down to posterity as too good to be true, Pope has come down as too bad. In most accounts the

[135

little monster of Twick'nam seems bound up with everything that is waspish and malicious and deformed — an incorrigible mischief-maker with venom enough in his heart
to poison the whole atmosphere of the age. His malice, indeed, has descended as so unremitting that, by blackening
so many lives, it eventually blackened none; Pope's victims,
not Pope, have always received the benefit of the doubt. For
generations, despairing commentators seized on Pope's
wonderful devotion to his parents as a triumphant proof
that he was not *all* bad, and as a last-ditch argument that he
should be thought better of. Fascinating as Pope's lifetime
history is, much the more fascinating part only commences
at his death. For then the evidence started piling up, the
contradictions multiplied, the treacheries grew manifest,
the conspiracies turned multiform: the man's reputation
went bankrupt, his poetry was put in escrow; and he enjoyed a posthumous notoriety even greater than his living
fame.

And his fame while alive was very great: besides standing
high among its social personages and first among its wits, he
was the supreme English poet of his age. He made implacable enemies, but he had very distinguished friends — Swift,
Gay, Bolingbroke, Peterborough, Arbuthnot, Buckingham.
In spite of towering disadvantages of every kind, Pope managed, with little to assist him save genius, to outpace the
record set by any previous poet in the English calendar.

His parents were Roman Catholics not above the middle
class; his schooling was desultory and almost furtive; sickly
as a child, he became deformed as a man. Everything —
even, one would think, the respectable family means which
for a normal youth would have opened up many pleasant
prospects — contrived to intensify a morbid and introverted
nature in a coarse and extraverted age. Fortunately Pope
knew what he wanted to be as quickly as he knew that he
could be almost nothing else. He had lisped in numbers; suc-
cessively, then, he stuttered, spoke, sneered, and screamed

in numbers; numbers, from the point of view of a temperament finding its objective, were his life. Before he was twelve he was crouched in a coffee-house, gazing at Dryden from afar; before he was eighteen he was exchanging letters and compliments with the aged Wycherley. Whatever other sufferings Pope endured, he was never troubled by a choice of profession; and never opposed in that choice by his parents.

Of his blazing career a reminder is hardly necessary. While in his teens, he was already sought out by a publisher; while in his twenties, he wrote such classics as the *Essay on Criticism* and *The Rape of the Lock*, and for an imposing subscription list translated the *Iliad* at an unprecedented price. At thirty he was in command, standing on the threshold of the great world, with the fear of his enemies adding almost more to his fame than the favour of his friends. At thirty he settled down, for the rest of his life, at Twickenham; and there he busied himself with his garden and his grotto; took care of his mother; entertained his friends; wrote his poetry; wrote, rewrote, and doctored his letters; nursed his feuds; and squirted his poison. From time to time he appeared in London, or went on visits to lordly houses — a " valetudinaire " always, an invalid usually; and ended " that long disease, my life," at the age of fifty-six.

He had very hateful qualities. He was vindictive beyond credulity, and upon his just, his unjust, and his imagined malefactors alike he took every manner of scathing revenge. He was all the meaner-minded for being so keenly sensitive, since pettiness upset his feelings no less than great provocation. He lied, he slandered, he falsified, and — in paying off his co-workers on the *Odyssey* — he seems to have short-changed. His gallantries, in word and presumably in deed, are so many sniggers and palm-twittings and winks. Grub Street he sneered at without even pitying; and of humanitarian instincts in general, as we conceive them, he had almost none. Beyond all that, his unbridled denunciations in

[137

verse are as wanting in charity and dignity as a superb knowledge of words can make them.

But if Pope's badness is both glaring and repugnant, it is only his vanity and not the malice which fed upon it that is continuous in the man; he was quite unlike a monster. He needed affection and sympathy and deference, as most men need them and are in some way warped if they do not get them; but Pope needed them the more because, besides being inordinately vain, he was chronically sick and defensively insolent and a half-Luciferian, a half-sycophantic parvenu. It was his instinct to take offence, and he made it his trade. It is throwing no sop — as it once was to dilate on his wonderful devotion to his parents — to say that alongside the list of Pope's faults, there goes a list of far better qualities: affection and crooked loyalty towards his friends, playfulness, a charming social self, and — cramped in between the soiled gallantries and the shrill hates — an instinct for Mozartean grace. These do not redeem Pope; they deepen him. They reinforce modern belief that evil is better called pathology, and they make us see that the eighteenth century had no data for understanding him, and the nineteenth century not the right data.

One might, if one chose, draw many ingenious, if not too accurate, parallels between Pope and Proust. Enough do exist, at any rate, to bring home to us the one valuable fact that the Frenchman, coming two hundred years after the poet, lived (and died) in much less danger of being misunderstood as a man. Each mirrored the decadent high society, into which each threaded his way, of his era; the one suffered from being a Catholic and a hunchback, the other from being a half-Jew and a homosexual; each was morbidly sensitive, each a distressed invalid, and each had an abnormal attachment to his art. (Where Proust gasped for breath in a cork-lined room, Pope had to be helped in and out of grotesque clothes, and always required a servant within call.) In character Proust had little in common with Pope, but in temperament he had a great deal. But Proust lived in an age when that temperament received thoughtful handling, and was saved by other men's courtesy from excesses and malformations. Pope lived in an age of high language and low sensibilities and, though certainly not more sinned against than sinning, was prodded into malice as often as he found it companionable. Had he lived two centuries later, his supreme talent for vituperation might have been balked of an outlet, but his character must have been modified for the better.

It must always, however, have had repellent aspects, because they were deep-seated ones. There is no point in not accepting the fact: throwing up one's hands was never a solution, and shutting one's eyes is not one either. From any point of view Pope is too interesting to be sacrificed to the moral fervour of the Victorians or the sentimental fervour of Bloomsbury.[1] And his poetry — that second hollow battleground never evacuated from Johnson's death to Swinburne's — should cease to be a commodity in quest of a name and become the more valuable, not the less, for being unique.

Is it " poetry "? After a century of wrangling, brought to a head by Arnold's decision that Pope " is a classic of our prose," the common verdict now is that if it isn't *quite* poetry, it deserves the same standing. In my own way of throwing the apple of discord, I am not sure that it is poetry, if arbitrary distinctions (and to be useful, distinctions must be arbitrary) are to count. But the name is immaterial in the presence of the thing. Call much of the two *Essays* aphorism, call parts of *The Rape of the Lock* wit, call the *Epistle to Dr Arbuthnot* autobiography, call the portrait of Addison innuendo, or the portrait of Hervey slander: all, whatever you choose to call them, are brilliant and astonishing. After two centuries perhaps it is still

[1] Edith Sitwell's biography (1930) seems more interested in reversing past opinion than in elucidating Pope.

permissible to point out that it is less important for something to be " poetry " than for it to be literature. Whatever it was he wrote, Pope wrote it with startling and lasting success; well over half of him can still be read with delight. He still holds the fort; he still, no matter how unscrupulously he obtained it, has the last word. Addison, for one, must lie very uneasy in his grave. And, however many libelling and twisted and mendacious utterances Pope devoted his life to making, his most unmodified one was perhaps the truest of all:

> *Yes, I am proud: I must be proud to see*
> *Men, not afraid of God, afraid of me.*

Swift

To treat of Swift is to grapple with a personality not only singular and great, but profoundly mystifying. He has been harshly attacked and fanatically defended; no man's history has been more closely scrutinized, and no man's reputation more at the mercy of conjecture. He has revealed himself, consciously or otherwise, in a hundred ways, yet only to create a conflicting portrait, and to baffle us the more by his revelations. After two centuries we still feel the man better than we understand him; and know, whatever else eludes us, the force of his ego, his suffering, and his genius.

Behind Swift is an overwhelming drive; and the madness in which his life ended is foreshadowed in the ferocity with which it was pursued. His energies were too great — it is highly Swiftian that even his supreme ability to express himself was not enough to relieve his mind of what he wanted to say: after saying it with finality, he was frustrated still. His feelings were perhaps too intense to find an outlet in *any* form of expression; beneath their savage explosiveness lay something that would not explode.

Sprung of good English stock, he was born poor, in Ireland. He refused, however, to be considered an Irishman: do you call a man a horse, he asked, because he is born in a stable? A posthumous child, he grew up rather meanly, but not in want: he had a sufficient home and the opportunities of a good education. For Swift, however, these were not enough. Shabby gentility, if a good background for his genius, was a bad one for his character. By intensifying his natural discontent and accentuating his pride, it got him started in life on the wrong foot, and he never regained his balance.

His earliest employment was as a kind of secretary to Sir William Temple. His patron, following a career as the friend of kings and the maker of treaties, had seized on a setback as the pretext for withdrawing from politics, and proceeded to live a life of high-toned philosophical retirement. In addition to a small salary and an ambiguous social position, he provided Swift with oceans of worldly wisdom. Swift seems to have been grateful and resentful by turns, and in after years sometimes sneered at Sir William's memory and sometimes honoured it: he probably cared more for the man than for what he represented. As for existence with Temple at Moor Park, it gave Swift an admirable chance to catch the hang of things, and to read and study; and it was there he first knew Esther Johnson — " Stella."

Swift now entered the Church and received an Irish living; he was to serve the Church with fighting zeal for the rest of his life. That is one of the anomalies of it.

Another of its anomalies is that, in contrast to his formal declarations as a churchman, he never acknowledged himself, in the professional sense, to be a writer. In the artistic world, though he knew his own genius, he had few ambitions or vanities. He let some of his work lie unpublished for years; he published almost all of it anonymously; he was paid for almost none of it; and though determined that his writings should accomplish their immediate purpose, he

cared little about their ultimate fate. He had quite the opposite of an artist's aloofness: he was of the battle, not above it.

It was inevitable that a man of Swift's strong views and
bursting energy should want to join the battle where it raged
most fiercely; and he was soon in London. He came pleading the cause of the Irish Church and dreaming of preferment for himself; and by embracing the Whig cause when
he got there, looked to the Whig chiefs for help. They promised him both help and preferment, and provided neither.
So far as Swift's personal future was concerned, the tone of
his *Tale of a Tub* had permanently injured it. An archbishop
and the Queen were forever to oppose the prize which, always splendid, at length became symbolic to Swift — a
bishopric; they felt that however militant a churchman he
might be, he was not a right-thinking one. The sop that
was finally thrown to him — an *Irish* deanery — was thrown
much later, and not by the Whigs but by the Tories.

It was little enough reward, when it came, for the magnificent services Swift rendered the Tory Party as pamphleteer.
In winning him over with bland words from the ungrateful
Whigs, Harley and Bolingbroke knew, even better than,
for all his self-esteem, Swift did, what a writer they were
getting. The *Examiners* he wrote, the pamphlets he reeled
off, tremendously fortified their peace policy. Swift's price
was characteristic. He repudiated pay — it stank of hirelings and Grub Street; he disdained vulgar fame. He wanted
Harley's and Bolingbroke's intimacy — the run of their
houses, a seat at their private dinner-tables; and on achieving this, he flattered himself that he was privy to their
secrets. They took him in, in a double sense. But, for all that,
never before nor since has any writer, solely by his writings,
occupied so great a place in government. For several years
Swift was kotowed to by the men who were ruling England.

It was a great hour. He moved among the biggest names
and best minds of the day, in coffee-houses, in mansions, at
court. Bishop Kennett wrote in his diary:

Alexander Pope by J. Richardson, the elder

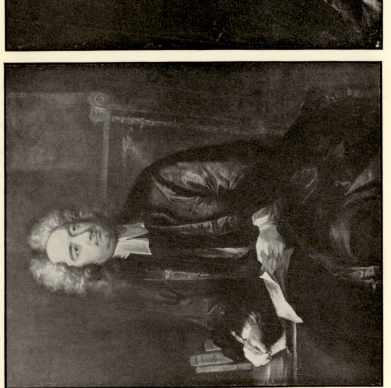

Jonathan Swift by Charles Jervas

When I came to the antechamber to wait before prayers, Dr Swift was the principal man of talk and business, and acted as minister of requests. He was soliciting the Earl of Arran to speak to his brother the Duke of Ormond to get a chaplain's place established in the garrison of Hull, for Mr Fiddes, a clergyman in that neighbourhood. . . . He was promising Mr Thorold to undertake with my Lord Treasurer that according to his petition he should obtain a salary of 200 pounds per annum, as minister of the English Church at Rotterdam. He stopped F. Gwynne, Esq., going in with the red bag to the Queen, and told him aloud he had something to say to him from my Lord Treasurer. He talked with the son of Dr Davenant to be sent abroad, and took out his pocketbook and wrote down several things as *memoranda,* to do for him. . . . Then he instructed a young nobleman that the best poet in England was Mr Pope (a Papist), who had begun a translation of Homer into English verse, for which, he said, he must have them all subscribe. " For," says he, " the author *shall not* begin to print till *I have* a thousand guineas for him." Lord Treasurer, after leaving the Queen, came through the room, beckoning Dr Swift to follow him.

Then the seeker of a bishopric was dished with a deanery, and his hour was over. He went back to Ireland to defend the liberties of a country he detested and be hailed as the saviour of a people he despised. He went back, too, to play the village despot, to dominate rustic salons, to pursue his never quite comprehended relations with one woman until she died, and to be followed there by another woman whose passion he trifled with to the point of killing her. He went back to write the *Drapier's Letters* and *A Modest Proposal* and *Gulliver's Travels;* to pun, to exist in self-conscious exile, to complain wrathfully of life, and at last go mad.

There is no proper summarizing of Swift's career. His actions do not stand by themselves, his words are not confined to his books; both, far more than is usually true of men, are tangled up in his character. That character impresses us more than his achievements, fascinates us as much as his books. It is a mesh of fighting opposites. He hated oppression, yet was violently intolerant. He could be very tender, but was less tender than brutal. Too proud, as he said, to be vain, Swift's pride had sillier aspects than most men's vanity. He saw, with terrible lucidity, all the blundering chaos of life and smashed its pretensions to pulp; yet he was not always emancipated or even cynical enough to free his mind of petty thoughts and contemptible desires. Perhaps he preserved his reason as long as he did by revenging the Lilliputian insect-bites in his life to forget, for a moment, the intolerable pain of his Brobdingnagian wounds. He swore he hated mankind but loved John, Thomas, and Peter, yet it was rather mankind that he helped than John, Thomas, or Peter he made happy. It is easy to say that such a mass of contradictions is only Everyman. But it would be difficult to find elsewhere *any* man in whom the contradictions are so tremendous, or the characteristics so intense. Swift went mad, not by having too much mind, but by having too violent a nature for even so strong a mind to cope with!

And singular though he was in so many respects, it is not the oddity but the deep-thrustingness of the man that most fascinates and baffles us. There are perhaps as many eccentric stories told about Swift as about Dr Johnson, but where Johnson was only, in a very great sense, a " character " whose crotchets adorn a substantial Englishman, Swift is a dark and knotted genius unformed in the national, or in any national, mould. That a good deal must be set down to Swift's lifelong ill health, to his deafness and giddiness, is perfectly clear. It was a further cause — it may have been the original cause — for distorting his view of life; and it must have had a great deal to do with making him hate life as much in practice as the usual misanthrope does in theory. Indeed, there is a kind of double-distilled hate in Swift, something in excess of a misanthrope's philosophical needs and of a human being's defensive cursing. It was a hate rich in self-replenishment and incapable of catharsis; and the worst thing of all, for Swift himself, is that he got no enjoyment out of hating.

The tenderness which is the other side of the man, and which, when you come right down to it, existed only toward Esther Johnson, was genuine and deep, but it was not counterbalancing. And it was a little whimsical, a little impure: Swift could not bestow his tenderness without tinkering at it. Whatever he felt toward Stella, he treated her too specially to treat her altogether naturally; and one makes very severe demands (if only to oneself) on whomever one grants a place apart. There was something at once too good and not good enough about Swift's tenderness to Stella. Certainly in the constrained, faintly self-conscious pages he wrote in praise of her just after her death, there is a crushed-out note of remorse and of regret; while the famous words he scrawled: " Only a woman's hair," mean less to me, for all their terrible sentimentality of cynicism, than that any word was scrawled or hair preserved.

On the gossipy side Swift's relations with women have perhaps been too much enlarged upon, but they are too deeply embedded in the unpenetrated darkness of his life to count only as gossip. Whether Swift and Stella ever were married, whether Stella was ever his mistress, or whether Vanessa was ever his mistress are less interesting as facts than as manifestations. The real mystery is psychological — not what it was Swift concealed, but why he chose to conceal it. For we must start with the assumption that it was not posterity he was keeping in the dark, but first Varina, and then Vanessa, and finally Stella. Was there ever such a letter as his second one to Varina? Three years earlier he had made an extravagant avowal and been turned down; now he writes in answer to overtures from her side. He does not say yes or no in any of a dozen fashions for saying either; instead he lays down insulting terms for marrying her. But something beyond an insult must have been in his mind — he could have insultingly rejected her!

In the case of Vanessa, Swift's actions border on the disingenuous. Here was a girl much younger than he was, and much in love with him; he would not marry her, he would not (it is usually supposed) satisfy her without marriage, but he had not the brutal grace to break with her. Where he was curiously insulting to Varina by laying down terms for marriage, he is curiously cruel to Vanessa by laying down terms for friendship. He seems to have played the game with all possible perversity, turning discreet whenever the relationship turned dangerous. There are grounds, of course, for believing it had passed beyond that point, but they are uncertain ones. In any case the girl was kept miserable, as the man well knew. " The tragedy of Vanessa," says Carl Van Doren, " was that Swift saw their drama as a comedy." That is true; but it is true, after all, of many brilliant middle-aged men who have fascinated young girls — only they usually show more heart, and less wit, than Swift did. His chief contribution to the affair was a long poem, intended for Vanessa's private ear, which makes distinctly odd reading.[2]

But if a kind of desire to insult with originality can account for Varina, and a kind of amused and drifting come-hitherness for Vanessa, the principal mystery, Stella, remains unsolved. That all his strange love-making or absence of it has not a psychological but a simple sexual explanation — namely, that Swift was impotent or diseased — is a possible theory; but there is no real evidence to support it. It is possible, also, that ill health, producing a hatred of his own body, instilled in Swift (as John Hayward has remarked) a repulsion for the body's uses. That he loved Stella and loved her deeply, and that he altogether dominated her, can scarcely be doubted. He had known her since her childhood, supervised her education, moulded her taste, brought her to Ireland: in all this there is perhaps less a lover's than a father's hand; and in one sense the document

---

[2] A recent critic, W. B. C. Watkins, has compared Swift's " cruelty to women " with Hamlet's.

he wrote at her death shows a father's pride. But if he thought of her as a child, sometimes he courted her as a woman; and his tone toward her is deeply possessive, not just proprietary. In refusing, after she came with Miss Dingley to Ireland, ever to see her except when a third person was present, Swift must almost certainly have been thinking of something beyond Stella's reputation: of some weakness, some shadowy fatalism, some formal decision long arrived at. The child-fixation occurs to me as at least suggestive: a fatherly feeling on Swift's part too inwoven to permit his becoming Stella's lover with peace of mind; and, again, a symbolic idea that, the world being a bestial and filthy place, Stella must be kept free from its bestiality: in the letter, a virgin; in the spirit, a child. Yet there is something far too fine-spun about such theories once one thinks of a vigorous, brutal, butting man like Swift in the company of the woman he loved week after week, year after year. Such restraint, such sublimation, seems hard to believe of a man who, to speak plainly, would be likelier to rape a woman than patiently court her. Yet of sex itself, quite apart from Stella, we cannot plumb Swift's experience. Others have noted that while he is so often foul-mouthed and filthy, he is almost never obscene. And Stella, whose letters to him Swift destroyed, has tendered posterity not a scrap of evidence. She too is mysterious, and whatever we may choose to believe, the truth about her and Swift can never now be known.

The filth in Swift is, of course, an accessory of his violence. His almost fanatical personal cleanliness is historic, and the dunghill and the latrine did not fascinate but revolted him — yet his writing abounds with references to them. Leslie Stephen is almost surely right in saying that Swift's " intense repugnance to certain images led him to use them as the only adequate expression of his savage contempt." For a man who loathed the world as Swift did, no milder language could begin to express such loathing. But as Stephen also says, so recurrent a practice cannot but indicate a " diseased " mind.

Yet that mind overtops in fascination even the vital, strong-edged, self-consuming personality that sought always to be master, yet was servant of odd causes; that while flaying mankind, assisted obscure and defeated people, and while scorning it, attracted and retained noble friends. Swift is the last person to sum up in pat phrases, yet it is perhaps possible to say of his brain that, even in his prime, it was the brain of a madman. Neither his extraordinary sanity in public affairs nor the very strictness of his logic gainsays this. For they have often a madman's logic, a madman's shrewdness, a madman's insight. Perhaps no one in history has argued more brilliantly and unanswerably, *from false or grotesque premises,* than Swift. And this applies as fully to some of his plain pamphleteering, the *Drapier's Letters* for example, as to his fantasy and fiction. Swift did not have a deep or even a good philosophical mind; nor, when it came to challenging facts or assessing beliefs, an open one. He espoused wrong causes, upheld quibbling doctrines, denounced wise projects, simply because he was a mass of prejudices. He was honest but not enlightened. He had a grammatical mind in an idiomatic nature: that is what makes his thinking so fraudulent in one sense, so magnetic in another, and what assigns him a place with the masters of fiction and not of fact.

Swift's living brain was akin to other men's in dreams. They there, and he in waking, posit an unreal predicament, and act it out with all possible gravity and logic. That is obvious; but they there, and he in waking, enrich the unreal by drawing on their own concrete experience. It is this *concrete,* personal quality, issuing out of our memory rather than our wits, that makes certain dreams so terrifyingly actual; and it is this same concrete quality, made up of all the shreds and patches of life, that distributes Swift's waking brain to such marvellous advantage. It is in his cunning workaday detail that Swift, somewhat like Defoe, is triumphant: Emerson said that Swift always described his fictional characters as if for the police.

Such an approach is a special one even for satire, and it was of special advantage for the kind of satire Swift wrote. He saw nothing that dignified or ennobled life, but only what poisoned and tarnished and degraded it; so that of the world's resources he chose for mention little but the vicious, the shabby, and the commonplace. His plain literal detail is always the detail familiar to the dullest human creature; his success is arrived at, not merely by turning things inside out in the manner of all ironists, but by examining the reversed world with the eyes of John Jones — or call him Lemuel Gulliver. Swift is capable of a complete identification with Gulliver's outlook; he steps perfectly into the shoes of the soulless mediocrity. For understanding or identifying himself with a great nature, an Othello's or a Lear's, he has no equipment at all. He is unpoetic, nonphilosophical, anti-mystical. For revealing the blind blundering of the universe, the commonest of common sense is not only his disguise, but also his weapon. He so managed his revelation as to make it lasting and tremendous; but it is the product of a mind of intense thrust, yet narrow gauge, a mind mimicking sanity, not diffusing it, a mind punishing a world that pretends to be better than it is by making it worse.

Swift's undoing was that he allowed himself nothing to fall back on: beyond even rejecting the world with his mind, he recoiled from love, and in friendship he gave but would not ask or accept. (Consider how, when Stella lay dying and Pope and others put out tentacles of sympathy, Swift utterly ignored them; nor did he ever, after her death, mention her name again.) His pride completed what his hate had begun, and his bitterness became absolute. In his extreme moments, such as the Voyage to the Houyhnhnms in *Gulliver*, we are close to raving, as in Pope's to screaming.

[149

At such moments the satire can have no possible tonic power because it has shot beyond the mark. One can no longer be supposed, as could nineteenth-century writers beginning with Scott, to object to parts of the Voyage through prudery or squeamishness; but for different reasons one must object equally. The magnificent method breaks down, the enchantments of the story dissolve, and despite some superb touches, Swift's inventiveness as a whole grows coarse and iterative. The artist as well as the moralist has lost his grip; Swift becomes more like a Yahoo than he imagined.

By shooting beyond the mark too often and too wilfully Swift, for all his brilliance, must be content with a great special place in literature rather than a great general one. The sum of all his preaching is that only wisdom and virtue should have any credit in the world; the sum of all his experience is that wisdom and virtue barely exist. He might exempt from his harsh indictment an Esther Johnson or an Arbuthnot or — of all people! — a Harley; but of what account are they, set in the scale against the rest of mankind? Swift was left not only without hope but without pity. Even so great a thing as *A Modest Proposal*, blazing with indignation beneath its icy words, has got beyond compassion. It was not out of a great heart but out of a tormented mind that Swift waged the battle that morally elevates his name. In an age of injustice and cynical corruption he fought against man's oppression, against his poverty, against his outrageous toiling and bog-trapped helplessness. A magnificent combat; yet Swift struggled half in darkness, warring against his own resentments as well as other men's, and rose rather above his age than above himself.

We see certain sullen beasts, scattered over the country; they are male and female, dark and leaden-looking, tanned by the sun, and chained to the earth, which they are always digging and turning over with invincible doggedness; they have voices almost articulate, and when they raise themselves on their feet they show human faces, and in truth they are men. They retire at night into their dens, where they live on black bread, water and roots; they save other men the trouble of sowing, toiling and reaping for their livelihood, and thus do not deserve to lack the bread which they themselves have sown.

These words are not Swift's — they are La Bruyère's; and even under the handicap of translation they move us in a way that Swift's do not. Not only because we feel the pity in them, but because without being dispassionate they are impersonal — La Bruyère does not divide his emotions between other men's sufferings and (the point is important) his own very different ones.

Swift's mind was deformed and had in it something contemptible. We can understand, but we must not overlook, his petty side. His Church views were narrow and unconciliatory, the stuff of bigots; and the more oddly so in that he quite lacked religious feeling. It has been plausibly suggested that Swift clung so hard to his dogmas " because they provided him with some sort of fixed convictions in this strange and disastrous muddle . . . and justified him to himself for going on living " when " suicide seemed to be the most reasonable course." If so it was, then indeed the more uncompromising his beliefs, the better. But it does not exonerate him from a rabid intolerance of people who thought otherwise — and often not very much otherwise. " Dog! " he wrote of Bishop Burnet, and lived to call him worse names. Nor can we much tolerate the determined way in which Swift knocked people down, rode roughshod over them, and was childishly high-and-mighty. The showy, parvenu bluster of the scene called up by Bishop Kennett's diary, which I quoted earlier in another connexion, is the action of a man who has turned his back on sensibility. Swift had, besides, too strong a love of fraternizing with the great and of noisily bullying them. He wanted to be " treated like a lord " because, unfortunately, he was not one. We may put that down, perhaps, to the odd streak in so many first-rate people who, knowing their merit in their own field is apparent, try to shine where it is doubtful. And we may put *all* these things down to Swift's being at war with himself; he could not find his equilibrium. A lesser and more careful man, like Addison, could; or pretended he could. We are reminded of Sir James Mackintosh's remark that Addison should have been the dean, and Swift the Secretary of State. So highly placed as that, Swift might have come to terms with life.

Bolingbroke called Swift an inverted hypocrite, implying he was the kind of man who sought to put himself always in the worst light rather than the best. It is a shrewd comment — Dr Johnson made one much the same — and less mystifying than most other things concerning Swift. For, since he could get no real rewards from life, he was reduced to getting perverse gratifications. With all the logic-proceeding-out-of-grotesqueness that he went to Lilliput, he went to Bedlam.

Swift's violent nature has provoked violent partisanship. Many, attracted by his uncommon virtues (or dazzled by his mind), have refused to make much of his faults. Others, like Thackeray and Macaulay, obsessed by his faults, have grudged him his merits and regarded his genius as a high explosive best looked at from afar. Of the genius there is certainly no question. As for the man, he was not so much good or bad as indomitable and fiery on the one hand, and sick and mistaken on the other. He fought well, but not too wisely. For life was hardly what he conceived it to be, and his conception lives on not because of the vigour of his reasoning but because of the greatness of his falsifying — a falsifying still bold and awful, and stamped with the language of a brilliant artist.

Defoe

DEFOE wrote everything that contributes to his lasting reputation inside the space of a very few years. They were not
the years of his physical prime: he was near sixty when he
produced *Robinson Crusoe,* near sixty-five when he produced *Roxana.* Yet these remarkable books did not result
from any sudden or mystic release of energy, or still less
from a long and selfless dedication to art. Defoe had spent
a lifetime practising his trade, and at the end merely practised it to greater advantage. He discharged his masterpieces in the same mood and by the same methods that he
reeled off his pamphlets and hoaxes; and the great works
are set apart from the grubby ones largely because indura-
tion to hackwork gave Defoe the skill to rise above it.

Defoe was less of an artist — by circumstances, temperament, or aspiration — than almost any other great writer in
the range of English letters. From his youth he was caught
up in the practical affairs of living — business, politics, hard-
fisted journalism; these employments kept him on the run,
put him out at hire, exposed him to the pillory, hounded him
to prison. He never lived among writers or reflected about
writing; he merely sat down, in indecent haste, and wrote.
But the need to earn a living, whatever other difficulties it
created, did not lacerate his sensibilities or harrow his soul;
he had no soul, even though as a Dissenter he was forever in-
tent upon saving it. He had instead the most concrete and
empirical mind of the great writers of his age; he trafficked
incessantly in the commerce of life; he seized, with the dispatch of a census-taker, on facts. There was hardly a politician in Defoe's time who did not care more for culture
than Defoe did. Harley collected a superb library; there is
no evidence that Defoe ever dreamed of a modest one.
Bolingbroke became a lord of style; there is no evidence that
Defoe ever interrupted his writing to hunt for a word. No
doubt Defoe would have welcomed a literary patron, but

[153

given his choice, he would have taken, any time, a business backer.

If Defoe was sixty before he wrote anything great, he was quite thirty before he wrote at all. Son of a Nonconformist tradesman, he was bred up to trade; and it was only the political and religious ferments of the late seventeenth century that turned the industrious Dissenter into the path of the pamphleteer. By the end of William's reign Defoe was prospering in William's service; but after William's death, when the Tories were swept into office and dissent fell upon evil days, Defoe swiftly got into trouble. His celebrated *Shortest Way with the Dissenters,* the irony of which first misled and then enraged the high-flying Tories, sent its author to the pillory and Newgate. Released some months later, he went into Harley's pay and founded his *Review.* For some ten years he was to edit England's first sustained journal of opinion; and concurrently, for the pay of a servant, to do the work of a spy.

It would be hard to exaggerate the extent and effectiveness of Defoe's labours during this period. At a time when the pamphlet had as widespread an influence on public opinion as the radio has today, Defoe was the most influential of pamphleteers. At a time when the hired political snooper served the purpose of a Gallup Poll, Defoe snooped indefatigably. The five-thousand-odd pages of the *Review* which Defoe wrote single-handed are not only a contemporary record of immense value, not only evidence of his enormous journalistic industry, but proof in a dozen ways of his journalistic genius. The long article with which each issue of the *Review* opened is clearly the ancestor of the modern editorial. The pieces relating to manners and social life led within a few years to the *Tatler* and the *Spectator.* The gossip items in the *Review's* Advice from the Scandalous Club may claim a certain share of credit in the career of even our present-day columnists. Later in life Defoe was to contrive still other devices of journalism, notably the personal interview; and it is fitting that the first English novel ever serialized in a newspaper (to be sure, it was almost the first English novel) should have been *Robinson Crusoe.*

The man who took to the road in quest of copy, who hung out in alehouses eavesdropping for Harley, who was Whig by inclination but often Tory by trade, who dissected politics and dispensed morality, who could lie his head off and give the impression of speaking gospel truth — lower middle-class to the roots of his nature, hard-headed, sharp-tongued, frank, ingenious, hypocritical — formed no part of the literary life of his day. Despite Swift's dismissing him as " an illiterate fellow whose name I forget," he was well enough educated and certainly well enough known; but as temperament had granted him no feeling for art, so circumstance granted him no share in its spoils. In point of fortune, his practicality served him less well than a feeling for culture served Addison or Prior or Pope.

Defoe was still a hack when late in life he sat down and wrote novels; and he addressed the novels, not to cultivated readers, but to greengrocers and scullery maids and all other plain folk who could read. Defoe wanted fame and fortune clearly enough, but he looked to his own class — at least at the outset — to provide them. In writing *Crusoe* and *Roxana, Moll Flanders* and *Colonel Jacque,* he stuck to his plain, inelegant style, kept in view the public's love of adventure and sex, forestalled censure with glib and solicitous moralizing. The books caught on at once, as well they might, for they must rank with the liveliest narratives we know, and they treat of people who, though they dip into their Bibles when they are about to be undone, lead anything but pious existences. In them, moreover, Defoe roamed the globe: followed Moll Flanders to the Virginia plantations, crossed darkest Africa with Captain Singleton, was shipwrecked off South America with Crusoe. The life of all his characters is hazardous and hard, but their capacity to endure it is British and muscular. Crusoe and Singleton, Moll and Roxana are among the great extraverts of English fiction; they have no time for sensibility since their whole struggle is toward survival. In one sense Moll and Roxana are as crass as Alger heroes in wanting to rise in the world; but actually they are spurred on much less by love of success than by fear of failure. If they are constantly counting their money, it is because they feel constantly insecure: they fear the gutter much more, really, than they do the gallows.

The real stock-in-trade of Defoe's characters is what happens to them, not what they are, as it was Defoe's great gift, not to dissect them, but to drive them on. If his people are real, it is from the vigour with which Defoe could implant in others what was true of himself, or what would have been true in the circumstances, or what was generally true of their kind. Psychology with him seldom went farther than to ask himself what it would be sensible for the average thief or pirate or castaway to do in a given situation. And in a way this is a type of insight not usual among great novelists, since most of them can much better divine the secrets of love or pride or suffering than the operations of common sense.

In the typical Defoe novel the story-telling emerges, in every case, as episodic and picaresque. It could hardly not be, since in every case Defoe was writing about people who led wandering lives; but one may still ask whether Defoe suited his method to his people or found people to exemplify his method. If he had known how to contrive a compact, centralized plot, would he, as a champion of morality, have turned to scenes of domestic happiness? One doubts it. One doubts whether he had the same interest in housewives and shopkeepers that he had in sluts and rogues; and one feels certain that, even if he did, he knew his readers didn't. Being essentially a hypocrite, Defoe may have reasoned that in order to castigate sin you must first uncover it; but whatever his reasoning, almost certainly the desire to chron-

icle free-and-easy lives came first, and the free-and-easy
chronicling came afterwards.

Hence there are no carefully worked-out plots in Defoe;
we simply go with the story. We really care less how Moll
or Roxana will react to a situation than how she will emerge
from it. Experience, to be sure, accentuates the characters
of these people, but it almost never transforms them. All
that really concerns us is whether they will prosper or fail.
This is not because they are one-dimensional characters,
but because they inhabit a one-dimensional world whose
values are altogether mercenary. Among Defoe's many
criminals it is impossible to find even one great character
of evil. Hardened by profession, they remain singularly
easy-going by nature, and as they never struggle violently
against themselves, so they are not embittered or enven-
omed by others. Theft or prostitution or murder is simply
their vocation, and like Falstaff they believe (though they
will not aver) that to labour at one's vocation is no sin. When
they get into a tight place, they hastily thumb their Bibles,
but it is not their peace they want to make with God; it is
a bargain.

But just as too much practicality worked against Defoe's
living fortunes, so it has lowered his posthumous fame. He
is, to be sure, much more than a good story-teller; he is a
convincing realist and a vivid historian whose novels paint
a powerful picture of the disreputable life of his age. That
they are utterly wanting in sensibility, in exaltation, in tragic
force, is inescapable when we consider the temperament of
the man who wrote them. Nevertheless the man would have
been far greater had he not been so crudely moralistic, so
inveterately philistine. He was certainly no Nonconformist
as a novelist: no other writer of his day pandered so much
to popular convention and vulgar morality. He kept shop in
a nation of shopkeepers, and the things he wanted in life,
the things he honoured, lacked all largeness and nobility.

It is going too far to say of Defoe that he knew the price of everything and the value of nothing; but it is going, certainly, in the right direction. He most detested the English workingman because he was not thrifty! And yet, deep down, he knew how tame and dull and safe his values were: there was far more breadth and health in him than suited his ambitions. If he shrewdly grasped the commercial possibilities in picturing the racy side of life, he nevertheless had a persistent interest in it, a strong enjoyment of it. He was a great vulgarian, but an even greater adventurer; and he became, in his field, a great pioneer.

It was Dickens who remarked that *Robinson Crusoe* is the only great novel which never moves the reader to either laughter or tears. The answer is that Defoe was at once too earnest and too easy-going — with a Nonconformist's incapacity to flood his mind with laughter, and a trueborn Englishman's inability to exult or despair. Defoe's novels are like bottled water, which keeps fresh and unadulterated for a very long time. But greater novels are like casked wine that imperceptibly ferments, adding a new quality, which becomes the essential one, to the juice of the pressed-out grapes.

PART II

Provincial Sketches

CHAPTER I

COUNTRY MATTERS

Country Life

WHEN AN EIGHTEENTH-CENTURY STAGECOACH left London behind and lumbered over bumpy uneven roads, it was on its way to a world of different inspirations. A Roman citizen quartered in some remote province of the Empire could hardly have complained more of life there than would an inveterate Londoner in the age of the first Georges who withdrew to a Yorkshire hamlet. For while every new king — and every fresh war — brought to the capital a new existence, with all the lively twists of fashion, the horizons of the countryside were almost as fixed as they were narrow. Before 1750 the death of feudalism was the one profound change — and in practice it was sometimes not profound — that had come over the countryside during hundreds of years. Generation past generation a man lived rooted as his father had done. Traditions reaching back to pagan times, merged with centuries-old traditions of the Church, still dictated the tenor of life. You lived wherever it was that you farmed, or fished, or wove, or tended sheep. Travel was cumbersome and dear, so that men stayed home; communication irregular and slow, so that men stayed largely uninformed; education, if easier than of old, was

[161

still not easy to come by; and to rise in the world, unless in some sense you had already risen, came close to resembling a miracle.

It is only at London and some of the watering-places that we encounter the alternation of pace, variety of manners, currency of ideas, and gloss of personality that offer the historian an almanac. Rustic life has much more of a sameness about it. Yet it was not the mobile face of London that was greatly altered during the eighteenth century; it was the heavy, stocky form of England. Bolingbroke and Marlborough, at one end of the century, might with a little coaching have stepped into the shoes of Fox and Pitt at the other. But changes came over rural England which were permanent and final, and in many respects the villager of 1700 was less close to 1800 than to the Middle Ages. The movement of that hundred years is gradual, orderly, unconfused; there is none of the boiling flux of nineteenth-century activity; but it is none the less a movement whose changes were irrevocable.

The life outside London was, after all, the life of four fifths of the population of England. And in 1700 this four fifths was still largely an agricultural people, living either in deep country or clustered round villages and towns. Every settlement had its lord of the manor, still exercising — or allowed to exercise — some of the prerogatives of feudal days. Villagers and country folk alike tilled the soil: " wheat for export and for bread for the bettermost people; barley for the brewers and for the poor man's loaf; and oats for the horses and, in the north . . . for cakes and bannocks." There was as yet no modern machinery; the farmer did all his work with the scythe and the sickle, and the whole village turned out for the haying and the harvesting. At such seasons extra hands were put to work — discharged soldiers in need of jobs and poor rustics in search of extra shillings. In most communities every commoner had his piece of land, or might draw for it every season; but in an age of large families and crude agricultural methods it seldom yielded enough to keep him going, and he had to eke out his income by serving as a harvester or by having a trade, like carpentry or smithing. In those days the common field system still obtained, so that each man shared to some degree in the common yield; joint ownership extended so far, indeed, as to make the bulls and rams the property of the parish. Life was not plentiful in the rural England of which I write; but except for the aristocracy, all classes stood closer together, and as most men were never extremely rich, so few were extremely poor. And life was to continue thus until, after 1760, the Enclosure System came into more general use; then farming methods much improved, but the small farmer's position greatly declined. The big landlords and " capitalist farmers " began squeezing out the yeoman and turning him into a labourer.

But in those days everything was still simple and not very efficient — life had been worn smooth by centuries of custom, and newfangled things won no welcome because no credence. As men worked, so they governed themselves. To be sure, village life by 1700 had overthrown the jurisdiction of the manor courts in favour of that of magistrates. Crimes and disputes were settled now in the vestries. Generally once in the year the rate-payers came to a vestry meeting (labourers, not paying taxes, were excluded) and elected officials: churchwardens, constables, surveyors of the highway, overseers of the poor, and such outlandish public servants as dog-whippers, hog-wardens, and town scavengers. They levied taxes and passed by-laws, regulated charity and relief, imposed fines and offered rewards. Every settlement, in other words, exercised self-government on relatively democratic principles. Where keeping the peace and putting down crime were concerned, the self-government worked smoothly enough. Where it least succeeded was in taking care of the poor. In England it was not a philanthropic age, and in country parishes it was not a prosperous one. As a result, village officials were for the most part close-fisted in matters of charity. People seeking relief were apt to be sent for their pains to the workhouse; or, if helped, were not relieved. They had, however, one point in their favour. If left stranded, they could appeal to the nearest justice, usually a country gentleman; and since the gentleman was not financially involved himself, he often forced the vestry to spend more on the supplicant than it need have spent in the first place. Records of eighteenth-century charity survive: " Given to Widow Parry to go to the doctor with her sore eyes and a horse to carry her "; or " The Vestry also ordered that Gowlatt's Boy doe have a pair of breeches and a fear-nothing coat."

Town officers, sluggish about helping people, were alert about punishing them. As we know already, the English penal laws were disgraceful; how disgraceful we can judge by seeing what befell those who were not criminals. " Paid Thos. Hawkins for whipping three people y^t had the small pox 8d." Someone else was paid for finding out whether or not a woman was pregnant. Whippings went on at a furious rate and for a variety of reasons. To us they cannot but seem like violent remedies; yet, to do the times justice, perhaps they were substitutes for even stronger measures, as though the community chose to handle its errants like children rather than visit upon them the full severity of the law.

Perhaps we best enter the world outside London not by riding over country roads, or traversing the parks of historic country houses, but by following our nose down the High Street of an eighteenth-century village. At one end probably stands the market-place; and from old engravings we can recall the dun- and brick-coloured shops with their bellied windows, the arches over the alley-ways, and the wooden signs flapping in the wind. Tradesmen go by names that today seem quaint — wheelwright, mercer, mantua-maker. In the smallest villages there might be simply one general dealer: such a man was Thomas Turner of East Hoathley in Sussex, whose *Diary* is a valuable expression of middle-class village life. But what is worthiest of note is that during the very years of which I write, the tradesman's status changed, and changed greatly for the worse. Before 1750 trade bore no great stigma, and younger sons of good family went into it on as honourable terms as they went, a century later, into uniform. It was not odd for a carpenter to be styled a gentleman. By way of trade many men rose from obscurity to power. But around 1750 a change of attitude began to prevail; it was said to have come from Germany with the Georges; it spread fast and soon loomed large. Thereafter the word *trade* stank in English nostrils, and the tradesman's status sank so low that, at the century's close, there is record of exactly one merchant becoming a lord — and he at the cost of an outcry.

Nothing is here for tears, however. The tradesman for the most part did pretty well for himself. Defoe, early in the century, set four hundred pounds a year as a very usual tradesman's income; a descendant of Thomas Turner's, late in the century, had an annual turnover of five thousand pounds. These were very large takings in view of the value of money in those days. Turner himself confesses, and others refer, to much good eating and drink; such a man might go to the races on his own horse, own the house he lived in and his neighbour's to boot, give his children excellent schooling, clothe his family in some style, and — though this does not prove very much — gamble inordinately. Nor were country tradesmen without education. Crabbe's father took in *The Philosophical Magazine;* a tailor's widow boasted of having read Milton; Turner himself constantly read good books. It is easy to see how, where feudal conceptions had long given country people either a quite lofty or a quite lowly station, these tradesmen who made up a rising middle class might become figures of some importance.

[165

They voted and held office; lent money and owned mort-
gages; and were in a fair way to becoming village benefactors or village despots. The poorer villagers, on the other
hand, had neither means nor education. The painted sign
outside a shop was not an ornament merely. The barber's
pole (originally intended as a limb swathed in bandages),
the chemist's coloured jars, the banker's three gilt balls,
were marks of identification for those (and they were most
of the village) who could not read.

The tradesman worked for his money, often performing
all kinds of jobs. A smith, for example, might be also a
metalworker and hardware merchant; now and then he
would even make andirons or grills. Shops opened at day-
break and closed long after nightfall. They never shut down
during the week, and though only " macarel and milk " were
supposed to be sold on Sunday, even Sunday, as time went
on, became something of a trading day. There were a few
holidays — not those we might expect, such as Christmas
or Good Friday, but rather Guy Fawkes Day or the anni-
versary of the beheading of Charles I. Fairs might end in
a flush of gambling or a debauch of drink, but the trader
seldom threw caution to the winds before he had got most
of his business transacted. Not all tradesmen, of course,
were shopkeepers: there were wool, linen, and cotton weavers, cattle dealers and corn factors, sawyers and millers.

The employer class — to which we subjoin the lawyer,
doctor, clergyman, and schoolmaster as socially on the same
or a slightly higher level — went its own way, essentially
removed from gentry and workingman alike. They were
middle-class enough, though not in the rigid sense that
prospering provincials were soon to become so. Morality
obsessed but did not discommode them; their habits, formed
on old country traditions and the coarse idiom of the times,
were at obvious variance with their ideals. Thomas Turner
is our best index to the tradesman character. A rustic Pepys,
he is not so ingratiating as his predecessor, but just as

frank; and quite comparable to Pepys as a repenting sinner. His sins, however, are not comparable at all. He was no wencher; it was drink that made all the trouble for him. Ceaselessly he laments having taken too much and then gone on to act the fool. After two hundred years, his hang-overs give you yourself a touch of headache; his *What else can I do when others drink?* strikes a sympathetic chord; his good resolutions, hardly kept from one journal entry to the next, induce a smile. Surely drink was the great social in-dulgence of these provincials; upon it apparently depended their goodfellowship; and from it arose such capers as soon turned into brawls. The pastor himself might play a part in these goings-on. There was gambling too, at small stakes, throughout the night, the bottle always on the table.[1] Turner went with other men to fairs, to neighbouring towns, to race-meets; he was constant at funerals; less constant at church; and sometimes watched a cockfight or played in a cricket match. Business had its ups and downs: he grum-bles over debts and a need for cash; then, as trade gets brisker, spends money more freely and finds it good to be alive. There are numerous touches of home life in the *Diary* — hours spent reading poetry and sermons; heavy meals; lovey-dovey moments with his wife; quarrelsome hours, days, and weeks with her. Half-way through the *Diary* Mrs Turner dies; and Thomas, not at all a hypocrite but very much a sentimentalist, feels empty without her, sighs over the past, mistrusts the future; until, with the passage of years, he goes once more a-courting, once more marries, and on the occasion of his marriage (perhaps by mere accident) ends his *Diary* forever. It is a record that might commemo-rate many other lives than his own.

---

[1] Cf. Dr Johnson, speaking of his country youth: " All the decent peo-ple in Lichfield got drunk every night and were not the worse thought of."

CHAPTER II

THE COUNTRY GENTLEMAN

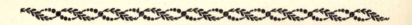

WHEN MENTION IS MADE of the eighteenth-century country gentleman, even the poorest of us is rich in memories, and may presume to speak, on *that* subject, with a certain assurance. For who has forgotten Sir Roger courting his widow, or Squire Western abandoning the hunt for Sophia in favour of hunting the fox? These two Tories, the one benevolent, the other irascible, the first strained through the genteel cheesecloth of Addison's fancy, the other left robustly in the raw, would seem to light us home through an otherwise uncharted wilderness. There they stand like corpulent landmarks, and when we see them, we seem to see England in her prime.

During a century rich in " characters," the squirearchy were, it may be, richest. Of all those with the leisure to acquire mannerisms, the country gentlemen acquired the most vivid; even to their contemporaries they seemed a little quaint and odd. All the same, their picturesqueness can be over-emphasized, for they were born into a kind of slavery. For a squire true to type, do not look to the great manor houses of England; do not call to mind a great park, a blooded stable, a dashing foxhunt, footmen in brilliant livery. We are not at Arundel, or Blenheim, or Chatsworth, or

168]

Castle Howard. The run of eighteenth-century squires were of a lower, less affluent order. They were gentry — a word that forbade them to work for their living yet failed to assure them of one; that saved them from the opprobrium of being middle-class, yet withheld from them the cachet of being aristocratic. Some few country gentlemen were very wealthy, others became wealthy as time went on; but they were usually not wealthy at all, not well known ten leagues from home, not participants in the banking, the legislating, the empire-building of eighteenth-century England. They were simply lords of their neighbourhood — so long as no actual lord resided in it.

Those at the top, to be sure, for the most part led a life of pleasure and, if their means sufficed, they might avoid the provincialism to which by nature they were condemned. Years at a good public school and then at Oxford or Cambridge might instil in them, if little knowledge, a certain aptitude for the graces. Or, instead of studying at one of the universities, they might embark on the grand tour and learn how they order these matters better in France, might winter in Rome or summer in Avignon, put one foot before another in a great lady's salon, and catch sight — however bashfully — of music and art. As time passed, such men might sit in Parliament and so spend part of each year in London. A comfortable squire's son might marry a rich nobleman's daughter and rapidly acquire the entrée into the world of fashion. The intermingling of gentry with peerage was a common practice of the eighteenth century, and went far toward extending the limits of good society. It is to patrician and squire alike, where either man had means, that we owe so many of the beautiful manor houses built or restored in the reign of Anne or the Georges. The very best of such men filled their houses with superb furniture and plate; laid hands on old masters for their drawing-rooms and galleries; stocked their libraries with books, their greenhouses with flowers; and hauled up from their cellars

[169

the claret that brightened, and the port that shortened, their lives.

But this is the more romantic side of the picture. Far less attractive was the life of most country gentlemen; far less so, indeed, than the life of, for example, Squire Western. For Western had money, and the run of his kind had not. Where they did resemble him, for the most part, was in a boorishness, an obscenity, an immitigable coarseness that were extreme enough to disgust so case-hardened a man of the world as Fielding. By birth and insolence alone did they tower above the rest of the neighbourhood, for they were ignorant, stupid, loutish guzzlers, and little more. They gobbled up meat and swilled down liquor, played stable-boys' jokes, were seasoned lechers, bold riders, fuming Tories, and an example to the parish.

Such a life was more or less thrust upon the petty squire. Supposing his income to be a few hundred pounds a year, he might early in the century have thriven in some comfort, but as his income stayed the same and its buying power declined, he found the amenities passing beyond his reach. He could not travel or buy books or keep his house in repair or educate his sons. It was not uncommon for him to lose his status of country gentleman and drop to the level of a yeoman farmer. London might come to be as remote for him as a Virginia plantation: a rustic in his thinking and tastes, he became a yokel in his habits. The village fair, a neighbouring race-meet, a plebeian cockfight, smoking and drinking in an alehouse, some hunting and fishing, some local political gossip — these, together with his wenching, composed the sum of his pleasures. Also, as likely as not, he was the justice of the peace in his neighbourhood and could command small fees in payment for his work. But except where he exploited the job — and in an age filthy with corruption it is to the squire's credit that he almost never took bribes and often refused fees — his income was little increased by his service. Squires became magistrates partly through a desire for self-importance, partly through a smug paternalism; and the consensus is that they dispensed sound Tory justice.

But let us look at a country house maintained by neither a gentleman just a cut below an aristocrat nor a squire just a cut above a farmer. He himself will doubtless be more like Squire Western than like the estimable Coke of Norfolk; will take in one newspaper and no literary magazine; will speak the dialect of the region rather than the King's English (assuming the King spoke English); will be Stuart in sympathies but Hanoverian in deportment; and will carry into his drawing-room little more than muddy jackboots. He will preside over a large picture-puzzle house which keeps its hearth-fire roaring, will set a solid table, and with no misgivings bring up a numerous and obedient family. In winter, should he live too much outside the world, with wind howling round his eaves and snow blocking up the roads, he and his tribe will move to the nearest town or go to an inland spa like Bath or Tunbridge. Even during the summer it remains an age of deep-rutted highways and lumbering coaches, so that visiting among friends is no afternoon's outing. When friends come to see him, they will be urged — though it is no more than what they expect — to stay for months on end. The best bedrooms are swept out, a good cob is put at the disposal of the paterfamilias, a round of late suppers tops off days spent in the saddle, and it is no miracle for a country ball to be arranged. Civilized man can visualize nothing much duller, yet there are friendliness and stupidity to mitigate the dullness, and the men will go through it, for the most part, drunk.

In most respects we may draw a confining circle around an eighteenth-century country house, and espy inside it a quite self-sustaining little world. Over every estate there lorded it some petty absolute monarch. There has long existed a story of George III being told off by some such potentate for trespassing on his confines. " Do you know whom you address? " asked the King, more startled than stern. " Yes," replied his subject, " I know I have the King of England talking to me: but I, too, am king upon my own property." This attitude partook of more than arrogance. Virtually everything that made up a squire's life originated on his own acres. He was his own farmer, sowing his own grain, planting his own vegetables, and garnering his own fruit. He was his own dairyman and butcher; he might well be his own horse-breeder and have his own kennels. Though he had to buy his wine, his cordials were made in his own kitchen; though he bought his writing-paper, he made his own ink (still legible after two hundred years). And he made his own candles and his own soap; and with the help of an itinerant weaver, his wife made all his cloth.

Withal, considering how old-fashioned a life it was, there was a surprising amount of comfort. The times, of course, were changing: country life was not the same under the Stuarts as under the Georges. Where once all the boys slept any-which-way in one large dormitory, and all the girls in another, while the servants dropped down at night wherever they could find a pallet, within a generation it became the custom for members of the family to have private bedrooms, and for servants to have separate quarters. Where, under Queen Anne, country people might still be found drinking mead, a few years later they all drank port. Gout must have been even more widespread in the provinces than in town, for not only did squires constantly inflame themselves with port, but they were the most prodigious meat-eaters of modern times. Their bulging red faces and bursting fat forms are legendary. Only the saddle preserved them from complete bodily ruin.

As for the wives, theirs was a full life, bearing and bringing up children, humouring their husbands' whims, and managing the large, rambling, faulty, draughty houses. There were Gargantuan meals to superintend, seasonal washings of linen to oversee, cellars and pantries and wardrobes and lumber-rooms to keep in order. There might be many servants — but servants were only, in one sense, an added charge; and we must never forget that it was a period of everlasting illness. If the squire grew up to a life of leisure, not so his wife, and it is no wonder that she often had need of those " waiting gentlewomen "[1] who were a phenomenon of the times. These consisted, for the most part, of unmarried women from good but impoverished families who, though they dared not openly work, might condescend to " assist " in suitable establishments. Nominally they lived on equal terms with the families they served; actually they were treated with an insolence which the lower servants were spared. In most cases waiting gentlewomen seem to have hated their work, and as soon as possible abandoned it for the lesser humiliations of marriage.

Rustic marriage, even among well-born people, still smacked of days gone by. It was pastoral, if not perhaps in the best sense. During most of the century the parties involved were neither consulted nor considered, and marriages of convenience were quite as common as lovers' meetings. But in practice the English temperament rejected an idea that has always been taken as a matter of course by Continentals, so that young people frequently eloped, and old people frequently forgave them. Orthodox marriages were seldom very grand; there was much less to-do than in later times. A spinet, a tea-service, some old family furniture usually sufficed to indicate the family's pleasure in the event. But if parents were restrained, the countryside grew heady in thinking of the occasion: there were always feasting and toasting, dancing and drinking, and then the bringing home the bride to her husband's house, where, after supper, her bridesmaids put her to bed. Then the entire wedding party clustered round the bridal couple and indulged their high spirits after the hymeneal customs of centuries: which means in plain English that they said and did virtu-

---

[1] Of whom Fielding's Mrs Slipslop was a not very good example.

ally anything that might embarrass the bride and groom.
And when, at length, they withdrew, it was only until day-
break. Returning then, they serenaded the young couple
outside their window, not with song only, but with a clatter
of kettles and pans and a pounding of pokers and shovels.
These customs, which survived for generations among the
common people, and still survive in places extremely remote, gradually proved too much for the better-born, and
then and there arose the idea of a honeymoon. So now the
happy pair might venture as far afield as Scarborough or
Bath, though not alone: it was considered seemly for the
bride to take one of her bridesmaids with her.

It was by funerals, not weddings, that the gentry revealed
its love of show. Mourning — strict, deep, unequivocal
mourning — was *de rigueur*. Not only clothes, but furniture and household linen also, were draped and edged
with black. Funerals were elaborate and expensive, with
hired mourners carrying lights and branches, while the
bier, heavily tricked out in lugubrious velvets, was illuminated with a whole constellation of candles. It was customary to send valuable mourning rings, or other mementoes,
to near relatives and friends and to provide them, after the
funeral, with a magnificent feast. A hundred curious details
accentuated the pomp; nothing more ceremonial has ever
met the eye of man.

In such a fashion a life not otherwise ringed by splendour
went back to God.

CHAPTER III

OXFORD AND CAMBRIDGE

1

To PICTURE A CENTURY of life at England's two great universities would seem like a formidable undertaking. Even for the tough-minded, vistas open of grave application in a classical era, or at least an era that got the classics by heart. Never, one would suppose, were dons more donnish or was midnight oil more freely burned; never did men compose a more delightful society, growing discursive over a pipe and mellow over a bottle. And during a century which witnessed the overthrow of superstition and the domestication of sentiment, it would seem natural for Learning to live at home. But neither Oxford, "the home of great movements," nor Cambridge, "the home of great men," had any true vitality. The best minds that came in contact with them, far from coming of age within their walls, rejected them as stuffy, pedantic, and snobbish. The worst minds that came in contact with them, far from profiting by the introduction, suffered from it. Both universities were high-sounding but empty: Cowper's commentary sticks in the memory like a bur — "ignorance in stilts."

There was more than one reason for this lack of light and air, but the decadence of society was surely the most

[¹75

important. Like most institutions that are the badge of a special class, the universities defended that class more, even, than its own members did. The powers controlling Oxford and Cambridge were the aristocracy and the Church. In times past it had been the great merit of the aristocracy to maintain learning, and of the Church to uphold morality; then, though the universities might be exclusive, they conferred a real superiority on those whom they did not exclude. But by the early part of the eighteenth century the great world simply regarded Oxford and Cambridge as places where young gentlemen might go to amuse themselves; and the Church, whose object might once have been to obstruct depravity, was satisfied now to obstruct progress.

Thus to the stodgy clerical traditions of the dons was added the frivolous nonchalance of the students. Those whose home Oxford was for life jealously guarded their proprietorship against invaders, but were glad to help young worldlings, whose home it might be for a year or two, to enjoy their visit. And to be a gentleman commoner at Oxford or a fellow commoner at Cambridge was indeed to live in clover. The price came high, but it was worth the price. One might eat well, use poor students for valets, join good clubs, smoke and drink at one's ease, and be under not the slightest obligation to work. There were instances of young men who never went to lectures — indeed, of professors who never provided any lectures to go to. There were young men who never opened a book — worse yet, who never *met* their tutors. Historians contend that toward the middle of the century things had begun to improve, yet Gibbon, who entered Oxford in the spring of 1754, draws a picture of carousing students, condoning tutors, and fellows who had absolved their conscience " from the toil of reading, or thinking, or writing "; and others — Adam Smith for one — chime in with what he had to say.

The attitude of the universities toward their students was not the result of laxness only. It was the accepted attitude toward young men of fashion. Privilege was their birth-right and pleasure their destiny, so that tutors, with the thought of preferment ever in mind, did all they could to please. One Oxford don, for example, used to sit up till two in the morning drinking with an adolescent duke. And if the young men were under no academic orders to study, they had no worldly incentive either. So long as they ac-quired the *leniores virtutes* with which Chesterfield was always haranguing his son — so long as they learned how to bow and strut, wear a coat, dance a minuet, gamble with sang-froid, drink with poise, philander with grace, insult with style, they were well on their way toward success. The failure of the universities to teach them anything more (if *they* can be said to have taught them *that*) was due, not to any mitigating lack of ability, but to a thorough lack of demand.

Poor students, to be sure, inhabited a different world. The sizars at Cambridge and the servitors at Oxford did not eat with young lords, though they sometimes ate what the young lords had left on their plates. Nor did they pitch upon whatever adventure or amour might lie in wait; or go to bed drugged with port or claret. Rather were they waiters, pressers, barbers, jacks-of-all-trades, living and learning as best they were able. Such was the college life pursued by men like Dr Johnson — though Johnson himself was not a servitor — and its makeshifts and insecurity made men like Dr Johnson bitter and rebellious. Yet such men had to face the fact — as no doubt they must in any age — that this was their one way of getting ahead in the world. That many of them, offended in spirit and sorely taxed in endurance, left without taking a degree is not surprising. What is surprising is that some of them, like Johnson, re-mained faithful to the Tory scheme of things.

When we turn to the life of the professors, we must free our minds of the notion that academic men gave over their days and nights, with cloistral aloofness, to study. Oxford and Cambridge were in only one particular to the eighteenth century what the monasteries were to the Middle Ages: more than a touch of monastic mustiness, and hieratic formality, adhered to the college walls. The sequestration of the dons was great enough to provide a short trip to Epsom or Tunbridge with all the adventurousness of the grand tour. There were men who spent their entire lives in a single place, snobbishly glad to be there; but it is another matter to suppose that they strove incessantly after wisdom. Many of them were bigots, many others pedants, many others wranglers, and not a few all three. The atmosphere was clerical without being Christian. At Oxford the statutes of Laud governed the university, unaltered, until 1760. The Cambridge statutes went even farther back, to Elizabethan times. At both places the scholars were pre-eminently politicians, seeking promotion and preferment. Otherwise they were singularly inactive. There were men who never lectured from one year to the next, and those who did were for the most part backward and unenlightened. At Oxford in particular the faculty showed a pronounced hatred of new ideas. Now and then somebody might make a contribution to pure scholarship, restoring a corrupt Greek or Latin manuscript to its proper form, or dabble with the punctuation in a garbled edition of Hooker or Andrewes. But in their thinking the universities, far from taking the lead, straggled near the end of the procession. They were chiefly lethargic. But they were hardly more lethargic than they were parochial. Hedged in from life, fellows and dons meddled in one another's business, talked one another's (and nobody else's) language, joked at one another's expense.

Yet it is only fair to say that some heads jutted up above the crowd and began a renovation that with time would disturb and even abolish the worst practices of the past. Self-centred academic oligarchies, setting the pace from on

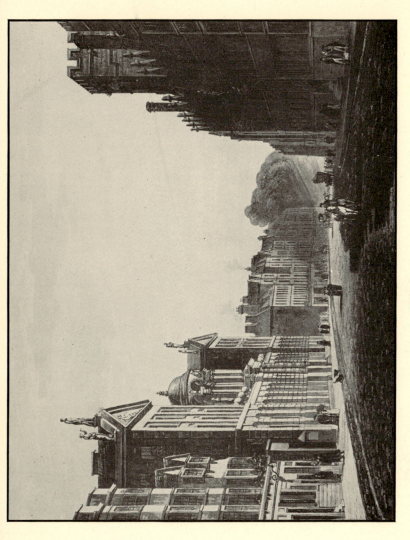

High Street, University and Queens, Oxford by Pugin

high, could not have their way forever; and now and then somebody appeared who was more than not lazy — who was actually not dull. Such a man, by his rarity, attracted a following and exerted an influence. In the matter of progress, however, we must differentiate sharply between Oxford and Cambridge, for the latter surpassed the former in every way. Cambridge had felt, for one thing, the impact of Newton's mind, so that all through the eighteenth century she revealed a great aptitude for science. Between 1702 and 1727, chairs were established at Cambridge in astronomy, anatomy, geology, and botany; and it was during those same years that Dr Bentley rejuvenated classical learning. Such not wholly forgotten names as Covel, Sherlock, Law, and Milner also throve during the century at Cambridge and did something to dissipate the old sluggishness.

The chief reason why Cambridge outran Oxford is clearly a political one. Oxford was overwhelmingly Tory, Cambridge predominantly Whig. And Whig sentiment was relatively progressive. There was a certain amount of truth in the famous Cambridge epigram:

> *The King to Oxford sent a troop of horse,*
> *For Tories own no argument but force;*
> *With equal skill to Cambridge books he sent,*
> *For Whigs admit no force but argument.*

Oxford, indeed, was not merely a Tory stronghold — it was " the Jacobite capital of England." Following the accession of George I, thither went a good many disaffected adherents of James III, non-jurors and High-Churchmen. Nor was it at Oxford a mere matter of political sympathies. Hundreds of scholars whose opinions had cost them their jobs saw in the restoration of James their own restoration to office. It was at Oxford that some of the most influential Jacobites conspired; indeed, at only three colleges were the heads anything less than rabidly disloyal to the Crown. When

[¹79

Sacheverell came to Oxford after his trial, he was received
hysterically; on the Pretender's birthday almost everybody
got drunk; and on one birthday of George I a Jacobite mob
turned a skimpy Whig celebration into a brawl.

Jacobite sentiment persisted at Oxford long after Jacobitism had become a hopeless cause. While the Whig power
held — and it held unbroken until after the accession of
George III — Oxford, however reactionary in belief, was
revolutionary in spirit. But once the Tories returned to
power and Tory scholars obtained fat jobs — once, that is,
a Guelph king summed up all that one might ask of a Stuart
— Jacobitism melted away. Successful themselves, the Oxford Tories no longer demanded success for their cause. As
for Oxford itself, no comparable intellectual stupor has visited it since.

2

ANY search for a representative university figure must end
in the choice of a singularly unrepresentative one. Once you
think of Dr Bentley, no other candidate will serve — just as,
in any real sense, no other candidate has survived. Bentley's
academic career is comedy of the first order, and nowhere
can scholarship produce a doughtier, more high-handed,
more overpowering figure. Richard Bentley is one of England's true claims to a place in scholarship. He changed the
face of classical learning not only by his brilliant research
but by his triumphant introduction of method. He con-
founded, he emended, he contradicted, he restored. Quite
often he improvised: he would take a garbled Greek frag-
ment, untwist what he took, and adduce what was lacking;
years later the whole passage would come to light, and
Bentley be proved correct to the last detail. Upon his foundations, faulty though they sometimes are, a totally re-
freshed modern scholarship has been erected in the classics;

and his name must always be a synonym for enormous and prodigious learning.[1]

But Bentley was more than a scholar. For forty-two years he was also Master of Trinity College, Cambridge. In the frigid computation of posterity those years stand for no more than a certain increased prestige for Trinity College. But in their own lifetime those years represent the equivalent of a dozen stormy parliaments: they bristle with academic feuds, break out into a rash of mock-heroic scandals, splutter with defiance, and leer at the law. By sheer nerve Bentley converted himself into a modern political boss, and at the expense of all custom, courtesy, law, and reason, he domineered over the fellows of Trinity and whipped them into submission. He bullied men into resigning and browbeat others into thinking they had been expelled; he pocketed Trinity's money and got Trinity to satisfy his exorbitant demands; he broke rules he was supposed to follow, he made others follow rules they were supposed to break. Nothing could put Richard Bentley out of countenance. Nothing, time proved, could put him out of office. The attempt was made for nearly thirty years: recourse was had to lawyers and law courts, bishops and cabinet ministers, and even Queen Anne herself. But if Bentley was often the defendant in lawsuits, he was even oftener the plaintiff. Nothing seems to have given him greater pleasure than the sight of a courtroom. He flung out suits, appeals, counter-charges, pleas for writs, anything that would give him redress if the fault was another's, or respite if the fault was his.

Meanwhile his victims persisted in trying to oust him. One bishop got so far as to write out Bentley's expulsion, but died before he could pronounce it. At length a second bishop plainly expelled him; but for many years Bentley

---

[1] " Bentley's faculty for discovering truth," said A. E. Housman in that terrifying introduction to the Manilius, "has no equal in the history of learning."

stayed in office simply by refusing to let the official bearer of the tidings deliver them. To Dr Colbatch, Bentley's most relentless enemy, this came as the bitterest blow of all. Colbatch had spent his entire life at the one job of trying to get Bentley dispossessed as Master of Trinity; and now that he had succeeded, he found that he had failed. The bishop's decree came as an irresistible force. But Bentley chose to be an immovable object, and in doing so, supplied an answer to an age-old question.

Yet in this comedy of men getting gouty and grey, of men dying and turning to dust, while pursuing a rugged, redoubtable tyrant, we must discern more than a monumental joke, more even than the eighteenth century's mania for litigation, more than disrespect for the law and a complete disregard of ethics. Bentley himself was an impressive figure. He was a born executive if a brutal one. He awakened a parochial Cambridge not only to the uses of study but to the power of learning, and though he abused his position, in the end he justified it. If posterity does not place quite the lordly opinion on Bentley that he placed with supreme egotism on himself, it concedes that he knew his business. He was very likely one of those men who run things because they have no confidence in the judgment of others, and who are as often found in universities as in corporations and governments. If they are not always so successful as Bentley was, they are seldom so able. But it would be difficult to find one anywhere among them who was so passionately disliked.

CHAPTER IV

BATH

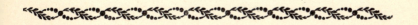

BATH, LIKE POWDERED HAIR and the minuet, seems peculiarly the bequest of the eighteenth century to those for whom memorials must be glamorous. Though it antedates the Roman conquest of Britain and may still be looked upon virtually intact, the real Bath belongs — as any one with a historical sense is aware — to the days of Pope and Johnson. It awoke under Anne and went back to sleep during the Regency. One visits it today largely for its past alone, as one visits Treves or Carcassonne or Pompeii. What it was still can be descried, though I would dispute that any ghosts now walk there. For Bath had pomp and elegance and a kind of magnificent dullness, and they are preserved in its stone and its gardens and its crescents. It had, too, just a touch of absurdity — of that absurdity implicit in a reign of reason and decorum. But the Bath dear to sentimentalists, a city ripe for gaiety and pleasure, very likely never existed.

Queen Anne gave it currency by visiting it during the first year of her reign. Others soon followed, and by 1704 it boasted its first Pump Room, by 1707 its first theatre, and by 1708 its first assembly. But it was not until Beau Nash set up as Master of Ceremonies that it caught the light it

[183

was so long to hold. Nash and two others, Ralph Allen and an architect named John Wood, were the city's patron saints. Allen financed a scheme for converting Bath into a true capital, and Wood converted it. Wood, with a light, sure, classical touch, satisfied eighteenth-century taste and, which is perhaps less to his credit, satisfies ours. Only when he spread himself over Prior Park, where Allen chose to live, did Wood come to grief. Prior Park is architecturally monstrous; its prestige lies elsewhere, in having dispensed years of hospitality to the great.

For soon enough after Nash set up as drillmaster — previously he had been a gambler — the great invaded Bath. They came for a dozen reasons: to take the waters, to change the air, to embrace (or forget) matrimony, to be with friends, to gamble, to enjoy a round of ceremonial pleasure; and if that were not enough, they came because Bath was the rage. No sooner had they arrived than the Beau, immaculately turned out, would call upon them. And no sooner had he called than they realized into what hands they had fallen. For Nash brooked no disobedience; he was King of Bath, his word was law, and the way of the transgressor was hard. He could petrify a mere gentlewoman, triumph over a Duchess of Marlborough, tilt swords with even a princess of the blood royal. He abolished duelling; he made clear how one should dress, when one might dance, where one might bathe. And under such an autocrat Bath bloomed, and everybody regarded it as a sort of privilege to obey his orders.

There was a good deal to do at Bath, provided you were willing to do it when it could be done. You might get up in the morning, for example. And then you might go take the waters. Gentlemen in drawers and ladies in brown linen shifts pushed themselves around the baths, their basins, which contained handkerchiefs and powder-boxes, bobbing up and down like corks. (Once the villainously tall Duchess of Norfolk commanded that the water flow in till it reached her chin, thus half-drowning all bathers of short or middle height.) After bathing, one went — if one were fashionable enough — to a private breakfast party. Then one might dance, out of doors, a minuet; or go to the Pump Room; or attend morning service — morning service was a kind of fashion show. Then followed concerts, lectures, visits to the lending libraries, shopping tours, stops at coffeehouses. All this was marking time before the high point of the solar day — the pompous promenade at four o'clock in the afternoon. It was the hour when cats went to look at kings, when ladies loaded themselves down with finery, when Pope or Addison, and later Smollett or Fielding, might stroll by, when the very great advanced with their retinues and passed on. After dinner came further promenading; and at last the sun went down, the theatres opened, the unwearied card playing began, or perhaps it was the occasion for a ball. An account of a ball over which, with infinite punctilio, the Beau presided, would be very tedious. The balls themselves can hardly have been lively or have continued very late. At Bath, we are told, there was "not a fiddle nor a card after eleven."

It was for this kind of life that the upper and middle classes of eighteenth-century England flocked to Bath. The drowsy watering-place of 1700 had become by 1750 a capital of fashion, never rivalled in England and scarcely rivalled abroad. The reverberating voice of Bath affected the fate of a book, a play, an actress in London. Even after the new laws put an end to gambling at Bath, the splendour of the place remained unclouded. It was rather Beau Nash, who had enjoyed a share in the gambling receipts, that fell thence into a decline. The courtly martinet, with his humourless pomp, his generosities, his good intentions, his meddling puritanism, who by means of a formula had created a kingdom, fell into an impecunious old age; but was never, till the day he died, without honour. He had shaken the hand, and refused to shake the hand, of the most illustrious men

and women in England. He had seen a scrawny town trans-
posed into a paradise for classicists; he had lured healthy
people to sick men's haunts, and prescribed for them; he had
seen fortunes made and lost, and had made and lost his own;
he had witnessed, at Bath, the most curiously snobbish of
democracies. For people sojourning there took up with one
another regardless of social standing, and a duchess might
drink the waters out of the same glass as her dressmaker.
But afterwards, in London, a great lady would cut dead
the same merchant's wife with whom, a month earlier, she
had exchanged confidences. Bath, for all its correctness,
was the eighteenth-century equivalent of shipboard inti-
macies.

It was also a great hive for gossip. Nothing went unde-
tected, nothing there went unsurmised. Where the world
flocked in search of diversion, where match-making mothers
brought marriageable daughters, where gallants pitched
camp and fortunes changed masters, was bound in no time
to be the stronghold of scandalmongers. But in spite of
appearances, knowing people insisted that Bath was unrea-
sonably virtuous. " Farewell, dear Bath! " a lady of fashion,
turning in her coach, apostrophized it: "nowhere so much
scandal, nowhere so little sin! "

Among the countless extravagances that cropped up at
Bath, perhaps historically the most interesting concern the
doings of Selina, Countess of Huntingdon. This woman,
a convert to Methodism, was sunk so deep in piety and
raised so high by fervour that quite single-handed she
turned her religion into a fad. She began with all the assurance of a peeress, respecting neither persons nor occasions;
Methodism was her life, Methodism was her (and your)
salvation; she talked — it would be truer to say she preached
— religion incessantly; she issued invitations in order to
preach it; she accepted invitations in order to preach it; she
harangued sinners in ballrooms, waylaid them in gambling
saloons; she railed — successfully — even against frivolous

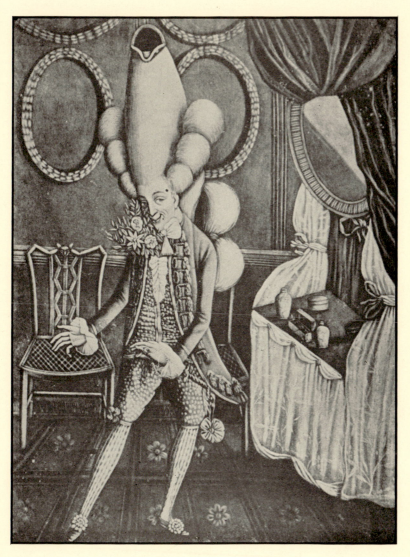

Fashions of the Macaronies — mezzotint, c. 1780

archbishops. A gaunt hideous woman, Lady Huntingdon must have looked as she acted, like the Voice of Conscience. She has been condemned, as a pious woman, for living out her life at Bath; but surely an evangelist should set up in the centre of pleasure, should, as Charles Wesley said, attack Satan " at his headquarters." She lived quite properly among sinners, and brought within their hearing not only her own fulminations, but every mouthpiece of Methodism she could lure to Bath. Wesley himself preached there; it was the occasion for his famous contretemps with Nash. *Nash:* " Your preaching frightens people out of their wits." *Wesley:* " Sir, did you ever hear me preach? " " No." " How then can you judge of what you have never heard? " " Sir, by common report." " Common report is not enough. Give me leave, sir, to ask, is not your name Nash? " " My name is Nash." " Sir, I dare not judge of you by common report." But this victory was almost Wesley's only one at Bath, though later the Countess made Wesley's doctrines into a nine days' wonder for the bored.

Bath, after Nash's heyday, by no means at once declined. Its glories lasted out two more generations, and we are on the whole more impressed by life at Bath after the drill-master's eclipse. The spa of later in the century was a city which, freed of compulsions, more truly possessed style: a city where Herschel, while discovering Uranus in his spare time, conducted the band; where Mrs Siddons acted; where Gainsborough became the rage; where the eccentric Beckfords moved into Prior Park; where Horace Walpole and Sheridan and Fanny Burney and Mrs Thrale and Dr Johnson and Nelson and Goldsmith and Lawrence and Clive and Burke and Pitt and, at length, Jane Austen achieved for Bath that brilliance never quite to be obtained by lineage alone. We can see Bath at length, before it sinks into a stupor brought on by too many colonels' widows, enhanced by maturity and tradition, and from being a health resort and a hub of fashion, becoming a safe retreat for culture. We can see there what was enduring as well as what was transitory about the eighteenth century. But it was after all an insulated world. Its horizons were contracting, not expanding ones. Culture's citadel, always a very superior place, will feel self-righteous even when it is not right. And Bath enclosed, perhaps, something else than culture: it was the guardian of a dream, an eighteenth-century dream of elegance and style. In the end, as can scarcely be a surprise, Bath did not wake from its " fat slumbers " but sank deeper and deeper in them, and expired.

Probably Bath was dull.[1] But it was dull in a lordly way; and only absurd because it kept so painstakingly a sense of proportion. It represents the triumph of a second-rate idea. But the triumph itself was a singularly great one: Bath made all England its dupe. England believed, while she so stylishly vegetated, that she was living life, the very best sort of life, up to the hilt.

---

[1] Horace Walpole said it did him ten times as much good to leave Bath as to go to it.

CHAPTER V

THE WESLEYAN MOVEMENT

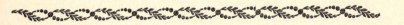

ALTHOUGH THE REIGN OF ANNE was rampant with religious controversy, actually it witnessed a falling away in religious zeal. By 1700 it was politics, not piety, that led to violence in matters of faith. By 1700 Puritan fanaticism had died out, and mystical devotion had dwindled. A modern world was dawning, and with it a rational and almost humanist attitude toward religion. One believed in the Trinity, one forbore from scrutinizing the Gospel narratives too sharply; but otherwise what engaged one, at the very behest of the Church itself, was the pursuit of the good life. Conscience, to a large extent, had superannuated creed. Do good in this life and you shall be saved in the life to come — this was the clear-cut and consolatory injunction of the Church. Gradually doctrinal absolutism had been allowed to lapse, for men insisted now on the use of their own minds, and the Church respected "the test of private judgment." As for mysticism, it was uncongenial to a society that had been influenced by the school of Locke, and abhorrent to an age dedicated to moderation and elegance. During half a century no word was more often excoriated than "enthusiasm": did not the great lexicographer himself define it as "violence of passion"?[1]

---

[1] A gravestone of the time, seeking to perpetuate a woman's virtues, described her as having been "pious without enthusiasm."

[189

There was spreading, of course, a far greater freedom of thought than that which circulated as " religious rationalism " inside the Church. Men were everywhere becoming outright sceptics. The advance of natural science which began by discrediting witchcraft and astrology went on to undermine man's belief in the supernatural generally. Many if not most educated eighteenth-century Englishmen were really not Christians at all; if they supported the Church it was from their feeling that Christianity, though untrue in itself, was cardinal to society. Montesquieu observed that when religion was mentioned in cultivated English circles it provoked nothing but laughter; that not half a dozen members of the House of Commons went regularly to church; and that, though in France he was thought to have too little religion, in England he was thought to have too much. All the same, freethinkers in England were usually outlawed and sometimes persecuted, and proved the particular prey of the very Churchmen who strove to free the Church from dogma. The Church had too much at stake, in a material way, to risk extermination.

The truth is that the growing latitudinarianism in religion was the result of a growing laxness toward it. The age was worldly, cynical, opportunistic, and corrupt. Most people would have felt certain that a good deed sprang from a bad motive. Most people, in the struggle for survival, had to suppress their better instincts, lest they be overwhelmed. The age, being — however unprincipled — not a crude one, men everywhere dissembled in their dealings; and the great curse of religion, hypocrisy, soon pervaded it. Middle-class Nonconformists were in the main, no doubt, sincerely pious. But the great world, living for pleasure, was bored with religion; and the poor — miserable, desperate, and sodden with gin — were contemptuous of it. Certainly they never saw the spirit of it among their betters; never was there a less philanthropic era. That Addison should have regarded the charity schools which sprang up in the reign of Anne as "the glory of the age" only suggests how inglorious an age it was.

Those who *were* religious in the early eighteenth century were inclined to be so with a vengeance. Numerous societies arose "for the reformation of manners," and though their members were militantly devout and often truly charitable, their principal labour was to go around discovering brothels, arresting swearers, and having the law upon Sabbath-breakers. Inside forty years — by 1735 — these societies, in London and Westminster alone, had brought about ninety-nine thousand prosecutions for debauchery and profaneness. Unfortunately their work proved the worst possible incentive to the good life. The masses detested such people as snoopers and spies, and could even attribute some of their prosecutions to personal vindictiveness. And not the masses only, but many magistrates as well, felt that swearing and failing to come to church were not matters for the law. By the middle of the century the societies had died out.

But by then something far more formidable had come into being. An apathetic England was rousing to the fervent evangelical voices, the flooded hearts, the blazing spirits of John Wesley and George Whitefield. By force of will and vigour of oratory these men had brought into the fold thousands of sinners, and were soon to bring thousands upon thousands more. A great movement was afoot, and the Wesleyan revival not only wrought greatly for God, but released the mighty floods of emotion which an Age of Reason had so long pent up.

John Wesley was that fascinating type of fanatic — the "rational" one. No mystic who responded to voices, no visionary before whose eyes came angels dancing, from childhood he looked at things with unremitting logic: "I think," said his father of him as a boy, "I think our Jack would not attend to the most pressing necessities of nature unless he could give a reason for it." In early manhood, as a brilliant young don at Oxford, he became extremely pious: he and his brother Charles were members of a small band who, to the amusement of the university, practised the greatest rigors of living. A few years later the brothers went with Oglethorpe to Georgia, John's chief desire being to convert the Indians. He found few to convert, and by his officious and implacable piety so infuriated the whites that he had to clear out for England. Soon after, in London one evening, came his own " conversion " — he was flooded with the true light and his heart caught fire. Thereafter his duty was plain, and he spent the rest of his long lifetime bringing the light to others.

As to Wesley's exact faith in a denominational sense, we need not linger over it; though it is worth noting that to the end of his life Wesley regarded himself as a clergyman of the Church of England. What the loose latitudinarian spirit of the age preached up was salvation by works. But Wesley would have none of this: he preached salvation by faith alone. Men were in a state of damnation and could be saved only by a " true trust and confidence of the mercy of God through our Lord Jesus Christ." Certainly men should live as usefully and uprightly as they knew how, but unless they suffered a sudden and overwhelming spiritual awakening — a kind of convulsion — no manner of unselfish deeds or lofty thoughts could avail. Wesley's coadjutor Whitefield insisted that *The Whole Duty of Man,* the accepted Anglican devotional work of the time, had, by putting emphasis on good works, " sent thousands to hell." Hence Wesley's mission lay in bringing men to Jesus, and that mission rang out in all forty thousand sermons that Wesley, traversing a quarter of a million miles, preached during half a century.

If victory came at last, it was yet slow, and difficult, and extremely perilous in coming. It could never have come at all had not Wesley and Whitefield been men of fire, fearless men, men drunk with God, who renounced all worldliness and rejoiced at danger, " crying ha! ha! amid the trumpets."

As it was, they had to face not only grim opposition inside the Church, being refused pulpit after pulpit to preach in; but the fury of ignorant and howling mobs who closed in upon them, beat them, trampled them down, pelted them with stones, dragged them along highways, and not once but a dozen times threatened them with death. Not the least argument for their faith was the recurring miracle of their deliverance; yet it was decidedly their own demeanour that saved them. Assaulted, Wesley would face his attackers with marvellous fortitude; then, raising his voice against the uproar, or waiting, before he spoke, for it to subside a little, would work a gradual spell upon them. " My heart " — to quote at random from his *Journal* — " was filled with love, my eyes with tears, and my mouth with arguments. They were amazed, they were ashamed, they were melted down, they devoured every word." How often did those who came quite literally to kill remain to pray.

It was not least these mobs of the poor and hungry, the brutal and licentious, that Wesley and Whitefield burned to bring into the fold; and it was most with them that they succeeded. When church doors were locked against him, Whitefield went into the open fields and preached; and Wesley, though at first revolted by the idea, later followed his example. In time thousands upon thousands gathered in the open to hear them — to hear the simple, colloquial, somehow instantly effective preaching of Wesley, or the incandescent and irresistible eloquence of Whitefield. And oftener and oftener, sometimes in the fields, sometimes in meeting-houses, now with a tiny band, now among multitudes, God's fire scorched and purged His children's hearts; people groaned in agony or shouted hallelujah for joy, swooned away, fell down in fits, pawed their clothes, foamed at the mouth, tore their hair. Night watches were frequent also, when those already converted renewed their devotions from dark to dawn. Commonly, too, small groups met and confessed in public as unreservedly as Papists did in the privacy of the confessional. "What known sin have you committed since our last meeting?" these people were asked. "What temptations have you met with? What have you thought, said, or done of which you doubt whether it be sin or not?"

The leaders never relaxed for a moment. At every season, in the blackest weathers, from town to town and from county to county they rode; into Wales, over to Ireland, north to Scotland; thirteen times the unwearied Whitefield crossed the Atlantic. As the years went by, the movement prospered. The angry mobs turned into eager crowds, the church doors swung open, the hordes who came to hear Wesley and Whitefield preach mounted to eight, to ten, to fifteen, to twenty thousand. Among the ignorant and poor Wesleyanism had the effect of a revolution; and though Wesley noted how seldom his preaching roused the educated and wealthy, in time it converted such persons as Lord Chesterfield's wife, Lord Dartmouth's wife, Lord Dartmouth himself, and the poet Cowper. From being vilified, Methodism at last became fashionable; long before he died Wesley was held in honour, and at his death he numbered seventy thousand followers in England alone. Late in the nineteenth century he might number more followers in the New World than belonged to any other denomination.

What the Wesleyan revival represents historically, beyond the founding of a new and powerful sect, is first (for all its faults) a cleansing influence upon the life of its times, and second (for all its excesses) the bringing to birth of a vivid life of the emotions. It left England less sinful and less shallow. Though in many ways a shockingly inhuman creed, yet both in reducing apathy and in suppressing evil it must be judged a notably humanitarian force. And culturally too it has its importance. In impulse it predates, in activity it coincides with, the growth of "feeling" in the eighteenth-century temperament: to its triumphant release of emotion, quite as much as to the love of the sentimental

in Richardson or Sterne, or the love of the romantic in Ossian
or Walpole, must we attribute the groundswell of the Romantic Revolution. Besides opening men's hearts to God,
it helped open them against a dead régime of decorum, and
the long sovereignty of empty " reason."

But its founder was concerned with God and God alone.
And his mission, having but one motive, could only be fulfilled by one means: fanaticism. In strength of character,
force of direction, power of will, John Wesley was an extraordinary man. His endless *Journal* is one of the world's
great revelations of personality as it is one of the great records of achievement. Leading his horse through a blinding
snowstorm, standing up to his attackers in defiance of their
blows, preaching unweariedly and incessantly, hovering
about deathbeds, reasoning with sinners, driving his dis-
ciples forward, he remains always himself, blunt, passionate,
vigorous, sincere. Though he threw multitudes into hyster-
ics, there was nothing hysterical about Wesley. He was
rocklike even when he seemed most on fire, for he had that
rare intensity which is so inwardly complete that it is never
outwardly frantic or wasteful. No doubt this stemmed in part
from his indestructible will, which from always refusing to
give way made him not only a great reclaimer of souls but
a superb administrator. Inside his movement his will was
absolute. He directed the movement's labours, established
its laws, tested its zeal, answered its calumniators, deposed
and dismissed its transgressors and weaklings. Humble toward God, toward mankind he was intransigent and peremptory. Yet he possessed great patience, and in such matters as controversy with his detractors he shows poise and
reasonableness, and even wit. He begins an answer to a
newspaper attack: " What, my good friend, again! only a
little disguised with a new name and a few scraps of Latin! "
The easy, dancing contempt of this suggests one of Whistler's squibs against Wilde rather than the immitigable
founder of a rigid sect. He was canny too: " I do not see how

it is possible in the nature of things for a religious revival
to last long. For religion must necessarily produce industry
and frugality. And these cannot but produce riches. But as
Riches increase, so will Pride and love of the world in all
its branches."

It was his essential clearsightedness, his grasp of worldly
psychology, his efficiency, his ability not only to handle situations but to shape and assert them, that enabled Wesley
to reap a spiritual harvest. As a speaker he was no match for
Whitefield. Whitefield was an astounding actor, with wonderful histrionic instincts — the choked voice, the convulsed
body, the stamping foot. His language was often excessive
and even absurd, but as Bernhardt could throw splendour
over tawdry roles, so Whitefield could give melodrama the
look of revelation. Everybody knows what Garrick said of
him: that he could pronounce the word Mesopotamia in a
way to move an audience to tears. Everybody remembers
how Franklin, going to hear him, resolved to put nothing in
the collection plate when he should have finished; how,
as Whitefield began to soar, Franklin " softened " and decided to part with his coppers; how, as Whitefield soared
higher, Franklin relented in favour of his silver also; and
how finally he turned his pockets inside out and thrust into
the plate all his coppers and silver and gold. Even Chesterfield, prince of cynics, succumbed to his spell. Whitefield
was picturing a sinner as a blind old man tottering over a
lonely moor, moving closer, and ever closer, to the verge of
a precipice; and when finally he reached it, the overwrought
Chesterfield exclaimed hysterically: " Good God! he is
gone." Such powers as these John Wesley lacked.

He lacked also Whitefield's tender, unrancorous, unde-
nominational spirit, his charm and amiability as a man. But
he lacked Whitefield's weakness, his impulsiveness, his
highstrung and emotional nature — qualities that were fatal
for keeping God's armies, once they were collected, on the
march. Only a man like Wesley could have kept them march-

John Wesley by N. Hone

NATIONAL PORTRAIT GALLERY, LONDON

ing: a man who could plan, who could give orders, who could strike down, who with the utmost certainty could see every habitation along the way as a snare, and the city of heaven bathed in blinding light at the end. It only helped that such a man was a martinet and a bigot, and it did not hinder that he subscribed — in spite of his logical mind — to the wildest and most appalling nonsense. He believed in divine intervention in the minutest particulars. He believed in the work of the devil. He believed in miracles. He believed, with all his heart, in witchcraft.

His intense singleness of vision produced a faith that was not simply oppressive, but that — in his own day — was dangerous and harmful. If certain of his followers were exalted by a knowledge of their redemption, others, constantly exhorted to find the true light, were forever terrified that they had missed it. A man who loved his family, or his friends, could only suffer incessant anguish over their sure and eternal damnation. Amid the frenzies of revival meetings, hundreds of people gave way to their emotions at the expense of their wits, and became hopelessly insane. For the too credulous or zealous, Wesleyanism meant a lifetime of torturing doubts and shuddersome forebodings.

For there was simply no pausing on the way to salvation. "No recreations, considered as such," said Wesley, "are innocent." Dancing and the theatre were plainly the devil's own mischief. But playing the violin was scarcely better, or going to the fair, or wearing jewelry or bright clothes. Wesley had real taste in secular literature, and read a good deal of it; but he frowned upon statues as heathen, and concerning the art treasures that were assembled for the British Museum, he wrote in his *Journal:* "What account will a man give to the Judge of the quick and the dead for a life spent in collecting all these?" One's feet were set on the right path early: in the school that Wesley founded for the children of miners, the pupils got up, winter and summer, at four in the morning, and were never allowed to play, for

" he that plays when he is a child will play when he is a man."

If Wesley rejected worldly pleasure, he no less rejected worldly gain. A man must not even put aside, for prudence' sake, a certain portion of his income. Wesley never sanctified wealth: he never preached that God intended some people to be rich, and others poor. He never genuflected to rank: after the proud Duchess of Buckingham went to hear Whitefield preach, she wrote indignantly: " It is monstrous to be told that you have a heart as sinful as the common wretches that crawl the earth." Wesley was constantly concerned for the poor: besides founding his school for the children of miners, he set up a dispensary in London, he inveighed against the slave trade, he helped relieve the sufferings of French prisoners of war, he protested the outrageous conditions of the jails. All this had its value, while of far greater value was the powerful example which the Wesleyan movement set the Church of England. Before the century was out, the Established Church had been reanimated: it preached a more fervent gospel, it fostered a more responsible attitude, it displayed a more genuine philanthropy.

Hence the Wesleyan movement stirred up the waters of a morally stagnant age. Nevertheless it cannot be called, in the most important sense, an instrument of enlightenment. For this we must blame the harsh self-righteousness of the faith itself, and the political backwardness of its founder. From being a religious bigot, Wesley opposed such a vital reform as Catholic emancipation. From being a political dullard, he opposed the right of Wilkes to sit in Parliament after the Middlesex election, and objected to offering concessions to the American colonists during the Revolutionary War. He believed, and not sanctimoniously, that all men were equal before God, but he never formulated a program for making them equal before the law. The reason, no doubt, was that he attributed men's iniquities to their not being in a state of grace rather than to the dislocations imposed upon them by society. But there was another reason for failure. A straitlaced religious movement full of intolerance and fanaticism — condemning, let us say, the ideas of a social liberal because he was also a religious sceptic, or blasting the discoveries of science because they plainly menaced the future of faith — was bound to be a reactionary one. A man who detested both Hume and Rousseau, as Wesley did, must perforce be a hindrance to enlightenment. The miserable and exploited, the ignorant and credulous among his followers who, from the purity of their faith, were saved for heaven only prolonged and intensified their bondage on earth.

PART III

Heyday

CHAPTER I

EMPIRE AND REVOLUTION

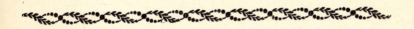

1

As the 1750s approached their close, England's fortunes seemed in desperate decline. Dribbling ministries could not cope with the most serious of national problems: war. Byng's tactics had lost Minorca, creating a situation in the Mediterranean. In America the French had defeated Braddock in Pennsylvania and were inflicting fresh defeats in Canada. The long odds of the Seven Years' War were growing longer. At home there was faction, incompetence, unrest; the old King could not look forward to an honoured grave.

Then matters took a story-book turn the fame of which has scarce diminished since, and one man, after a chequered career spent chiefly in opposition, was hoisted into power. " I am sure," said William Pitt, " that I can save this country, and that nobody else can." Despising half-measures, disdaining caution, flouting economy, he fell to, sending forth fleets and armies. There was plenty of opposition from the ignorant, the timid, the disaffected, but Pitt went ahead with his plans. He saw that the struggle was one, between two fiercely hostile nations, for empire; and he realized that it would be decided on colonial shores. The grand issue was America, but England and France were clashing all over

[203

the globe. Pitt threw all he had into the struggle: his genius for instant decisions, his half-instinctive knowledge of foreign affairs, his arrogant bent toward dictatorship, his tremendous talent for inspiring those he led. With a high but marvellously firm hand, he dispatched his orders — detailed, closely reasoned, *final* orders — to generals and admirals on three continents, and on the seas dividing them.

The year 1759 brought all Pitt's enterprises to the boil. And by Christmas England knew such victories as she had not known since the Middle Ages: Ferdinand of Brunswick in alliance with the British had scored superbly at Minden; Hawke had shattered the French fleet in Quiberon Bay; Madras had fallen, Guadeloupe, Lagos; and at Quebec, Wolfe had outgeneralled Montcalm and given Canada to Britain. Such were the triumphs which George II, whose throne had been secured to him by England's greatest peace minister, survived to see under her greatest minister in war.

They brought his reign to a dazzling close, for in the next year he died. His successor was his grandson, George III, who came to the throne at the age of twenty-two. He came to it loaded down with blessings: England was at the summit of her powers; he himself was a King whom his subjects delighted to honour, whom even the Jacobites were pleased to obey. He was young and good-looking, he was moral and proper. Things augured well.

The new King had been brought up in strict seclusion by his German mother, and no day could have passed when he was not reminded of the vastness of his destiny. He had been brought up, moreover, at an opposition court, where people out of favour and out of office, where Tories, where Scotchmen, where opportunists abounded; and certain things were dinned into his ears which were not to lack consequences.

We must recall that for over forty years the great Whigs had ruled the country. They were a clique with a fabulous patronage at their disposal, and they had converted that patronage into absolute rule. They had overpowered George I and George II; for, though neither was a supine king — George II in particular had tried to be assertive — each had kept his throne through Whig support, which in turn meant Whig domination. From Walpole onward there had been government by faction, and by faction so powerful that it did not so much coerce public opinion as create it. The Whigs ran no risk, for they controlled all the machinery: voting strength, immense private wealth, power of combination, and all manner of patronage.

All this George III had been made to realize. All this he had been educated to rebel against; and his education fitted his temperament to a T. He not only intended to be no figurehead; he was determined, stubbornly determined, to be a king. At his parents' court Bolingbroke had been both an ornament and an influence, and the philosophy of kingship he espoused in *The Idea of a Patriot King* had trickled through young George's brain, changing course and colour as it ran. The cracks in Bolingbroke's reasoning George widened into gaps, but the central idea persisted — that the monarch should be above faction and party, and that he should have power enough to subdue faction or party in Parliament.[1] " Measures, not men," was the bland, altisonant motto by which the disaffected Chesterfield adjured a king to govern; " Measures, not men," was the congenial slogan through which George III . . . intended to get rid of the Whigs.

From the outset George had their successor already groomed. This was Lord Bute, a Scotch Tory who had long been of the court party and who had latterly been George's principal adviser. As to talents, George's father had remarked that Bute would make a splendid ambassador at some petty court where there was nothing to do. But George

---

[1] It is worth noticing that the Hanoverian kings owed their thrones to the party principle: had George III come to the throne twenty years earlier and opposed the Whigs, he would have quickly lost his crown.

quickly insinuated Bute into the Cabinet, and contrived that as soon as possible he should come into power. Pitt was still indispensable to prosecute the war; but it was Bute's ambition, when the war had reaped all possible glory, to negotiate the peace. Pitt was all too soon in difficulties: his strenuous policy met opposition, and he at length resigned. Pitt, it is worth noting, was himself not a party man: he disliked government by faction quite as much as the King did; he had a strong regard for the Crown; and it was actually with the help of the Whig oligarchy that he was driven from office. Yet the King disliked him, for Pitt was a commanding leader, and George wanted complaisant servants.

Bute now went ahead to negotiate peace with France. The one he negotiated was good but, in view of England's amazing successes, it was not good enough. Yet on getting his peace terms ratified hung both his own and the King's political future; and at this point nothing was left to chance. Charles Fox's father, a highly corrupt but highly efficient manager of the House of Commons, was bribed to use his influence, and bribes were freely bestowed on many whom Fox was to persuade. The peace — the Peace of Paris, which Wilkes called " The peace of God, for it passeth all understanding " — was ratified. " Now," said George's mother, " now my son is King of England! " The Tories at last had power. They had got it corruptly and now they proceeded to exploit it vindictively. Not only were the important Whigs dismissed, but every petty official, every cook or bottle-washer who had obtained a job through Whig channels, no matter how respectably or how long ago, was flung downstairs.

If the peace was intensely unpopular with the nation, the ministry was even more so; and as soon as he could, Bute, who was most unpopular of all, resigned. Meanwhile the King himself was open, on many sides, to attack.

Very sharp attack, ignored for a while, came from a newspaper called the *North Briton*. Matters came to a head when the *North Briton,* in its famous forty-fifth issue, violently denounced the King's speech praising the Peace of Paris, and accused the King of lending the dignity of his name to the degrading work of his ministers. This insult George III would not let pass: he ordered everybody connected with the article arrested. Illegally using general warrants, the constabulary seized the evil-doing printers and wormed out of them the information that the author of the piece was one John Wilkes, a member of Parliament. Wilkes was now arrested and confined to the Tower, while his house was entered and his private papers were confiscated.

Thus began the greatest *cause célèbre* of eighteenth-century England, which, in a succession of chapters, extended over a period of many years, roused the nation to riots, threatened it with revolution, and all but toppled the King from his throne. It is impossible here to do more than enumerate the sequence of events and then briefly discuss the business as a whole. Act I ended with the acquittal of the printers, the order (frustrated by the mob) to burn all copies of No. 45, the refusal to let Wilkes plead parliamentary privilege against arrest, and his flight to France, which rendered him an outlaw. The curtain banged down amid extraordinary excitement, with Wilkes a national hero and " Wilkes and Liberty " a national cry. By its unscrupulous use of general warrants and its vindictive withdrawal of parliamentary privilege (however objectionable parliamentary privilege was in itself) the Government had badly blundered.

Act II opens with a bold stroke: Wilkes, *in absentia,* is expelled the House of Commons. The people counter with a bolder one: they re-elect him. The election is thrown out; at the same time the decision that Wilkes is an outlaw is reversed, he returns to England and is sentenced to twenty-two months' imprisonment for having written No. 45 and for having privately circulated, years before, a bawdy satire. His imprisonment is not merely an effective martyrdom; it becomes the social event of the year. (Wilkes in prison was visited and waited on by the most illustrious people of London.) Meanwhile the King's unpopularity grows. Twice more Wilkes is re-elected for Middlesex; twice more the Commons throw out the election. Then a Colonel Luttrell decides to run against Wilkes; he loses, but is declared the winner. This is the climax: the nation is beside itself. Had Wilkes enjoyed a seemlier reputation, or had he but pressed his advantage instead of good-naturedly neglecting it, anything might have happened: dethronement, revolution. Wilkes, however, was weary of the contest and eager for security and peace. Let Time vindicate him, he murmured. And Time did: it not only gave him back his seat in Parliament, but made him Lord Mayor of London.

The Wilkes case survives today chiefly as a monument of blunders and presumptions, wherein a stupid Government outrageously supported an arbitrary King. Wilkes had a case — the use of a general warrant had violated his civil rights; but if Parliament had not behaved so shockingly, he would never have had a cause. Wilkes himself is unimportant, not just because his attacks in the *North Briton* made him really guilty of criminal libel, but even more because, on his own confession, he was himself "no Wilkite." He was not a republican, and the best thing about him is that in the thick of his misfortunes and at the height of his popularity he never pretended to be.[2]

What *is* important about the case is the temper displayed by the common people of England: their sensibility to the infringement of political rights; their perception that once this went unchallenged, worse would follow; and their spontaneous opposition to a repressive policy and a despotic King. "That devil Wilkes," as George III called him — that

---

[2] He did, however, afterwards plump for democratic processes and reforms and, as the result of his own difficulties, strove successfully to enlarge the freedom of the press.

John Wilkes by William Hogarth

squinting, ribald, witty man who, though all politician, somehow never turned demagogue — became the battleground for the trueborn Englishman who was not to be balked of his rights. Otherwise the Wilkes case is half a comedy of poor tactics; it meant no more than what comes up in a court of law a dozen times a week; it meant nothing noble, or revolutionary, or tragic. But what it seemed to mean, and so in a sense what it came to mean, produced an unparalleled convulsion of national feeling, and leaves Wilkes's name still vaguely celebrated, like that of some patriot or martyr, a William Wallace or a William Tell.

2

LORD NORTH'S name is most commonly associated with the American war — a war he bears the discredit for prosecuting and the blame for losing. In many respects North was a scapegoat, though one of the most spineless on record. He was an agreeable and honest man, a clever and competent politician, but with the most damnable good nature he allowed himself, for upwards of ten years, to be the mouthpiece of the King. He scarcely wanted to be minister from the outset, and he repeatedly begged George III to let him resign. George as repeatedly refused, and North could not bring himself to defy him. Nor would he defy him concerning the policy of the war, which clearly arose out of historical forces which that policy could only intensify.

The origin of the American war lay in the mercantilist policy of the day, especially as applied by mother countries to their colonies. The Americans had to import either English-made goods, or foreign goods by way of England; and had to export their own goods either to England (when they were not competing with the English market) or nowhere at all. As a result, the colonists had successfully resorted to contraband trade, which — no doubt more because it was

successful than because it was contraband — angered the
mother country. After 1759 the strongest tie that bound
the colonies to Great Britain — their fear of a French invasion from Canada — was severed, and the remaining ties
were imponderable ones. It was only, however, after the
Peace of Paris — which left England's finances shaky — that
a first real crisis arose. Grenville decided on a colonial stamp
tax to defray part of the cost of maintaining defensive troops
in America. The idea may have been reasonable enough,
since the colonists, not England, were to benefit most from
what was paid out; but the method was incredibly fool-
hardy. To tax people without their consent was a menace
to their liberties; but, worse yet, it was a slap at their pride.
A quarter of a century before, when the colonists were much
less powerful, Walpole had seen the folly of adopting such
tactics. Now there was downright danger in doing so. But
Grenville pushed his Stamp Act through Parliament. The
colonies ignored it, stormed and rioted, boycotted English
goods; and even though the Stamp Act was soon revoked,
the stage was set for trouble.

There is not space — nor, in view of the limelight which
those events have always held, is there any need — to trace
the steps which led in the end to war. In brief, the colonies,
chafing under an obsolescent economic policy (and prosperous in spite of it) were over-ready to resent any bullying
from the mother country. England, on the other hand, once
she had blundered, felt she must back her blunders up:
give in now, the argument ran, and you must continue to
give in. This was true, but it did not point the way to success; it merely prefigured an ultimate failure.

Nevertheless, England did all she could to speed failure
on; and all the wise statesmen of the day, notably Burke [3]
and Chatham, pleaded for conciliation. (A wise policy, they

---

[3] "The question with me is not whether you have a right to render
your people miserable; but whether it is not in your interest to make them
happy." — *Speech on Conciliation.*

felt, might at least preserve America to England as independent colonies — much as Canada and Australia were to become.) But the North ministry allowed itself to think that if it came to war, England could whip the rebels hands down; and so it came to war.

At the start the King and North had the bulk of the nation behind them — all those people whom Burke excoriated for referring smugly to "*our* subjects in America; *our* colonies; *our* dependents." But on few things in history have the enlightened members of a country, even those habitually conservative, been more fully agreed than on the folly and injustice that provoked the American Revolution. Charles Fox, when the English had won a crushing victory over the rebels, wrote concerning "the *bad news* from Long Island." Horace Walpole thought that victory over the Americans would rivet English chains at home. The best minds felt that the colonists, in their rebellion, were actually defending the principles of the British Constitution. To oppose the struggle Fox, Burke, and the elder Pitt used every argument they could draw upon. They were not all of one mind, however, as to what policy England should pursue. Burke and Fox, as time went on, wanted to recognize American independence; but Pitt, who had a sentimental interest in America because of 1759, and whom the Americans looked to as their spokesman in England, sought for reconciliation. Indeed, it was to urge, to plead for this that Chatham came for the last time to the House of Lords — came in on a crutch, heavily supported by his son and son-in-law; and at the conclusion of a historic scene was carried home to die.

The later years of the war increased England's risks and diminished her hopes, for France — helping the Americans in order to hurt the British — also went to war against England; Spain followed France, and Holland, Spain. Thereafter the war became ever more disastrous abroad, ever more unpopular at home. But the King and his shackled minister persisted, with gross mismanagement of money and men, as long as they could; until, following the news from Yorktown, North threw up his hands and cried out: " Oh God, it is all over! " The King showed better poise, but the game was up.

Great Britain, by her senseless tactics, had lost America, and by her obstinacy had lost it at a staggering cost; but the outcome of the war may have saved her from something worse: from the peril of complete engrossment by the Crown. With his wilfulness, so notably abetted by bribery, favouritism and cool usurpation, George III was pretty well qualifying for the title of despot. Had he beaten the colonies, his popularity with the masses (who always rejoice over a successful war, though they never share in the spoils) combined with his increased self-assurance must sooner or later have forced a crisis. From subjugating America he would have confidently advanced toward subjugating England; and England would have had no choice, whatever the cost in blood, but to subjugate the King. Instead George III suffered a setback from which he never recovered. John Morley said that " a patriotic Englishman may revere the memory of Patrick Henry and George Washington no less justly than the patriotic American." For, as the war proceeded, George became ever more unpopular; and already in 1780 Dunning's famous motion: " That the influence of the Crown has increased, is increasing, and ought to be diminished," was carried by a narrow margin in a Parliament where the King's own party had (otherwise) a majority.

The end of the war saw the hurried exit of the Tories, but not the triumphal entrance of the Whigs. The Whigs came in to make peace for the country, and at length they did; but, being divided among themselves, they failed to hold their advantage. The first Whig ministry, under the Marquis of Rockingham, was dissolved at Rockingham's death; the second, under Lord Shelburne, was weakened by lacking a majority in the House and ruined by lacking the support of Fox; the third, the unholy coalition between Fox's Whigs and North's Tories, was destroyed by the King's enmity toward Fox and disgraceful coercion of the House of Lords. But the King did less to ruin Fox than Fox, by coalescing with his avowed political enemy, did to ruin himself; and when Fox fell, the Whig fortunes collapsed.

England, during such quarrelsome years, was a battered realm. She had lost a war, been lowered in prestige, milked dry of money, torn apart by internal friction. Tories and Whigs were alike in bad odour; neither good statesmen nor bad had the means of preserving power. The King in his extremity now turned to a young man not yet twenty-five, whom already two years earlier he had turned to without success, and asked him to take over the government. This time Chatham's son assented. And with everything against him at the start, he succeeded marvellously.

The younger Pitt did for the third George what Walpole had done for the first and second: he stabilized the country. When Pitt came in, England's worst troubles were financial, and Pitt was at much his greatest in the role of financier. But as an administrator in general he was eminent; and though he took office as a nominal Whig, with Whig aspirations of reform, from the outset he excelled at promoting a Tory ideal — the ideal of security and order. The other, the Whig ideal, he failed at. In the eighties, years of peace and prosperity though they were, the old political vices, the old social restrictions, were very little improved.

Pitt encountered only one real crisis during those first years of peace. In 1788 the King went mad, and there was need of some kind of regency. The young Prince of Wales disliked Pitt and hobnobbed with his enemies, Fox and Sheridan. Should the Prince come in with full powers as Regent, almost certainly Pitt would be turned out; and at once a battle raged over just how mad the King was. Fox, whose worst political weapon was his vehemence, as his worst political fault was the ambition that caused it, never behaved worse, Pitt never better. Pitt's skill at length bound the Prince to act as Regent with extremely limited powers, and actually the Prince never acted at all, for at this juncture the King regained his sanity. He now returned to the throne in a great burst of popularity.

Under such a smiling eye of Providence, England began life in the year 1789. Before it ended, the world of Gainsborough and Chesterfield and Johnson might see the beginning of its doom. What, spiritually, was the eighteenth century had drawn to an angrily vibrating close. Yet the early effect of the French Revolution on England was to put the clock back, not forward. As France went from liberty toward anarchy, England — in an access of panic — went from liberty to reaction. England's early joy in seeing the empire-greedy Bourbons balked of their ambitions was soon succeeded by a distrust of where the republicans were heading, by a dislike of where they soon arrived, by a horror at where they might next advance. For not only did France go too far, but she encouraged other nations to do likewise, and she promised them help if they did it.

Such circumstances split even the Whig Party in two. Burke fell back, while Fox continued to go forward. The past and the future were grimly confronting each other.

CHAPTER II

KINGS AND COUNSELLORS

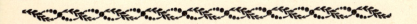

George III, His Consort, and His Court

MANY ADVANTAGES ATTENDED George III to the throne. He was the first native-born monarch to occupy it in fifty years, the first youthful one in a hundred. His name was not burdened with the crude stamp of Hanover; his person was not linked with beefy German women; his manners were not earmarked with a fatal lack of charm. Like his subjects, he might have felt that there was much to be thankful for.

But George III was not of a mind to be thankful for what he considered his due. Mama and Lord Bute, in their different ways, had seen to that: Mama with her blunt "George, be a king!" Bute with philosophical circumlocutions that advised the same conduct. George may have had an inadequate education — at eleven he could not read a word of English — but in what would nowadays be termed vocational guidance his education was far in advance of the time. The boy made a good pupil; like the last of the Stuarts, he was serious and moral, zealous for the Church, and terribly bent on doing his duty.

His duty, when he reached the throne, seemed plain enough: to dislodge from their high seats those few and

[2 1 5

powerful Whigs who owned so much of the wealth and determined so much of the policy of England; and then, by constantly exerting the power of the Crown, to keep England free from faction and usurpation. Certainly no advocate of free or honest government could defend the Whig manner of governing, which was one of self-interest maintained through corruption. But on strictly practical grounds there was something to be said for it — it had made England freer, richer and healthier than she once had been. Yet no doubt the King was perfectly right to want to raise the moral tone of politics and to transfer power to higher levels; it is not every king who tries to be a reformer.

In any case, we do not begin to understand George III until we grasp that the undermining and routing of the Whigs, like every other great project he embarked upon, was conducted as a moral crusade. There was nothing irresponsible about George's attitude toward affairs; there was scarcely that which in ordinary men would be called ambition; he simply felt the need of enforcing on the nation whatever Providence had confided to him; and he saw readily that to carry out his designs would demand all his energy and all his guile.

Men of vision must usually face the hardship of standing alone, but George positively welcomed it. He wanted no one else around, not even Tories. A true king did not solicit advice; he issued orders. The times, it is true, were not what they once were, say in the days of Lear before his retirement. There was now a constitution, and a parliament, and something to the effect that the King reigns but does not govern. Well then, as a recent biographer put it, " he would be constitutional. . . . He never intended to rule without Parliament; he merely intended to rule Parliament."

In a moral crusade the means are not important; only the end counts. George therefore quite cheerfully condescended to stoop. In the interests of his own morality he dispensed with all other and entered upon a campaign of lies and broken promises, of treacheries and insults, of bribery and blackmail. He blandly told Bedford or Grenville or Rockingham whatever they wanted to hear, so that he might quickly get on with whatever he wanted to do. He confided in people, though he could never quite manage to confide the truth. He expressed regret for his mistakes, but was not prevented from committing them all over again. He flattered the Whigs he had ruined by adopting their methods — by buying up votes with money, jobs, sinecures, pensions; or, should the voters prove refractory, by withholding money, by revoking sinecures, by cancelling pensions, and by terminating jobs.

The system worked. The Crown became extraordinarily powerful. Corruption became extraordinarily efficient. Men like Chatham and Fox were brazenly ousted; progress was humbled and common sense ignored. The system was not, of course, infallible. Wilkes finally won out over Parliament; the Americans finally won out over the English; Pitt finally won out over George III. Lord North was even finally allowed to resign. But no king had as fully ruled England since William III, if even he had; and in consequence, no king was henceforth to rule England at all. In his greatness George III dragged down with him to the grave the whole surviving machinery of royal power. But it is to be observed as a finishing touch that when George had been despoiled of all else, he found a final weapon. He went periodically mad, and in his saner moments realized how scared the nation was of driving him mad again.

George III was never a comedy figure. He was a very shrewd and dangerous man, a political sharper who outwitted some of the cleverest men of his time. His manœuvres had grave consequences, and had they gone much farther must either have upset the Constitution or overturned the throne. Politically, it is true, George III had no policy —

only prejudices and obsessions. These weaknesses alone prevented him from carrying out his despotic designs, for it was not the nature of his marksmanship that was faulty, it was only the nature of his targets. He attacked everything good and defended everything bad. It was the sheer stupidity of his demands that put an end to them, and it required a Pitt to do it. If George III was the worst of modern British sovereigns, he was also the most cunning.

Set off against his public performances, the King's private behaviour offers a great contrast, but not a contradiction. He had no social vices — did not drink, or gamble, or carry on with women. He had been reared in retirement, had doubtfully succumbed to one amour, had briefly indulged in one romance, then quietly acquiesced in the wishes of his mother and Lord Bute by marrying a homely German princess. He got up at dawn, rode horseback for an hour, ate a frugal breakfast, and by eight or nine o'clock was working away at the tonic business of appropriating an Empire. At the end of the day, after another frugal meal he went for a walk and came back to play chess or backgammon with an equerry. Disliking London, he led the life of a farmer. Kew he found preferable to Buckingham House, and Windsor to Kew; almost all his later years were spent at Windsor.

For the arts George III had scarcely more feeling than George II or George I, though a trifle more respect. Like most Hanoverians, he really liked music, particularly Handel. He founded the Royal Academy and wanted to found a literary tribunal to be called The King's Order of Minerva. He patronized Benjamin West and collected drawings. His bent for literature was expressed in his remark to Fanny Burney, that most of Shakespeare was " sad stuff — only one must not say so! " [1] Though he read very little, he had a good library, which was freely used by men like Dr Priestley

---

[1] He was in better company than he knew; Sheridan, Byron, Hume, Tolstoy, and G. B. Shaw have more or less shared his opinion.

and Dr Johnson. His stealing in upon a rapt Johnson, and the talk between them, make up one of the most justly celebrated passages in Boswell. It should be added that George III was himself an author, contributing, under the name of Ralph Robinson, articles on turnips to Arthur Young's *Annals of Agriculture*. Indeed, it was as Farmer George that the King played the most agreeable role of his life; for as a simple country squire, full of " Hey, hey "s and " What, what "s, he shed both his dangerous political inclinations and his repulsive moral *bêtise*.

His consort, the crocodile-mouthed Charlotte, who had grown up in her small unaffluent duchy resigned to entering a Protestant convent, was all the King asked for, and as much as he deserved. She bore him many children and was a dutiful though hardly an understanding mother. She deferred to George absolutely; she seems to have asserted herself conjugally in no way whatever, except somewhere to remind him that her lineage was hoarier than his. Her revenge for such deference was to exact it for herself of all the rest of the nation. No man except the King was *ever* permitted to sit in her presence, which was either the reason or the pretext for her sons' avoidance of court. She was ridiculously prudish, but not very discriminatingly moral: she merely accepted any woman whose husband accepted her, and repudiated any woman whose husband repudiated her. Charlotte had a taste for needlework and for fireworks and for finery. Like her husband (who spent all his money on political bribes), she was reputed a miser. It is told, however, that she was modestly charitable. She must have been a very tiresome woman, and serving her, as Fanny Burney did for so many years, must have been a very tiresome business.

It was beyond all doubt a very tiresome court. One must somehow comment on the fact that during a century of conscious glitter and factitious elegance, a century of high living played out against a lordly background, four successive

English sovereigns presided over courts either brutish or tarnished or tame. But George's and Charlotte's was in most respects the worst of all. As seldom as possible the Court contrived an evening of stiff dancing and strangled talk, after which the guests were sent home without any supper. The King and Queen, as a matter of fact, did not care for " society people," much preferring those with the moral grandeur of the middle class. Gambling was not allowed: first hazard was outlawed, then cards. If Horace Walpole is to be believed, Lord and Lady Holdernesse received court posts, not because of their rank, but because they were recommended by a chaplain and a governess.

But the example of the King and Queen could not prevent other members of the royal family from misbehaving. There was a scandalous succession of scandals. First the King's brother, the Duke of Cumberland, was named in a divorce case, and then showed his contrition by marrying a lively and unroyal widow. The King was furious and Cumberland was in disgrace. At this juncture another of the King's brothers, Gloucester, was driven by conscience to own up that he too had taken a bride, the charming but unroyal Lady Waldegrave. The King was even more furious, and Gloucester in even worse disgrace than Cumberland. Nor did sister Matilda, the Queen of Denmark, lag behind: she was taken in adultery and banished her husband's kingdom. As each of these scandals occurred, the atmosphere of the court, as might be surmised, became increasingly suffocating and moral.

But the greatest family misfortune came later from the usual family source, the royal firstborn. The future George IV, who had received a deputation at three and held a drawing-room at seven, continued to be socially precocious. In spite of the most careful home influences, he glided easily into the role of a fribble, a spendthrift, and a rake, ridiculing his father and making fast friends of all his father's sworn enemies.

At seventeen he became infatuated with one of his sisters' maids of honour, and at eighteen he became the lover of the beautiful " Perdita " Robinson, an actress of easy morals whom the King, to his great annoyance, had to buy off for five thousand pounds. The Prince would have married either lady had he been able; his constant desire to legalize his dalliance was the least rakish thing about him, though the reason may only have been that such a marriage was forbidden fruit. Some time in 1784, when he was twenty-two, he met the young, twice-widowed, lovely, and ladylike Mrs Fitzherbert. They fell deeply in love, but her person was a hopeless stumbling-block to their happiness, for besides being a commoner she was a Catholic. She was also a virtuous woman who held the Prince off as long as she could. True marriage was out of the question: under the Royal Marriage Act George needed his father's consent until he reached twenty-five, and under the Act of Settlement he could never, at any time, marry a Catholic without forfeiting the throne. He did the next best thing — went through a form of marriage with her that might at least bind them in the eyes of God. They lived together, in London and Brighton, during many years; then, at what seemed the height of their happiness, he broke with her in favour of the middle-aged Lady Hertford.

When not yet out of his teens, George met and was captivated by Fox, which did much to turn him into a sturdy Whig and to widen the breach between him and his father. Fox, Sheridan, the Duchess of Devonshire — the whole imposing Whig connexion — became his close friends, a fact which had serious political repercussions, notably at the time of the Regency crisis of 1788.

The more important half of George's life — his terrible marriage, his later liaisons, his fat and infamous middle age, along with the matter of his arraignment or vindication — must be sought elsewhere. In his youth, at any rate, he was not without attractive qualities. Selfish, spoiled, extravagant, and capricious he was from the outset; but from the outset he also provided an enjoyable contrast to the Georges who came before him. He was the first of them to have charm, and the only one to possess the social graces. A good guest and a splendid host, he lent to society that glitter and dash which it always expects from royalty and almost never obtains. And he did something for the cause of peace, for he never had a son.

Parliament

THE CLASH between Parliament and King, with the ultimate victory of Parliament, was the grand political issue of seventeenth-century England. Yet the character of Parliament in the eighteenth century was for a long time impure and indistinct. By strict Whig tenets Parliament was a holy place, dedicated to defending the Constitution and creating law. But when we come to examine this high-sounding creed more carefully, we find it restricting the influence of the Crown rather than extending the powers of the people. The Whigs, true enough, favoured greater religious tolerance and were politically susceptible, at least in moderation, to change; but it was late in the century before the most liberal-minded among them made any effort to convert Parliament into a truly representative (and not noticeably corrupt) assembly.

The House of Commons in the eighteenth century was at the mercy of numerous threats: the ambitions of the Crown; the influence of party leaders; the grip, often amounting to a stranglehold, exerted by those who owned votes; the unsuppressed trafficking in every species of jobbery; and the patrician nature of the parliamentary rank and file themselves. Queen Anne had the power to make and break administrations; hence both Whigs and Tories were bound to solicit her goodwill, and in fact competed for it. George I and George II had this power much less — first because they were not securely enough established; again because Walpole and the Whig lords were immensely strong; finally because, being unpopular kings, they caused a vast decline in kingly sentiment, hence of kingly power. George III sought to regain that power and for a while succeeded. He did so, for one thing, by breaking up the Whig combination; for another, by making men dependent for their well-being on the royal favour: there were not only jobs to be won, there were also jobs to be lost. These usurpations were at last put down, thanks to a cabinet system which demanded that the " ins " must fall when they could not command a majority. Yet George III managed to govern Parliament, in one way or another, for almost a quarter of a century.

Equally, at other times, the Prime Minister governed Parliament — not nominally as its leader, but decisively as its boss. Walpole's colleagues were almost all negligible, as were the younger Pitt's: both men, once they became entrenched, had power far in excess of their office, and over long periods of time ran the government almost single-handed.

What made this possible — what could have made anything possible — was the wholesale bribery and jobbery that turned the Commons into a market-place. To begin with, there was neither universal suffrage nor proportional representation. Large towns like Manchester and Leeds were not represented at all. Sixteen thousand men in Yorkshire returned two members to Parliament; so did fifty men at Thirsk; so did one man at Bossiney in Cornwall; so did seven non-residents at the deserted village of Old Sarum. It was therefore quite simple for men with money to pay out four or five thousand pounds and come to own a pocket borough; now and then a borough would even advertise itself for sale. Thus almost all the seats were owned by wealthy lords or by the "nabobs" of the East India Company.[2] Such a system of bought seats naturally produced a parliament of bought men.

But the disease by no means stopped there. Voting power was clinched by every sort of bribe. Every nincompoop in the Commons, if the administration was to feel sure of his vote, had to be given some kind of pension or sinecure. Burke, when he sought to clean up the House and abolish the suppurating economic abuses of the kingdom, showed how England's finances must become desperate, England's justice become obsolete, England's foreign policy become paralysed, England's alliances become inoperative, because "the King's turnspit was a member of Parliament." Take away from this M.P. his sinecure of King's turnspit? Take away from other M.P.s their similar sinecures? How could you — when it required the vote of the M.P.s themselves! It was to clash with power at its source. All the same, though political reform had to wait till 1832, Burke's second (and emasculated) Bill for Economical Reform did pass Parliament in 1784 and destroyed a few abuses. And men of integrity, against their own interest, destroyed a few more — as when Pitt sacrificed the Clerkship of the Pells, conferring it elsewhere than on himself in exchange for calling in a needless pension; or when Burke, as Paymaster of the Forces, set its salary at four thousand pounds per annum and annihilated its huge perquisites of some twenty-five thousand pounds.

All these conditions were so chiefly because the Commons was almost entirely composed of members drawn from the ruling classes. As its seats were in the gift of men of wealth and rank, so its sitters were drawn from their own families, friends, and sycophants. Whatever his talents, no

---

[2] Wilkes once attempted to show that a majority in the House of Commons could be achieved from the votes of 5,723 persons scattered throughout the country. Its total population was around seven million.

political free-lance could dream of entering Parliament without patronage; though, if he was talented enough, patrons and parties might compete for his services.

The aristocratic nature of Parliament turned it, in some degree, into what has been called an informal debating society. There was much less to do than there is nowadays, and most of it was done, not through committees, but from the floor of the House. Proceedings were still largely private; the galleries could be cleared of visitors and were closed to reporters. In such an atmosphere manners were freer, though speeches were longer. Members joked, ate, stretched out on benches, brutally coughed down tiresome or uncongenial speakers, like footmen hissing at the play. There was, indeed, an air of the theatre about the House of Commons and, as time passed, an air of actors about its members. If the reason lies chiefly in the orators, it also lies somewhat in the taste of the times, which ran to the grandiose, and loved effect. The imperious presence, aquiline countenance, superb tones, and dramatic delivery of Chatham must have gone far to set the standard, but those who came after were able to uphold it. Nevertheless, it should be emphasized that long speeches predominated, not great ones; and that a well-bred Parliament, far from being enthralled, would usually have died of boredom. Happily Parliament was not well-bred — its insults often came to duels, and bunglers and bores were either silenced or shunned. But bunglers and bores usually knew their place. Those squires who, on the whole, were the most upright section of the House, and took their seats from an old-fashioned Tory sense of duty, seldom had any more desire to shine than they had ability. They spoke rarely; on the other hand they were most often affected by the speeches of others. Worldlings and politicians might dazzle one another with their rhetoric, but they seldom changed one another's votes; it was the country gentlemen, with their stronger principles and weaker minds, who could be swayed by great oratory; and great orators knew it.

The names of those great orators are household names, and a recital of their triumphs tends to degenerate into a collection of ana. We must remember, however, that behind their brilliant gestures lay towering events; that their showmanship was enlisted, not merely by love of self-display, but by serious and even solemn issues. They were defending the cause of war or pleading the cause of peace; they were legislating the life of continents; they were crusading for liberty, appealing for order, inveighing against oppression. The grand manner, on many occasions, was not in excess of what called it forth.

North, Townshend, Windham, Shelburne, Barré: orators obscure today, or unknown. Of some lesser age of oratory they might still form a living part, but theirs was the age ushered in by Chatham and set echoing by Fox, Pitt, Sheridan, and Burke. It opened with the events that led to one revolution, it closed with the events that proceeded out of another. The interval between heard these voices raised for the reform of Great Britain, the relief of Ireland, and the renovation of India; it culminated in the impeachment and trial of a man whom Burke hunted down and excoriated with fanatic fury, whom Sheridan denounced in the most effulgent of all orations.

In sustained eloquence, in immediate magnetism, Chatham probably excelled all the others; he was a man endowed with the greatest majesty, inspired by the strongest patriotism: a schoolboy's hero both for his aims and for his manner of achieving them. His patriot's dream of empire, his conqueror's strength in creating it, can scarcely call forth today the same praise they have called forth in the past: he was a great leader, but in a cause not ultimately enlightened. He is glorious only for his genius and his success; it is impossible to admire his philosophy.

But if none of the four men who came after Chatham had

William Pitt by J. Hoppner

NATIONAL PORTRAIT GALLERY, LONDON

quite his incandescence, the spectacle of all four of them in superb and simultaneous motion remains quite unmatched. Now rallying to one another's support, now retorting upon one another's demands, now lashing out in fierce rejoinder, now locking horns for a last and decisive struggle — what movement, what utterance were these! [3] Though the younger Pitt lacked his father's magnetism, he inherited all his authority and had a power to dominate not inferior to his father's power to arouse. Fox, with his warmth, his wit, his spontaneous rush of words that led him to speak as the author of *Tristram Shandy* wrote — beginning a sentence, and leaving it to the Almighty to finish for him — was a distinguished though hardly a great orator; but he was the greatest *debater* of all time. Sheridan's name, though inferior elsewhere, still blazes up for the part he played in impeaching Hastings in the Commons and trying him before the Lords. His five-and-a-half-hour speech in the Lower House, which kept it so breathless and aroused it to such a torrent of applause that Pitt instantly moved an adjournment before members could vote, is thought to be the greatest of all parliamentary orations.

As for the trial of Hastings itself, it seems — with its parliamentary dress parade, its roll-call of eloquent accusers, its audience as glittering as its stage, its conscious use of heraldic pomp — a kind of valedictory of the old order. For the last time, almost, powdered hair and buckled shoes were correct attire rather than fancy, or servile, dress; for the last time a Parliament soon to be reborn conducted on a great scale an obsolescent thing, an impeachment. Long before it had dragged out its seven years some of the principal actors had quarrelled, others had died, everyone was heartily tired of it, everyone knew that the " oppressor " of India would be acquitted. More than that one need not

---

[3] Nor must their powers of invective be forgotten. Oratory abounded in such touches as Burke's " If Lord Shelburne is not a Catiline or a Borgia, it must not be ascribed to anything but his understanding."

[227

add. The fame of Warren Hastings's trial owes to Macaulay what that of the Mona Lisa owes to Pater; and each, having been exalted by memorable words, has at length been vulgarized by them.

Burke

BURKE is certainly one of the great names of the eighteenth century; but just as he once asked of another political philosopher with a style: " Who now reads Bolingbroke? " so might we inquire: " Who now reads Burke? " For I suspect we might find, even among those who should know better, very few readers of Burke under the age of forty. However much his writings may abound in sententious wisdom and soaring eloquence, they are not congenial to modern liberals, nor very useful to modern conservatives; while even the student of pure literature must admit to serious blemishes in the style. Above all, Burke's personality seems to us not only unpleasant, but alien; from almost no one else of equal intellectual stature do we today feel more estranged. It is not merely that Burke lives inside an eighteenth-century frame; so does Johnson, so does Gibbon; but where their portraits retain a fine period quality, Burke's has only the dated sobriety (though Burke was anything but a sober man) of a steel engraving.

Burke's personal life need not detain us. He was a middle-class Irishman who early migrated to England, who came to politics by way of literature, and who remained to the end something of a literary politician. His public career is everything. It is linked with all the great issues and events of his time — the American and French Revolutions, Ireland, India, economic reform; it includes having been the advocate, the mentor, and at length the dissolvent of a great political party. It is a career which where it was distinguished had no lasting influence, but where it was misguided had a decisive effect. Burke the liberal was only a tonic moral force; Burke the reactionary shattered the Whig power and fathered the Conservative Party of the nineteenth century.

We must begin by grasping the fact that for Burke the Revolution of 1688 was a revolution, in England, to end all others. The Whig principles which promoted it, and the Whig policy which grew out of it — founded as both were on a championing of the English Constitution — Burke regarded as henceforth inviolable. The lines of government might be broadened, the needs of government might be enlarged, the machinery of government might — and should — be strengthened; but the Constitution must never be betrayed. Obviously, then, Burke, from being opposed to structural change, was not a true reformer. Wherever the political structure was more antiquated than in England, as in Ireland or India, he could honestly urge its improvement; wherever the political structure was endangered by England herself, as in the American colonies, he could honestly urge its defence; and whatever of it was diseased, whether through mismanagement, corruption, or neglect, he honestly sought to repair. To such a view Burke brought an unselfish zeal and a perfect integrity; to such a view he further brought a passionate hatred of injustice, so far as he could recognize injustice.

But Burke was not endowed with any pioneering spirit, any modern intuitions, such as among other powerful intellects of his age, in both England and France, were calculated to change the direction of history. It was entirely the other way round. He valued tradition far too much, so that he could not help valuing order at the expense of progress. If he loved a lord partly because he was a snob, he loved him also because a great name stood for a great past, and was privileged to the extent that it might claim a reward for past services. Democracy, to Burke, meant a mob, a turbulent ruthless majority ignoring the rights of the few. Moreover, his experience of mobs, during the violent Gordon Riots of 1780, was decisive: many writers have shown how his memories of a lawless London assured his verdict on a lawless Paris.[4] His Whig principles, sturdy though they were, were no match for his Tory instincts; and with those instincts to misguide him, Burke from the outset became the most unbridled, bigoted, and unrelenting of opponents to the French Revolution.

And certainly the most successful: his furious blasts made men quake for the future of Britain, helped force Pitt to suppress British civil liberties, gave the nation an appetite for war, inflamed the nation against signing a "regicide peace." Shrieking and imploring, Burke became a man possessed, seeing all mischief in a Paris mob, as Lear saw it in the world's daughters. Burke lived only to end the catastrophe in France and to avert a similar one in England. With amazing insight he predicted atheism across the Channel, butchery, the beheading of the King, the spread of republican propaganda, the advent of French aggressive warfare, the rise of a military dictator. It all came true and, thanks to Burke, England escaped with almost nothing of it.

There are men whose conduct history must morally indict; there are others whose conduct it can only deplore. Of these latter is Burke. His motives concerning the French Revolution, so far as he understood them, were honest ones: to him, all that he held sacred was being trampled down in a reign of lawlessness. He feared democracy, he loathed disorder, he abhorred atheism; besides, he was a sentimentalist about tradition, and to see it flouted, raped, rent in two, to think of queens and kings being brutally mauled — in Paine's famous phrase, he pitied the plumage but forgot the dying bird. Quite simply, he forgot the former life of the people of France; and at length, reasoning complexly, he

---

[4] But cf. Hazlitt: "It was Burke, who professed to despise mobs, who did more than any man to inflame mob fury in England " (at the time of the French Revolution).

denied their claims. It was not that he lacked feeling, but that he misapplied it; not that he consciously sought to perpetuate injustice, but that, caught in the meshes of his own conception of progress, he rejected any other. He " held fast to the doctrine that everything must be done for the multitude, but nothing by them." [5]

But whatever produced it, Burke's attitude made him the spokesman for all the viciously reactionary forces of his age. His old enemy, George III, said that the *Reflexions on the French Revolution* was a book that every gentleman ought to read. With his own hand Louis XVI translated it into French. The King of Poland sent Burke a gold medal. All the people he had spent a lifetime denouncing — the most backward, the most selfish, the most evilly entrenched people of England and Europe — now united to praise him. We may wonder that he could feel comfortable in such company, but we forget what a religion self-righteousness can become. And Burke felt that by his own standards he was no renegade: in supporting the American Revolution he had defended Britain's Constitution against itself; in opposing the French Revolution he was defending the same Constitution against anarchy. But nothing could have been worse than the *seeming* betrayal involved: when a great liberal, who has plainly not been bought, goes over to the other side, he wounds the old cause irreparably by seeming to stigmatize it as dangerous and rotten. In Burke's case he gave the Tories an opportunity that far outlasted the crisis which prompted it. He kept the old order in power far longer than it might otherwise have stayed, and his name is still invoked to defend indefensible causes. History can deplore few things more than Burke's wisdom as to the events and blindness as to the meaning of the French Revolution.

---

[5] As Leonard Woolf has said, Burke " stood for vested interests in civilization."

Charles James Fox

THE HEART warms in writing of Charles James Fox, for which reason the mind must sternly beware. Otherwise we shall be too indulgent toward the most delightful Englishman of his time. We can so quickly be swamped by his charm, dazzled by his talents, disarmed by his humanity, touched by his bad luck; or — worst danger of all — be merely dismayed, instead of moved to judgment, by his blunders. We know, without having been under it, what Pitt meant when he spoke of " the wand of the magician."

The tale strikes a romantic note at once: Fox's parents were the most spectacular runaway couple of their generation. Up-and-coming Henry Fox dared elope with the daughter of a duke, and the girl for a time was disowned in the very best style. Her husband, " the public defaulter of unaccounted millions," amassed a huge fortune and became the most hated man in England. A villain abroad, Henry Fox was idolized by his family, for the excellent reason that he idolized them in turn and showered them with kindness. Of them all, his favourite was the chubby and prodigious Charles, who, virtually in babyhood, assumed the management of his own affairs. He chose to go to Eton and hypnotized the school. He chose to go to Oxford and astounded it by the quality of his work and the quantity of his play. A dandy (though in later life he became a sloven), a wit, a rake, he was pre-eminently a gambler, and before he was eighteen had lost some hundred and twenty thousand pounds. He went on to become one of the great gamblers of history, and much the unluckiest. Throughout his life, though the son of one of the wealthiest men in England, he was almost never out of debt.

At nineteen Charles Fox entered Parliament. Filial-minded, high-spirited, abominably spoiled, he began his career in the worst possible way: as an instantaneous parliamentary success, pledged to the wrong party and the wrong ideals. He supported the King; he supported the oligarchy; he supported everything that betokened privilege. In rapid, high-flying, brilliantly impudent orations he denounced the plea of Wilkes, opposed the sovereignty of the people, defended the villainous claims of Sir James Lowther against the Duke of Portland. A reactionary ministry seemed to have found that greatest of treasures, a reactionary genius, and in no time Fox was rewarded with a junior lordship of the Admiralty. Then, for the first time, the wind shifted when the King introduced his Royal Marriage Bill, which Fox opposed from sentimental chivalry.[6] He at once resigned from the Admiralty, but hastened to insist: " I think myself very safe from going into opposition, which is the only danger."

This capricious move had the effect of deepening the King's dislike of him into intense hostility. The King had disliked Fox's father; the moral and frugal sovereign was bound on principle to dislike the dissolute and spendthrift son; now he had a personal reason to dislike him. But in those days, with his gusto and charm and immense adventurousness, Fox might almost have been pleased to have an enemy.

Truly, he did not go into opposition, and next year he returned to office as junior lord of the Treasury. With his eloquence and parts, he was necessarily an asset to administration, though administration could never for long be easy in its mind about him. Sooner or later so impetuous a figure must strike out on his own; sooner or later, for that matter, the King was resolved to be rid of him. The moment arrived when Fox voted against the ministry. He was handed a dry note from Lord North which read: " His Majesty has

---

[6] On coming to the throne, George III fell in love with Lady Sarah Lennox, Fox's young aunt. He proposed, she procrastinated; then she broke her leg, and while she was convalescing, George's mother and Lord Bute hurried him into a marriage with Charlotte. To Fox, the Royal Marriage Bill cast a slur on his aunt's romance.

[233

thought proper to order a new Commission of the Treasury to be made out, in which I do not see your name."

He did not enjoy his dismissal, but he profited by it. The moment was of itself an opportunity. Britain was on the brink of war with America, and the ministry was proceeding so as to make war inevitable. Luckily for Fox he had never, while perpetrating his Tory follies, committed himself on the subject of America: if he now defended it, he had no former words to eat. And so, passing from the Tory to the Whig contingent, Fox went into opposition and supported first conciliation and later independence. The American war cleared his head and fortified his character. He had done with being the cleverest of parliamentary fops; he henceforth became, by common consent, the greatest of all parliamentary debaters.

Before he was thirty, Fox was the acknowledged leader of the opposition, and, in spite or because of the King's hostility, an extraordinarily popular public figure. But his turn for power did not come until North fell in 1781. Three critical years followed, and Fox botched them. First he entered the Rockingham administration as one of the two Secretaries of State. The other was Shelburne, whom Fox did not like and would not trust. The business of the moment was peace with America, and a farce arose over negotiating it. Fox had charge of foreign affairs, Shelburne of colonial ones. Was America (whose independence was soon to be, but had not yet been, acknowledged) a foreign country or a colony? It could not have mattered had Fox and Shelburne co-operated; but Fox and Shelburne tried, instead, to outwit each other. At that point Rockingham died, and Fox petulantly resigned.

Shelburne and Fox, Rockingham's heirs of place, had need to unite; instead they divided. Shelburne became Prime Minister, and Fox misused his friendship with the Rockingham connexion by trying to oust him. As a result, the Rockingham party kept Shelburne and ousted Fox. Fox, having committed a blunder, went on to commit an outrage. The two groups opposed to Shelburne's administration were Fox's Whigs and North's Tories. Between them they could outvote Shelburne, and it seemed clear that sooner or later one of the two would coalesce with him. Instead they turned Shelburne out by coalescing with each other.

The Fox-North coalition was born a political scandal and remains a political disgrace. During the whole of the American Revolution Fox had denounced North, his party, his policies, his principles; had wanted to send him to the scaffold for his mismanagement of the war. As late as 1782 Fox had written of North's group: "From the moment when I shall make any terms with one of them, I shall rest satisfied to be called the most infamous of mankind." Now, in 1783, he advanced the excuse that his friendships were perpetual, but his enmities were not. Nobody believed him. He could have only two motives for the alliance: personal dislike of Shelburne, which prevented the right sort of coalition; and personal desire for power, which dictated the wrong sort. It was perhaps the most egregious moral liquidation, as it was the most unfortunate political blunder, of the century. Fox, so long adored, was now execrated: against almost impossible odds he had managed to get the people to agree with the King. "Nothing," Fox himself admitted, "nothing but success can justify the coalition"; and though success could not have justified it, it never had any. George III, defending morality by way of rancour, saw to that; and Fox fell, almost like Lucifer. Thereafter, except for a few months before he died, he was to be always out of office, ever in opposition. It was a very great opposition, levelled against a very great ministry; for the successor to Fox was Pitt.

Over many enlightened measures of Pitt's early years — parliamentary reform, abolition of the slave trade, Catholic emancipation — Fox, it should be emphasized, worked *with* Pitt; for both men in those days were servants of reform. And Pitt acquiesced in the impeachment of Warren Hast-

[235

ings, wherein Fox took part — though the chief glory of the trial, which turned out to be its eloquence, belongs to neither, but to Sheridan and Burke. But Fox, wherever possible, *opposed* Pitt; and in the matter of the Regency Bill, when the King went temporarily insane, Fox opposed him with loss of discretion and character alike. All he cared to understand was that if his crony, the Prince of Wales, took over the throne, Pitt would probably fall from power, and he accede to it.

But the notable part of Fox's opposition has mostly to do with his attitude toward the French Revolution. At the fall of the Bastille most Englishmen rejoiced, assuming that the French would now take to themselves a constitution and form of government minutely patterned on the English. But the pent-up passions, the accumulated abuses of many generations imposed a less graceful outcome. Excitement in France turned to confusion, and confusion to terror; the French encouraged other nations to revolt, and began a campaign of aggression which produced Napoleon and subsided only at Waterloo.

The mind of Burke could only deprecate from the outset, and soon enough denounce, what was happening. Pitt, with the instinct of cultivating his garden, sought to ignore the situation as long as he could. But Fox's pulses instantly leapt: " How much the greatest event it is," he wrote when the Bastille fell, " that has ever happened in the world! and how much the best! " Fox, at this point, may only have exulted at the declining power of the Bourbons, and the diminished danger of harm from the nation which he, like William III and Chatham, regarded as England's inveterate enemy.[7] But he was soon exulting in the cause of liberty itself; and though France plunged into deeper and deeper excesses, Fox's faith held firm. What he kept before him were the implications of the struggle; he regretted what they entailed, but his regret stopped short of condemnation.

---

[7] For this view, see *Fox*, by Christopher Hobhouse, pp. 223 et seq.

The French Revolution produced a crisis in English life, but it first produced a schism among the Whigs. It brought out everything latent in the opposition's two great leaders: everything reactionary in Burke, everything liberal-minded in Fox. The two men, bitterly divided in their opinions, had been friends of many years, and Fox — generous, if perhaps too easy-going — hoped they might continue friends. But Burke, inexorable, consummated the most celebrated of political quarrels against the historic background of the House of Commons; and their friendship ended forever.[8]

Burke, with many followers, went over to the side of Pitt; Fox, Sheridan, and the others clung, not always with a clear head, to the side of liberty. In England matters approached a crisis. France declared war, and promised aid to British insurgents. The nation, with its instinctive love of reaction and its instructed love of order — an order it preserved by means of mob violence — felt the onrush of panic. Just enough French agents were at work on British soil to give the anti-Jacobins a handle for their accusations; just enough, moreover, to seem like a great many more than there were. Pitt, with a certain preliminary reluctance, at length moved against the conspirators and firebrands. A policy of severe repression went into effect: the habeas corpus act was suspended, and seditious-mutiny acts and treasonable-practices acts made free assembly and free speech matters of treason.

Though Fox's later attitude toward the war against France was jointly founded on hatred of Pitt and misconception of events, his championing of English liberties was always much more than mere opposition to the Government. He had against him, not simply the King, not simply the ministry, not simply most of his former followers and friends, but the country itself; so that what he pleaded for was no less than a kind of liberty new to the eighteenth century: the liberty of the few.

---

[8] Burke, as a matter of fact, refused to speak to anybody who supported the French Revolution.

Fox's last years are a blot on the picture. His unquenched thirst for power and unsated hatred of Pitt led him, along narrow political lines, to commit fresh mistakes and reveal new flaws of character. When finally, a few months before his death, he came back into power, he offered no evidence of deserving it. For, with office attained, he did precisely what he had long denounced his opponents for doing; all of which, to be sure, belongs to the nineteenth century.

It is by no means easy to pass judgment on Fox. The social figure is all very well: *that* Fox had great charm and much picturesqueness. *That* Fox was a freely moving eighteenth-century aristocrat of irrepressible high spirits. Whether we catch sight of him at Brooks's, ruining himself at faro; or in the great Whig country houses of England, enchanting duchesses and shooting grouse; or dirty and hot, galloping toward the post at Newmarket and all but outrunning his own entries; or at his little villa at St Ann's Hill, content with gardening and books, delighted to welcome friends, overjoyed to be alone with the woman who in time became his wife — socially a man so engaging, so hearty, so versatile, is entitled to the appreciation he will never fail to get. That such a fellow could win the affection of Prinny or George Selwyn or the Duchess of Devonshire is almost too easily understandable. But Horace Walpole was hard to please, and Charles Fox pleased him; the Literary Club had high standards of membership, and Fox was admitted to it; [9] Gibbon was precise in his language, and Gibbon remarked of him: "Perhaps no human being was ever more perfectly exempt from the taint of malevolence, vanity or falsehood." Burke's panegyric of 1784 still leaves one breathless. Mme du Deffand, it is true, disliked Fox, but

---

[9] Curiously enough, Fox seems to have been completely cowed by Dr Johnson, and seldom dared speak in his presence. And Johnson found Fox a bore, who wanted to talk about such subjects as Catiline!

then, they had different vices,[10] and different ideas of the drawing-room. Yet Mme du Deffand was not altogether wrong, for socially Fox had faults. He was atrociously spoiled, and he felt excessively privileged. He could scarcely help knowing how charming he was, and though he did not consciously exploit his charm, he subconsciously depended on it. He could be rude and peremptory toward his friends, and was altogether irresponsible in the matter of his debts; and toward the few people he disliked, a Shelburne or a Pitt, he showed singular ill nature. But one can still feel the warmth and gust of spirit which made so many not inconsiderable men choose him for a leader, and follow where he led.

Fox was a very imperfect statesman; but it is only fair to emphasize how badly he was favoured by his background, his opportunities, and his personal habits. His first mentor was his father, whom he loved; and his father was one of the most corrupt and cynical men of his age. He indulged Charles to the hilt: far from trying to restrain his son's conduct, he sought to furnish it with incentives. Charles became a youthful leader of the last close-knit aristocracy in the life of England — a small body of men born to great wealth and title, bred to unbelievably high living, formed to regard themselves as a separate and special race. Moreover, they were talented enough to feel that, whatever their faults, their virtues were unexampled.

Charles Fox fitted in perfectly with all this. If it was his good fortune to be something additional, how better could he prove it than by entering public life to serve his country by serving his class? That is as much as his first performances in Parliament promised, and all that was asked of them: plainly he would rise, in time, to the top of a tree

---

10 Mme du Deffand was French enough, in matters of money, to be outraged by Fox's losses at gambling, and particularly so by the easy-going manner in which he bore them.

whose roots were rotten. If we rearrange his life a little — offer him, prematurely, more power than he had, concede him the friendship rather than the hostility of the King — we may shudder to think what might have happened.

Still, there was something ardent and rebellious in the man which must sooner or later have demanded a larger outlet. Descended from cavalier kings, he had a cavalier's spirit; and he had as well much of that recklessness which derives from having a perfect sense of security. Once his temperament found an objective, as it rapidly found one in the American war, he was bound to free himself from the worst disabilities of his background. The background left its mark, but the American war brought out the man and leader in him, and thenceforth what faults he had were the offshoots of his virtues.

The worst of these faults is the omnipresent vice of public life: the thirst for power. That thirst necessitated the indefensible coalition with North, the shabby scheming over the Regency Bill, the repeated blows at the head of Pitt,[11] the final tactics of a power-haunted politician. It entailed compromises, tergiversations, and bombast; it produced some unsound and erratic political friendships. It was the dangerous passion of a passionate man, as it was the costliest blunder of a blundering statesman. Among the men of his day who really count, Fox in his worst moments fell lower than any of them.

But at his best he rose above them all. He lacked Burke's insight and Pitt's integrity; he lacked a certain moral stamina, even a certain common sense. But his career is saved because, even if we ascribe the worst motives to his best performances (which it is not safe to do), the performances transcend what may have prompted them. Let us grant that in opposition he thundered more than he might have thundered in office, and that he thundered more against Pitt than

---

[11] Fox and Pitt, to be sure, expressed great admiration for each other, but that was in terms of their capacities, not their careers.

he might have against another man. Let us grant that bound up in the statesman of forward views there was much of the opportunist and something of the demagogue: in all this, were not his good instincts, as well as his bad ones, desperate? The man who is ahead of his time in thought will frequently lag behind his time in conduct, for he is frustrated. Fox erred, to be sure, from being frustrated in his ambitions; but he also erred from being frustrated in his ideals.

In the end, much remains to his credit. Burke was correct, was almost clairvoyant, concerning the particulars of the French Revolution: he anticipated all its evils and excesses. But the stupendous opportunity of the French Revolution Burke repudiated, while Fox understood and approved of it. From the standpoint of " public order," Pitt was well advised to clamp down on English liberties when there was danger of English revolution: he averted a crisis. But Fox (who was anything but a revolutionary) fought with great tenacity for a principle of civil liberties which most good minds of his day would have hardly even bothered to examine. And though it was partly owing to spleen, how satisfying to find in Fox an emancipation from misguided patriotism, a desire to see England *lose* two wars he felt were unjust! When everything has been deducted that must be — either as regards personal motives or political misapprehensions — there remains an honest and vigorous championing of the future against the past. It is imperfect and insufficient, but it is much.

Fox, to be sure, died what he was born — an aristocrat. He demanded political and, in some sense, economic reform; but for true democracy he had no sympathy whatever, and it could never have entered his head to question the class system. He was shocked to the core by the second part of Paine's *Rights of Man*. Late in his career, while naming certain other obligations, he stated that " something is due to one's station in life "; and in accepting his station, he accepted all the laxity and frivolity — though perhaps not the

[241

corruption, and certainly not the cruelty — that went along with it. If his instinct was toward the future, much even of what seems modern in him was an eighteenth-century attitude. Liberty, which he exalted above all else, was — just liberty; not equality, not opportunity, not security; it might mean the liberty to dissent or even to triumph; it more often meant the liberty to starve. But he was willing to follow wherever it might lead, into whatever regions of danger; and it was something, during thirty years, that he could never be accused of deserting.

William Pitt

THE MIND must beware in writing of Pitt also, not because he warms but because he chills the heart. The temptation is to pass a cold and flintlike judgment on a cold and flintlike man; apparently extreme virtue shocks mankind more than extreme vice, and we recoil from the Addisons, the Pitts, the Macaulays, out of instinct, seeing in them a polar race that only ambition succeeds in thawing out, condemning them for a refusal to acquiesce in the common faults of mankind. When Macaulay goes into raptures over Addison, our mounting distaste snatches at the chance to deflate them both. But Pitt, severe as a Doric column, the "watchman on the lonely tower," is hardly so intolerable; he comes closer to being tragic.

"Pitt," said Lord Rosebery, "was never young, and Fox certainly could never have been old." Much the same thing has been said of Bach and Mozart, and in passing from Fox to Pitt there is the same sudden change of music; or rather it is like leaving a lighted house where there was companionship and dancing and supper, to walk home alone through streets solemn with midnight. The two men, not unlike in distinction and opportunity, were fatally different in character and were born to be rivals. When Fox's mother saw the seven-year-old William Pitt — "the cleverest child I ever saw, and brought up so strictly and so proper in his behaviour" — she said at once: "Mark my words, that little boy will be a thorn in Charles's side as long as he lives." The little boy was never permitted, nor did he ever seek, his future rival's modes of pleasure; he was shy and studious, aiming from childhood at a career in the House of Commons. He was glad, he said once, that he was the second son of the family, for the smaller theatre of the House of Lords would never have accommodated him.

When Chatham's son entered Parliament at twenty-one, he was even more assured of a hearing than Henry Fox's son had been; and after his maiden speech he was assured of a hearing always. Full of high-minded endeavour, he began his career in opposition. But he had no intention of climbing to power through long years of subordinacy: at twenty-two, when North fell, Pitt announced that, if invited, he would join the new administration only in an important capacity. At twenty-three, as all the world knows, when George III was seeking any means to stave off the Coalition, Pitt refused an offer from the King to be prime minister of England. He knew he must run too great a risk of failure and shrewdly chose to let Fox and North run the risk instead. But after they fell, the situation was different; and Pitt, still not twenty-five, formed an administration. Most people gave it a month; it lasted for seventeen years.

By the time Pitt assumed office he had broken with the Foxite Whigs and become alienated from Fox himself. Two years earlier he had sought Fox out as Shelburne's spokesman, hoping to induce Shelburne's enemy to become his ally. Fox refused, then hinted that Pitt and himself might work something out from which Shelburne could be excluded. Pitt snubbed him in high priggish style: "I did not come here," he said, "to betray Lord Shelburne." He and Fox were never afterwards friends, and once Pitt took power, Fox became his most determined enemy, first scoffing

at his " schoolboy administration," and then, when it came
of age, denouncing it unweariedly.

Pitt took office lacking one of its requirements: he had
no majority in the House of Commons. What he did have
was the support of the people, who were furious with Fox;
and at the next election such of them as could vote revealed
their feelings at the polls. It was a great triumph, but Pitt
had still to perform an enormous task. He had to put an
England ruined by war back on its feet. And with remarkable administrative skill he did it — did it so well that within
ten years a nation that had been close to economic collapse
waxed fat and prosperous. The national debt was reduced,
systematic taxation was installed, graft and corruption were
curtailed, and the first important free-trade treaty — for
Pitt had read and approved Adam Smith — went into effect.

On taking office Pitt had hoped not only to stabilize the
country but also to reform it. He wanted to abolish pocket
boroughs, wipe out jobbery, destroy the slave trade, achieve
greater religious toleration. But during the early stages of
his administration, when powerful interests opposed all
these measures, he lacked the ability to bring them off. During the later stages he unfortunately lacked the inclination:
once the shadow of revolution fell across Europe, Pitt
sounded a retreat; progress was sacrificed to Pitt's conception of duty. It does not matter much whether Pitt, in his
heart, was a genuine reactionary, for he was always an administrator, and an administrator seeks to preserve his do-
mains at any price. So that, for all it mattered, Pitt might
have been as reactionary, at heart, as the King.

The remainder of Pitt's career was no more successful
than it was judicious. Forced — by French military, not
by French revolutionary, aspirations — into war, he clung
to his code; but having ceased to be the friend of progress,
he ceased equally to be the saviour of order. For directing
a nation at war he had none of his father's force and vision;
time after time he blundered. The star of England sank as

that of Napoleon rose, and the end was not yet. Suddenly, after seventeen years in office, Pitt resigned; not, as it happens, over the war, but over his failure to bring about Catholic emancipation in Ireland. That one liberal aim still inspired him, but the King was adamantine. Three years later Pitt came back to his old job, which this time killed him, for after Austerlitz he brokenly turned his face to the wall.

In terms of private character, the eighteenth century yields up no other statesman who ranks as high as Pitt. If all the world remembers that he drank unbelievable quantities of port, it may forget that drink was his only weakness. From the day he took office he raised the moral tone of the position of prime minister. Quite poor, and in danger of being rapidly ousted, he spurned a large sinecure which at that moment fell vacant and which any preceding statesman would have fallen upon. He was scrupulously honest in a corrupt age and intensely conscientious in a frivolous one. At times he showed animus, but never irritation. His patience was infinite — patience, he remarked, was the first requirement of a prime minister. Pitt lived in his work, partly from a love of power, partly from a dedication to duty. As an administrator he served his country well. George III chose Pitt with the object of finding a submissive servant; what he found was a master, equal in obstinacy, superior in insight. Could Pitt have lived out his life as the neighbour of an untroubled Europe, he might have given England unparalleled security and success, for he knew the way. He knew it, indeed, a little too well: as Professor Rose has remarked, the chief opponent of Pitt the reformer was Pitt the financier. But after 1789 the way was not open; France was not genteel enough to humour Pitt's ambitions.

So that after 1789 things went ill with Pitt; went very ill, even though, in order to save what he valued most, he sacrificed what he should have valued more. The liberal statesman perished, but in those years of danger the vigorous administrator fared little better. It is barely possible that Pitt saved England from revolution; but it is altogether clear that he failed to save her from want, dissatisfaction, years of defeat, and — so far as that goes — from mutiny. The times were against him, it is true. The pity is that he reacted to them so weakly, that — like almost all statesmen in power — he could find no wiser formula in a crisis than repression. The ultimate disparity in him is that between his virtues and his values. The latter are really much of a piece, and nowhere in advance of the age. The same man who combated Jacobinism with severe legislation believed in child labour and devised a Combination Act to stamp out trade unions. He had a sincere regard for the welfare of his country, but history offers abundant proof that patriotism is the first refuge of a reactionary.

In the end, the quercine steadfastness of a Pitt contrasted with the mercurial ardour of a Fox points no useful moral. A good man who is not forward-looking in his social thinking may easily do harm. Pitt performed useful services, not exemplary ones. As he lacked the human touch, so his policies ignored the human element. A man compounded of the Pitt hauteur and the Grenville starch necessarily was the victim of even his good qualities. If he had clean hands, they hardly compensate for a narrow mind. His aloofness, his celibacy of mind as well as body, were dangerous and tragic for the same reason: they kept him from understanding the people in whose interest he sought to govern. Pitt stabilized his country, and for that his contemporaries might admire him; but the important fact for us is that he left it no better than he found it.

CHAPTER III

THE GREAT WORLD

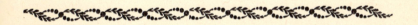

LASTING CHANGES came over London, as over England, as the century moved forward. The city that Swift and Addison had known and that Hogarth has partly preserved (where the Thames, spanned by but a single bridge, was still a great thoroughfare of travel) was fast dying. In the fashionable West End new streets, new squares, new mansions were everywhere springing up; May Fair, a region of fields behind Piccadilly, was becoming, in brick and plaster, Mayfair. The Russells were domesticating Bloomsbury, the Harleys laying out streets around the Tyburn Road. Westminster Bridge was opened for traffic in 1750, Blackfriars in 1769. The old City gates — at Temple Bar — came down, streets were new paved, roadways mended. To what extent crooked, airless London was improving we may gauge from the fact that, where in 1749 English visitors marvelled at Paris for being so clean, twenty-five years later they were scandalized to find it so dirty.

Change came too — though less noticeably — into the life of the upper classes, who strove increasingly after elegance. The Augustan age, except for its exemplars, was seldom either gracious or moderate: heady, violent, extravagant, it lived by pelting mud and driving home the sword. But from

[247

the time of Charles II onward, English society, whether authentically or falsely, became a good deal more frenchified. The demeanour of the French courtier and the French fop began having its English counterpart, and words like *ton* and *gout* soon acquired a scriptural importance. As time went on, sons of good family accepted the grand tour as part of their educations, and brought back from the drawing-rooms of Paris an attitude that they plainly overstressed and frequently caricatured. It was nothing for a young man to reappear in England with " a valet, a monkey, and a trunkful of laced coats," and to startle the rustics of Bury St Albans with the fopperies of the faubourg Saint-Germain. Indeed, worldlings of every age contrived to be at Paris whenever they could — the dandies to buy fine clothes, the rakes to seek new pleasures, the wits to make the circle of the salons. Furthermore, a man of reputation but no great social standing, a Sterne, a Hume, an Arthur Young, found himself idolized abroad where he might be neglected or condescended to at home. How deeply ingrained the Gallic tradition became with men of fashion we may note in the prose of a Horace Walpole, which is rather French than English, or of a George Selwyn, which is sometimes hardly English at all.

Elegance, at any rate, became capital to the English drawing-room, and produced in the school of Chesterfield a standard of polish and ease that would not tolerate the patrician grossness of an earlier day. This new standard was in some ways very little for the better. That, for all his true worldliness and sense of form, Chesterfield should have thought it unbecoming in a gentleman to play the violin, and vulgar to laugh, tells us how implacably exquisite the manners of the new generation had become. There were still, in descent from the hardy old line, the Bloods and the Frolics — gamblers, bullies, freethinkers and violent rakes; but the mincing fop of Queen Anne's time turned into the beau, or pretty fellow, of the Georges; scented himself, wore a fancy stick, and used girls' names in referring to his friends. There was also a tendency to be insolent and blasé:

Why [declares one character of another in Miss Burney's *Cecilia*] he's the very head of ton. There's nothing in the world so fashionable as taking no notice of things, and never seeing people, and saying nothing at all, and never hearing a word, and not knowing one's own acquaintance, and always finding fault; all the ton do so.

Along with such studied rudeness there went more " sensibility " than formerly: the rise of that squeamishness which Jane Austen would be swift to mock, of that prudery which would at length engulf the Victorians. Plain speech was clearly on its way out: Mrs Thrale, reading aloud from the *Spectator* papers concerning a woman who mentioned the stomach-ache, shocked her maid into insisting that no *lady* could possibly have used such a phrase. On the other hand, growing taboos offer no proof of growing taste: when a young French nobleman visited England in 1782, he found things mentioned in good society at which the French would have thrown up their hands.

Society itself, as the century wore on, became more, not less, of a rigid caste. To grow rich in trade, and marry or climb into the aristocracy, had once been fully possible; trade, as has already been said, then bore no stigma; and the whole age, from another point of view, was open to the adventurer. But the long domination of the great Whig clique went far toward consolidating the social world. It was a fixed group, a combination of the great landowning and the great political families who knew one another from birth and fortified their position by careful intermarriage.[1] At the accession of George III, when the Whig clique was finally dispossessed, there were only 174 British peers, and a

---

[1] There were, of course, some exceptions: some noble families married into trade, and a few high-born gentlemen married actresses.

[249

peerage consequently meant a great deal. Their number was much added to toward the end of the century, during the administration of the younger Pitt; but never to the advantage of the parvenu — it was upon statesmen and politicos, judges and ancillary connexions of the great houses, that the titles fell. It is worth remembering that in the sphere of politics itself Burke, from his inferiority of birth, was never granted high office by the Whigs.

What one finds, then, in the second half of the eighteenth century is an English society growing ever more ritualized and narrow, ever less feudal and careless and spacious in its expression of rank. For all its insolent condescension in the days of Anne, the great world had not been sheathed in that confining sense of snobbishness which traffics in such phrases as " the best people ": men of high birth had no hesitation in dropping down to the level of the coffee-house, in becoming intimate with men of talent, in refusing to conform. But in the next age the distinction was rarely overlooked: Wilberforce set down as one of his reasons for not desiring a peerage that it would deny his children the friendship of " private gentlemen of moderate fortunes, and clergymen, and still more, mercantile men." A Charles Fox or a Topham Beauclerk might take a broad or bohemian view of society and seek instruction or amusement outside the closed circle, but the typical aristocrat of parts, Horace Walpole or George Selwyn, was an ingrained or fussy snob who valued his place in life far too highly to step down from it.

The difference between the age of Anne and that of the later Georges is nowhere better revealed than in the creation of that ostentatiously exclusive institution, the club. This was, of course, not at all like the old Kit-Cat or Scriblerus; it arose when the gentlemen who used to gamble and drink chocolate at White's decided to take over the whole house and set up a blackball. Membership in White's, and to a lesser degree in Brooks's or Boodle's, was a badge of caste.

The New-Fashioned Phaeton — engraving, c. 1776

BETTMANN ARCHIVES

These somehow came to supplant the coffee-houses, by usurping for the few what had formerly been open to the many. Why the many let the coffee-houses perish once the few had disdained them cannot be wholly answered; but one reason, clearly, is that the classlessness of the old coffee-house had in it something disturbingly un-English.

The *primum mobile* of the clubs was the rage for gambling. The betting-book at Brooks's remains its central and most characteristic memorial; indeed, its political celebrity would never have come about had not Charles Fox been as great a gambler as he was a statesman. And though, in the seventies and eighties, White's and Brooks's were differentiated by their politics, White's being Tory and Brooks's Whig, it was never the Whigs' buff waistcoats, but always the table's green baize, that kept the clubs going. White's, the oldest of them, was always the most exclusive: clever and gifted men were often admitted to Brooks's, but almost never to White's. Colley Cibber, it is true, belonged; but Selwyn kept Sheridan out for years until (so the story goes) he was got in by a ruse. Selwyn himself had to wait nine years to graduate from White's Young Club to its Old one, and that was considered a very short time. So foremost was the Old Club at White's (Chesterfield called it the Established Church) that it was the one other club for which a member of Brooks's, then Almack's, was permitted to stand. If the roster of Brooks's had less blue blood, it had much more distinction: the original membership included Burke, Fox, Gibbon, Reynolds, Garrick, and Hume.

So overwhelming was the passion to bet in the clubs that some of their wagers sound today less like wagers than jokes. Members bet high sums that one woman would have a child before another ("N.B. Miscarriages go for nothing"); that a lord would outlive a dancing-master; that the Duke of Queensberry would die before half past five in the afternoon of June 27, 1773. Two men laid a bet that Beau Nash would die before Colley Cibber, but both bettors had committed suicide before either bettor was in a position to collect. Men even bet (and lost) that they wouldn't gamble in the future.

But it was at cards and dice that really great sums changed hands. Stakes, which had been growing prodigious all through the century, reached their peak — in the opinion of Charles Fox — during the three years preceding the outbreak of the American war. Fox himself boasted of having lost two hundred thousand pounds in a single night; a hundred and eighty thousand pounds were lost in one night at the Cocoa Tree; and it was nothing for an ancestral estate to hinge on the turn of a card — at the gaming-table the Duke of Devonshire, for instance, lost Leicester Abbey. " I tremble to think," wrote George Lyttleton, " that the rattling of a dice-box at White's may one day or other (if my son should be a member of that noble academy) shake down all our fine oaks." Horace Walpole wondered what Charles Fox would do " when he had gambled away the estates of all his friends." Virtually no one in the great world was exempt from the itch to play, or from the punishment of losing. It was the Achilles' tendon of even so disciplined a man as Chesterfield, who was as unlucky as he was intemperate: as the best way of getting their money back, the creditors of a notorious cheat used to let him out of debtors' prison whenever Chesterfield came up to London. In his will Chesterfield stipulated that his godson must forfeit five thousand pounds if he ever lost more than five hundred pounds at gambling in one day.

The less well off were as avid as the opulent, the women (playing at home) as avid as the men, the young as avid as the old. " The girls and boys," wrote Lady Hertford, " sit down as gravely to whist tables as the Fellows of colleges used to do formerly." An anecdote of Walpole's is famous: " Lord Stavordale, not one-and-twenty, lost eleven thousand last Tuesday, but recovered it by one great hand at hazard. He swore a great oath — ' Now, if I had been playing *deep*,

I might have won millions.'" The gambling rules at the
clubs were very strict: at Almack's "every person playing
at the new guinea table do keep fifty guineas before him."
A table displaying ten thousand pounds in specie was a
common sight. One man retired from Brooks's in disgust
because he had won only twelve thousand pounds in two
months. Hazard and faro (then spelled *pharaoh*) had been
made illegal by a gaming act of 1738, but that law and others
were flouted throughout the rest of the century, and many
society women who were convicted of running gambling
establishments narrowly escaped the pillory. Frances Pelham, a prime minister's daughter, wrecked her life by her
passion for gambling. The debts of the Duchess of Devonshire were once more than a million pounds.[2]

Drinking abated somewhat among men of fashion during
the course of the century, but none the less remained very
pronounced until the end. The modern jest of the French,
that water is very good to bathe in, was commonly made
during the eighteenth century by the English — though
there is no evidence that they bathed in it. The English,
moreover, did not drink light wines, but quantities of brandy
and port. A dozen-odd young bloods sat up after a ball
until seven in the morning, emptying (on top of what they
had already drunk) thirty-two bottles of wine. Dr Johnson
once drank thirty-six glasses of port without budging — and
with a lump of sugar in every glass. A Sheridan or Lord
Eldon was said to be able to drink six bottles at a sitting;
and Porson — after Bentley the greatest classical scholar
of the eighteenth century — drank as much as he could get,
went round draining the lees of other people's wineglasses,
and, it was said, when there was nothing else to swallow,
drank ink. Among writers Goldsmith and Boswell were
topers like Steele and Addison before them. What was true
of George IV's Mrs Fitzherbert's house at Brighton must
have been true of countless others: it contained an ale

---

[2] These, it is true, included other things than gambling.

cellar, a small-beer cellar, a wine-in-casks cellar, and a wine-in-bottles cellar.

By modern standards, almost all eighteenth-century men of the world drank well; all the same, many got drunk, and their drunkenness resulted in practical jokes, quarrels, duels, and the tormenting and assaulting of women. Certain hackney-drivers got most of their income from cruising about town late at night to pick drunken men up and carry them home. If they were too drunk to recall where they lived, the coachmen put them to bed in a tavern, then called on them next morning, certain of being handsomely tipped.

Throughout the century the wealthy continued to eat their great heavy meals. The dinner hour in society grew constantly later: from two, during the age of Anne, it advanced to four in the heyday of Horace Walpole, then to five, and at the close of the century had usually reached six. Tea was served as soon after dinner as the men reached the drawing-room; and with late hours becoming the rule, supper came to play as great a part in the social round as dinner. By the seventies Walpole was complaining of the late hours, with everyone thinking it chic to make them, if possible, later than they already were. " It is the fashion now to go to Ranelagh two hours after it is over. . . . The music ends at ten; the company goes at twelve." And Walpole adds that Lord Derby's cook had threatened to give notice, from being constantly worn out by preparing suppers at three in the morning.

Early in the century, when men and women went largely their own way, there appear to have been few formal entertainments for both sexes; but by 1740 we begin to read of a great number of dinner-parties and balls, of masquerades and ridottos. Perhaps the absence, during those years, of violent political stress contributed to the harmony of social life; but certainly the aspiration toward elegance contributed more. By the end of the century the London " season " was in most respects the same as in modern times.

Ranelagh (with its famous rotunda) was opened in 1742, to supplement Vauxhall as a public pleasure resort; and though both places, and Vauxhall in particular, belonged rather to the middle than the upper classes, the great world found it an agreeable condescension to visit them from time to time. In the seventies the Pantheon was thrown open in Oxford Street, as a winter Ranelagh, and for masquerades; while for a quarter of a century the polite world went to balls and ridottos at Mme Cornlys's rooms in Soho Square. At most parties a formal tone was scrupulously maintained, though the masquerades were thought, notwithstanding, to have very immoral consequences.[3]

The changes in dress during the second half of the century were many and extreme. No other age in English history has run to such gorgeousness and such extravagance alike: both for men and women, no colours were too rich, no fabrics too sumptuous. It was an age when physicians carried large gold-headed canes; when men as well as women tripped about on high heels; when women, at one time, laced themselves so tight they came near to fainting; at another, wore enormous hoopskirts and fantastically wide hats; and at still another, wore such piles of false hair as to tower ten feet high and be forced, when driving in carriages, to sit on the floor. Above all, it was the age of the fan and the snuffbox. Most of these eccentricities came late in the century, when taste in general had run to the rococo, and when a craze for fads destroyed much of the true tone that had earlier given upper-class life at least a surface elegance. In the course of the century first the full-bottomed wig and then wigs in general ceased to be fashionable, giving way to powdered hair. Then the high tax on hair-powder during the French Revolution (and in some quarters the republican gesture of leaving the hair unpowdered) combined to end what is perhaps the most familiar and pictur-

---

[3] Mme Cornlys was clearly a go-between for upper-class sexual intrigues.

esque custom of the times. In the same period men, who
had already abandoned dress swords, abandoned silk stock-
ings and buckled shoes as well. Trousers succeeded; and
with them — no longer bearing its old stigma of effeminacy
— the umbrella.

In Queen Anne's time, and for some time after, most of
the men who bore the title of wits were professional writers
who had acquired a certain position in society: Addison,
Steele, Pope, Prior, Gay. A Duke of Shrewsbury might stand
on his dignity and refuse to accept a Prior as his co-ambassador to Paris, but would have no objection to dining or drinking with him for the good things he might say. Indeed, aristocrats like Bolingbroke, Hervey, and Lady Mary competed
with the professionals in saying good things and helped create that atmosphere of wit which was never again exactly
recovered. But as time went on, though some writers might
still be taken up by society, they were not taken up as wits,
and the mid-century wit was a special product of society itself — someone who said his good things among his own
friends. Thus, however witty, Dr Johnson was never known
as a wit; nor were most of the writers — Burke, Gibbon,
Sterne — who moved among aristocrats. It was Chesterfield
who became the first great society wit, and George Selwyn
who became the second.

The shift was not entirely advantageous. The age of Anne
was an age of great talk in which the high-born shared; the
age of George III, though it possessed the greatest of all
talkers — and this means Burke as well as Johnson — was
nothing better, in the polite world, than an age of badinage.
The society wits, with their puns, their preciousness, their
family jokes, do not rank very high. Chesterfield, who possessed a literary sense, is very good at his best, but his best
is infrequent. One may still, perhaps, enjoy his description
of two persons dancing a minuet, looking " as if they were
hired to do it, and were doubtful of being paid "; and his

description of a certain marriage, sometimes attributed to Sheridan, has a cold malicious brilliance: " Nobody's son," he remarked, "has married Everybody's daughter."

Chesterfield, we may note, passed a cosmopolitan and public existence; but a mere fribble like Selwyn was no more than the classic diner-out of his time, and in him we encounter the inbred, second-rate jesting of a man who need not be on his toes for what a Pope or Johnson might retort upon him. Legend has it that Selwyn's tedious puns and stylish cackle gained greatly from the prim and melancholy look with which he uttered them. That well may be. Today his better remarks sound like mere pleasantries, as when, seeing a woman whose dress was covered with spangles the size of shillings, he said to her: " Bless me, you look like change for a guinea." His two best sayings are based on his notorious love of executions. Once Selwyn visited his dentist to have a tooth pulled, and said he would drop a handkerchief as the signal to begin. And once, when someone named Charles Fox had been hanged, the other Charles Fox asked Selwyn if he had gone to watch. " You know, Charles," he answered, " that I never attend rehearsals."

The wittiest man of the day, we may be sure, was no man of birth, but a parvenu and a professional — Sheridan.[4] His wit, like Sydney Smith's, Wilde's, Whistler's, Mark Twain's, and in our own day Dorothy Parker's, has become classic; and he probably never said a good many of the things attributed to him.[5]

The second half of the century brings on the social scene no women with the old force of character of Lady Mary or the Duchess of Marlborough; but in place of the high-handed aplomb of the one, and the unmanageable arro-

---

[4] His talk was good enough to keep the Duchess of Devonshire for two months at Chatsworth that she had planned (and paid for) at Bath.

[5] Wilkes, too, was a real wit, as is attested by several stories as good as that in which he asked a man to vote for him. " Vote for you, sir! I would rather vote for the devil." To which Wilkes: " But — in case your friend does not stand? "

gance of the other, we find women of greater grace and sensibility, and with talents that were creative as well as social. English society was never, in the strict sense, to accept the French conception of the salon: for the great salons of Paris — where an almost fixed group met at fixed intervals to range over fixed topics — imposed a regimen which few English people would undergo. Rather, in England, there were women whose houses became known for their hospitality and sparkle: first the lively, disreputable Lady Townshend and the charming Lady Hervey (formerly Mary Lepel, and the widow of "Sporus"), who had such men as Walpole and Chesterfield, Hume and Helvetius to dinner; later Mrs Montagu, the century's most impressive bluestocking, and Hetty Thrale, the century's most attractive hostess.

Mrs Montagu was singularly clever from childhood, and at fourteen was writing like this:

Your Grace desired me to send you some verses. I have not heard so much as a rhyme lately, and I believe the Muses have all got agues in this country; but I have enclosed you the following summons, which we sent to an old batchelor, who is very much our humble servant, and would die, but not dance for us. . . .

After her marriage she set up as a great London hostess at a time when other clever women — Mrs Vesey, Mrs Boscawen, Miss Carter,[6] Miss Talbot — were trying to refashion a social world in which card-playing had quite supplanted talk, and who were seeking also to make feminine brains, as distinct from feminine wit, respectable. Men, in those years, still seem to have shied away from intellectual women; indeed, Lady Mary herself was strongly insisting that her infant granddaughter be brought up " to conceal whatever learning she attains, with as much solicitude as she would hide

---

[6] By general consent, she seems much the most erudite of the bluestockings. In her way of waking up in the morning, as we learn from Boswell, she was a hundred and fifty years ahead of Rube Goldberg. She had her night-light burn through a string to which a heavy weight was suspended; the fall of the weight woke the lady up.

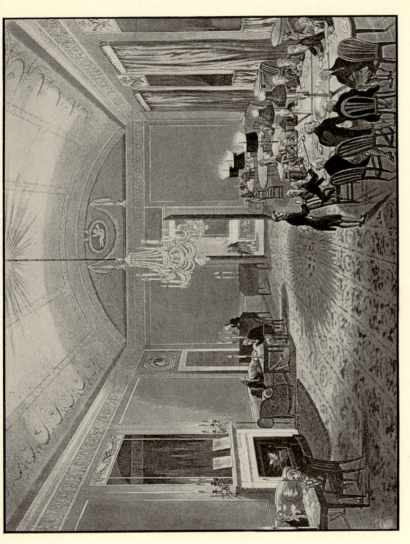

Great Subscription Room at Brooks's by Thomas Rowlandson

COURTESY NEW YORK PUBLIC LIBRARY PRINT ROOM

crookedness or lameness." Fanny Burney was not pleased when Johnson began teaching her Latin — she feared it would hurt her reputation to be known as a " learned lady." And Sir Joshua's sister, who acted as his hostess to many brilliant groups of men, gave out that " the most perfect feminine mind habitually aims at nothing higher than exemption from blame."

Now, under the leadership of Mrs Montagu, these defiant bluestockings managed to acquire distinction and draw round them many eminent men of the day. They were a mixed group, some of them great ladies like the Duchess of Portland, others hard-working middle-class women who lived virtually in Grub Street; but all were " modern" and all had pronounced ideas. They abused the butterfly existence of society women,[7] distrusted romance, denounced marrying for money, and excoriated the double standard. Some of them wrote, others became pioneer reformers and philanthropists. Each had a slightly different idea of the drawing-room. Mrs Ord, seeking a severe concentration, grouped her guests round a table, as for " a dinner-party without the dinner." Mrs Vesey, disliking the ceremoniousness of a fixed circle, pushed the furniture any which way about the room, breaking up the company into small groups; and " the instant any earnestness of countenance or animation of gesture struck her eye, she darted forward to inquire what was going on." But Mrs Montagu, with her princely house in Portman Square, desired a more formal atmosphere.

At Mrs Montagu's [wrote Fanny Burney in her *Diary*] " the semi-circle that faced the fire retained during the whole evening its unbroken form, with a precision that made it seem described by a Brobdingnagian compass. The lady of the castle commonly placed herself at the upper end of the room, near the commence-

---

[7] They would not have approved of their contemporary Lady Melbourne, whose attitude toward money-matters was revealed in her remark: " Lord, they say the stocks will blow up: that will be very comical."

ment of the curve, so as to be courteously visible to all her guests; having the person of highest rank or consequence properly on one side, and the person the most eminent for talents, sagaciously on the other. . . . No one ventured to break the ring.

With its Feather Room, its Great Room adorned by Angelica Kauffmann, its stately *conversaziones,* its teas for a hundred, its breakfasts for seven hundred — with such show of pomp, an aura of the great world hangs over Montagu House. Yet Mrs Montagu was not merely a wealthy woman who gave parties: her letters still make tolerable reading, her essay on Shakespeare makes good sense, she was the perennial toast of The Club, and Johnson himself said of her: "That lady exerts more *mind* in conversation than any person I have met."[8] Her definition of the tone is neatly achieved, and squares with that in *Cecilia:*

> I can never tell you what it is; but I will try to tell you what it is not. In conversation, it is not wit; in manners, it is not politeness; in behaviour, it is not address; but it is a little like them all. It can only belong to people of a certain race, who live in a certain manner, with certain persons who have not certain virtues and who have certain vices, and who inhabit a certain part of the town.

The bluestockings were the product of an artificial and self-conscious, yet not supine, age; and when they had run their course, they left no successors behind them. After 1800 we may suppose that the middle-class woman of parts became a writer or educator, with small place in high society; while the society woman of parts became a great hostess, but chose a discreet role in the world of intellect. It is true that eighteenth-century Montagu House, splendid as was its roll-call of names, cannot hold a candle to nineteenth-century Holland House, that " house of all Europe " which commonly entertained Fox and Sheridan, Byron and Talley-

---

[8] On the other hand, Johnson confessed he couldn't read the Essay on Shakespeare through.

rand, Canova and Mme de Staël, Sydney Smith and Washington Irving, Lord Melbourne and Macaulay; but master-
ful and imperious as Lady Holland was — in Greville's pages
she sounds dreadful, and even in Macaulay's much to be
disliked — she was never shown the same kind of respect,
or granted the same intellectual status, as Mrs Montagu;
and as a hostess she can have had none of the quickness
and gaiety of Mrs Thrale.

No one, of course, ever thinks of Mrs Thrale without
thinking of Dr Johnson; and her niche in history assuredly
derives from her having soothed and softened, as well as
vividly chronicled, the Doctor's life at Streatham; and from
her having — until near the end of his days — commanded
his admiration and love. But before Johnson was ever
brought to meet her, Hetty Thrale had contrived to be a
hostess, and without having been beautiful or notably brilliant, seems to have had a vivaciousness which made for
bright gatherings. Neither all her gifts, it is true, nor all her
efforts ever won her a secure place among the bluestockings;
but then, rattling away as she did, she never sought their
formal elegances. " Mrs Montagu's bouquet is all out of
the hothouse," she said, describing that lady's talk; " mine
out of the woods and fields, and many a weed there is in it."
Yet, while surveying her parties with a touch of humour,
she plainly took pride in them:

> Mrs Montagu was brilliant in diamonds, solid in judgment,
> critical in talk. Sophy smiled, Piozzi sang, Pepys panted with
> admiration, Johnson was good-humoured, Lord John Clinton
> attentive, Dr Bowdler lame, and my Master not asleep. Mrs
> Ord looked elegant, Lady Rothes dainty, Mrs Davenant dapper,
> and Sir Philip's curls were blown about by the wind.

Elsewhere we are told that at Streatham " dinner was sumptuous: tea was social." There, in the foreground, was the
blooming Mrs Thrale with her high spirits, her gay remarks,
her suspicious spontaneities — as when she wept over *Ce-*

cilia and kissed the book in her joy. And in the background was Thrale, handsome, hospitable, and frigidly correct, whom Hetty respected but did not love. Then Thrale died, and Hetty took up with Piozzi, her daughters' music-master, whom once at Dr Burney's she had cruelly mimicked; married him, shocked London, alienated Johnson; and passed into a new existence that proved far happier than the old one.

We can most suitably bring down the curtain on a vanished patrician world with that name, its brightness still not spent, which, like the glittering Chesterfield's, seems to sum up a whole frivolous, fictional, grandee society. Not much, it is true, remains to be told of Georgiana Duchess of Devonshire. With great good sense she demolished the hoopskirt ten feet round, but only to glorify the ostrich feather ten feet high. From reading Rousseau she was moved to dispense with a wetnurse and suckle her children herself. She adored Charles Fox and canvassed votes for him in the slums of London, visiting " the most blackguard houses in Long Acre " and, where nothing else would persuade, planting kisses on plebeian lips. Many ugly stories have been whispered of her; yet she seems to have taken the town by storm from the day she married and to have held it in fee till the day she died. At her death the Prince of Wales exclaimed: " We have lost the best-bred woman in England "; and Charles Fox added: " We have lost the kindest heart." And with her the music of an age — it was Mozart's age — had died away.

CHAPTER IV

THE WORLD BELOW

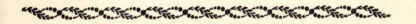

Lower-class England during the second half of the century was much transformed by the power of the Agrarian and Industrial Revolutions. But lower-class London was not. In some respects its circumstances were bettered, in others depressed, but there was as yet no radical change, and few of the things Dr Johnson saw would have startled Swift. The largely static condition of the eighteenth-century London poor resulted from the largely static eighteenth-century attitude toward poverty. In the benighted seventeenth century the chief explanation of poverty had been low wages. With the coming of the Age of Reason, however, this view collapsed, and by Queen Anne's time the cry had gone up that workingmen's wages were not too low but too high, and that poverty arose from the thriftlessness of the workers themselves. This widespread opinion — implying that labourers squandered their money in taverns and worked only when they had to — was promulgated by so observant a writer as Defoe. Certain theorists of the period even advocated raising the cost of living as a means of keeping the poor in tow; for, they insisted, so long as food was cheap, work need not be arduous. From all sides came pamphlets and tracts deprecating an easy life for those " not used to

[263

ease," and accusing such people, when their earnings were high, of living in profligate luxury. As late as the 1770s there was an excited outcry against the use of tea, sugar, and white bread in poor men's families.

At the beginning of the century the school of Locke was also arguing that society should not help the poor find work, but should force them to find it for themselves. Locke's contemporary, Dunning, suggested that if "help" were offered in the form of impossibly low wages, the workingman would then be compelled to look on his own for a more lucrative job; and Defoe chimed in, saying: " It seems strange . . . that it is our business to find them work and to employ them, rather than oblige them to find themselves work and go about it."

This laissez-faire attitude did not fasten itself, however, upon the nation, possibly because in an age deficient in police it would have proved too dangerous; instead a movement arose by which the needy could be at once cared for and coralled. The eighteenth century suddenly thought it had found a panacea for all its economic evils in the creation of the workhouse. Here, at any rate, was a way to salve the national conscience without draining the national purse, and workhouses sprang up everywhere. Anyone in need who refused to enter one forfeited his right to relief, and the community could wash its hands of him. For all that, many refused to enter: workhouse living was harsh and workhouse management corrupt, while vermin and jail fever were almost as common in the London workhouses as in the London jails. Instead of being maintained by the community, the management was commonly farmed out to a contractor who took over the job for either a lump sum or a fixed per-capita charge. He naturally made his best profit if he underfed and overworked the inmates. At Shoreditch workhouse, near London, it came to light that thirty-nine children had to sleep in three beds. Child labour, of course, was an accepted part of eighteenth-century practice, and one of the chief arguments for diminishing poverty.[1]

Much prized though the workhouse idea was, the number of London workhouses was inadequate to the problem of the London poor. As the century advanced, an increase in private philanthropy did something to mitigate the problem: five great hospitals were founded in London by 1750, and afterwards the dispensary movement began to make headway, so that poor people could get free medicine and advice. In 1769 an Act of Parliament made it compulsory for the London parishes to send infants into the country to be nursed. About this time the lower classes also benefited from London's new system of lighting, paving, and draining and from some early attempts at slum clearage. All this growing humanitarianism did something to aid the London masses; but it did not do enough, as a survey of the existing penal code will show.

The penal code had been shocking at the beginning of the century, and as the century advanced, it grew worse. Romilly, who strove to improve it and finally, early in the next century, succeeded, wrote in 1786: "Among the variety of actions which men are daily liable to commit, no less than 160 have been declared by Act of Parliament to be felonies without benefit of clergy; or, in other words, to be worthy of instant death." The number of such felonies had increased during the century. At no time do the nation's legislators seem to have reflected on the penal system they were creating, but went ahead piling up capital offences in a kind of brutal lethargy. And the penal code was not only harsh; it was also absurd. When the nineteenth century dawned, stealing a sheep or horse was still a crime punishable by death; so was taking linen from a bleaching-ground; so was cutting down trees in a garden; so was picking a

---

[1] Defoe, early in the century, noted with enthusiasm of the children in a certain town: " Hardly anything above four years old but its hands are sufficient to itself "; and Davies, a clergyman who had real feeling for the poor, recommended late in the century that no child over six should be given poor relief if he did not know how to knit.

pocket for anything above a shilling; so was breaking the border of a fish-pond so that the fish could escape. On the other hand, if a man attempted his father's life it was only a misdemeanour. And stabbing a man, no matter how dangerously, so long as he recovered; burning down a house, no matter who was in it, so long as you were its lessee; committing perjury that might send an innocent man to his death — these were only punishable by fines and imprisonment. Again, to steal fruit already gathered was punishable by death, but to gather fruit and then steal it was only a trespass. To break into a house at five p.m. in winter was a capital offence; but to break into a house at five a.m. in summer was not.

However much England might pride itself on its form of government, its penal code was the most vicious and sanguinary in Europe. On many parts of the Continent prison reform was already under way, but even in the most backward places, such as Russia, though torture might still be frequently inflicted, the general situation was unlikely to be so bad. Fortunately in England the disease was partly its own cure. The laws were too severe for juries to be willing to enforce them: rather than send men to their deaths for trifling offences, jurors — in the full sight of their guilt — acquitted them. And even of those convicted, by no means all were put to death: of 1,121 persons condemned to die at the Old Bailey between 1749 and 1772, only 678 were executed. Many prisoners with a gambling instinct preferred to be tried for capital offences rather than misdemeanours, since in the one case they were certain to go to jail, whereas in the other, though they might hang, they might also go free. Criminals were handicapped, among other things, by not being provided with counsel, except in treason trials or where a point of law intervened; though as time went on, this rule was more and more violated. The trial, in any case, seldom lasted long. One day, at most, was the general custom: the law could not be burdened with the cost of a long trial, and jurors could not be bored with the annoyance of it. They ate in the jury-box, and drank, and got drunk; drunk or sober, they fell asleep; and often woke up to be talked by their fellows into any sort of verdict. Many, though not all, were soft-hearted; few had any sense of responsibility: Pope, long before, had scored them off with " For wretches hang that jurymen may dine."

Legislators, busy piling up new laws, were much idler in abrogating old ones. As a matter of fact, they left the whole business chiefly in the hands of lawyers. Burke, who did not share the parliamentary apathy, who branded the penal system as " abominable " and urged its revision, used to tell the story of being stopped by the Clerk one night when leaving the House of Commons and asked to stay to make a quorum. He inquired what business was before the House, and the Clerk replied: " Oh, sir, it is only a new capital felony."

A few very bad laws were, however, repealed. Prisoners who refused to plead could no longer be pressed to death, and women who murdered their husbands were at length sent to the gallows instead of the stake. Further, as one of its few creditable acts, the Coalition Ministry of 1783 abolished that grisly march toward doom which had come to resemble a London holiday, the procession to Tyburn. All the two miles from Newgate to Tyburn the mob, of old, had lined the streets, cheering or taunting the condemned; while hard by the scaffold pressed thousands of other curious and callous spectators. And not the masses only, but great folk also — Selwyns, Walpoles, Boswells — had been used to come and gape. When the spectacle was stopped, from all sides there arose a cry of protest. Dr Johnson joined in with an indignant antithesis: " The public," said he, " was gratified with the procession; the criminal was supported by it. Is all this," he protested, " to be swept away? " The theory that public executions acted as deterrents against crime had long since been exploded. The bravado which most criminals displayed, far from filling the mob with any terror of death, had infatuated it with a kind of glamour. "The day of his shame," wrote Fielding of a criminal being led to Tyburn, "has become the day of his glory."

Prison life throughout the century continued to be brutal and unprincipled. There was seldom enough food, and not always enough water; there was usually no bedding, no ventilation, no protection from the cold. The smells were vile, and an indication of the filth. The prisons were bestially overcrowded — in one of them, fifty men were confined by night inside a space barely six feet square. Scorbutic diseases were rife; jail fever, carrying off more prisoners than the gallows, was rampant. All this was much intensified by the cruelty and corruption of those in charge. Whatever advantages a prisoner enjoyed he had plainly bought. For lack of money he might very well have been condemned to jail in the first place, since the city magistrates were more than open to bribes. As against one Henry Fielding who dispensed honest justice in Bow Street, there were a dozen "trading magistrates" who sold their verdicts to whoever would buy them. The necessity for this arrangement may be judged from the fact that one man received thirty-six pounds a year for being a magistrate, and paid forty pounds a year to be one. Jurors who often bilked the law through soft-heartedness, equally often bilked it for gain. A newspaper announcement of 1762 offers "an elegant dinner" and five guineas to any juryman bringing in a verdict for the Crown.

Inside the jails the corruption was even worse than without. To begin with, some of the jails were privately owned. All — whoever owned them — were improperly managed. Jailkeeper and turnkeys were in a position to be absolute tyrants. They extorted money, not simply for granting privileges, but equally for respecting rights. Depending on what you paid, you were flung into the swarming Common side of the prison, or established in far greater comfort on the

Masters' side.[2] Many jailkeepers ran pubs and sold liquor for profit. And besides having to bribe his warders, a new prisoner had to run the gauntlet of his fellows: on entering, he had either to hand them over drink-money (called *chummage* or *garnish*) or part with his clothes. This transaction was curtly summed up in the phrase " Pay or strip."

Though some few abuses were remedied in the late eighteenth century, and some few advances made — as in the building of livable penitentiaries — it was not before the nineteenth century that the English prison system was in any sense adequately reformed. But much of the credit for accelerating the process belongs to the indefatigable labours of an eighteenth-century penologist and reformer, John Howard. Howard spent the greater part of his life, as well as his fortune, in minutely studying prison conditions. His " circumnavigation of charity," in Burke's phrase, led him all over Europe, and he finally died, in fact, of jail fever in Russia. So physically filthy was his work that he had to travel from place to place on horseback, because he smelled too vile to go in a stagecoach; and the very pages of his notebooks were yellowed and coated from the air of the jails. His findings, brought together in an exhaustive treatise and finally published, exposed alike the backwardness of the English system and the evils of its administration. Though his indictment was not immediately acted upon, it became the text of later reformers and eventually produced powerful results.

Howard was in no sense a sentimentalist or hazy humanitarian. He strongly believed, on the contrary, that prison life should serve as a deterrent against crime, hence should in no way be made inviting; he strongly believed, for example, in hard labour. What he sought to abolish were the

---

2 Here, indeed, if you could pay for it, you could have virtually anything you wanted: tradesmen called in, private rooms were let, and dinners and drinking-parties could be arranged. But such prison life was the exception.

great positive abuses of his time; what he wanted was justice for the prisoner, not kindness. Curiously enough, the direction which English prison life was to take in the next century, though it remedied most of the abuses, carried with it one great hardship which the old system, riddled with abuses though it was, did not have. Nineteenth-century methods, involving regular hours, solitary confinement, and hard labour, might have horrified the typical eighteenth-century prisoner more, even, than the conditions under which he lived. For he, at any rate, despite the smells and filth, the vermin and disease, the cold floors and rank food, was given leisure and companionship. With a little money, he could drink and gamble as well in prison as out; in the end, he simply transferred his soiled anarchic life from the city's slums to Newgate or Bridewell.

The poor man's health, in prison or out, was threatened on every side. It was an age when wealthy and educated people were only coming to know something about sanitation; when the dinner-tables of Berkeley Square had a prejudice against fresh vegetables; when it was difficult, at any price, to get fresh meat in winter; when inoculation against smallpox was disputed among the few who had heard about it; when eczema and scrofula were endemic, and syphilis was widespread; when the Thames was a glorified sewer and the streets of London had only just ceased being. In such an age, what might be the probable fate of the poor? There were, to be sure, the hospitals; but Howard, who went on to study hospitals as he had studied jails, found them inadequate and even insanitary. Two patients (who might be suffering from two very different diseases) were usually put in one bed; and the patients were seldom washed, for washing was considered "weakening." The hospitals were not generous of ventilation, or sparing of vermin. The patients ate as they chose, and drank. The nurses did what they pleased, and were frequently drunken.

Children's hospitals, for either rich or poor, did not exist: it was considered cruel and un-Christian to separate an ailing child from its mother. There were two hospitals for the insane: St Luke's, and Bedlam. Even late in the century Bedlam — with its tradition of the raving mad — was one of the sights of London.[3] A conscientious visitor would no more have missed seeing it than he would have missed seeing the Abbey or the Tower. Some visitors gave out that it was well conducted, with comfortable rooms and properly tended patients. On the other hand, so model and domestic a scene would hardly have attracted quite so many sightseers. How badly the common patient was treated in the private madhouses, and till how late a date, can be inferred from the notoriously harsh treatment allotted to a *royal* patient, George III.

After the middle of the century one change for the better came into the life of the poor: gin-drinking greatly declined. This was partly owing to government intervention; partly to a rise in the standard of living (though toward the end of the century it fell off again); and partly, perhaps, to the terrible consequences of the habit, which even a lawless and desperate underworld could not but notice. The lawlessness itself, in any case, declined very little. Yet it was to some extent of a deceptive nature. That is to say that though riots were frequent and the London mob was easily aroused, still the crowd followed a certain instinctive code that served the general welfare. The streets, it was often said, belonged to the poor; and they behaved in them pretty much as they pleased. They jostled their betters and jeered at foreigners; they dominated Tyburn hangings and took charge of the pillory; they frequented hundreds of rookeries, cheap taverns, and underworld amusement places; they turned Sundays into "days of riot, excursion and dissipation." A cry like " Wilkes and Liberty! " could dump them pell-mell into the streets, menacing, vociferating, exulting; the thought of popery could drive them hot and heedless

---

[3] It enjoyed such popularity that tea was served there.

through the town with all the burning, butchering, and pillaging of the Gordon Riots. Yet, except in such times of crisis, the mob was essentially good-natured. Though lawless in the sense that it snapped its fingers at the constable — though, in other words, it was a rabble — it was not a stealthy and it was not a vicious one.

The records of the jail and scaffold prove that, even after we have deducted from their rolls those petty trespasses and venial acts which were swelled up by the age into hanging matters, it was really an age of crime. The age itself was shrewd enough to point out that if a man was to hang for theft, he had no incentive for forgoing murder. But it was Fielding, a practising magistrate as well as a great novelist, who wrote: " The sufferings of the Poor are indeed less observed than their misdeeds "; and who pointed out that, though " they beg and steal and rob among their betters," it was worth remembering that " they starve and freeze and rot among themselves."

CHAPTER V

THE WORLD WITHIN

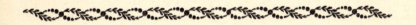

1

IT WAS A BRILLIANT PERIOD in the fine arts: nowhere else, and at no other time, did eighteenth-century England acquire so much of its elegance or its aura. Those who know nothing more — those to whom Johnson is hardly a name and Robert Walpole is a man who wrote letters — are familiar with one portrait or another of Lady Hamilton [1] and the Duchess of Devonshire, and with the stiff-legged Blue Boy and Sir Joshua's beautiful children. The period's well-bred ghost hovers about us in Chippendale chairs and Sheraton sideboards and Chinese wallpapers and Georgian plate, in Wedgwood and Worcester, in Bristol and Lowestoft. The miniature and the silhouette, which flourished under George III, seem most at home there. For better or worse, and whether false or true, the pictorial life of the period has come to be a synonym for charm.

Historically it was a period that witnessed many changes and much search for novelty. We tend to see it, not only as all of a piece, but in too romantic a light. We visualize eighteenth-century gardens and forget how few of them con-

---

[1] Romney painted a hundred in all, revealing his Divine Lady not only in her own person, but, among others, as Circe, Cassandra, Euphrosyne, Diana, Iphigenia, Ariadne, Calypso, Nature, Sensibility, Lady Macbeth, St Cecilia, a Pythian priestess, and Joan of Arc.

[273

tained any flowers. We think of great patrician dinners and forget that it was more the fashion to use the sort of Continental china we dislike than the Rockingham or Crown Derby we admire. We think of noble mahogany and forget how much furniture of the period was gilded. We think of Georgian country houses and forget that some of them were bastard Gothic. We think of Reynolds enthroned and forget about the up-and-coming Rowlandson. We think of the aristocratic rightness of Heppelwhite and forget that Heppelwhite catered largely to the middle classes. We think of impeccable taste and forget how often this art was capricious and even outré.

But since Hogarth's time England was not, at any rate, muscle-bound. Hogarth himself set no fashions: biting social satire was not to characterize the next era of painting; neither was the unfolding of drama in paint, nor a subject-matter that comprised all sides of London life. But as England's first great painter Hogarth had done something to shake off her slavish idolatry of foreigners. During the next age, painting was to drive the invader from her shores, and make Reynolds fully as fashionable as Kneller had been. Early in the century the massive baroque of architects like Vanbrugh had, under the leadership of the cultivated Earl of Burlington, been superseded by the classicism of Palladio; that too was to be scrutinized and dislodged with the coming of the brothers Adam. In the same age Gothic was to be a more or less preposterous foible, and chinoiserie to overrun houses and gardens. Fashion jostled fashion: Chippendale furniture, to use a familiar example, evolved from a Louis XV style to a Chinese one, and thence, ineffectually, to a Gothic.

Houses were at last not simply put up: they were really put together. Architects became embellishers as well: the fame of the brothers Adam survives as much in their interiors as their façades. Robert Adam, travelling on the Continent in the 1750s, turned away from classic temples to

study all manner of ruined baths and palaces and Renais-
sance mansions, and came back to England as fully equipped
for decoration as design. He came back with many more devices at his command than his predecessors had had, but
with the intention of subordinating them to details. His desire, as he expressed it, was to make decoration "more elegant and more interesting," and after working away with
his brothers at houses, he worked away at ceilings, mantel-
pieces, doorways, fanlights, *motifs* for furniture, besides
actually designing commodes and chairs and girandoles,
and even carpets and candlesticks. He directly commis-
sioned Wedgwood and Chippendale and Heppelwhite.
Seeking lightness and brightness, he preferred inlay to carv-
ing, and painted rooms to panelled ones; and achieved an
effect of spaciousness by having rooms open one into another. Although at their best these Scots were admirable architects, it is their creation of what has been called
a drawing-room style, it is their planning of the whole, that
gives them a special importance. Their arabesques and me-
dallions may seem at times too full of frippery, too much
given to what we, if not the specialists, mean by rococo; and
the detail may sometimes consume the design. But for the
most part their work combines greater variety of treatment
with greater unity of effect, achieving an elegance that only
the purest taste can deplore.

It was possibly the best age of Georgian houses, both in
town and country: not only of those palatial mansions and
noble seats which are not, in the end, the most satisfying examples of Georgian architecture, but — where box-styles
were avoided or Palladianism was tempered or the Adam
manner controlled — of lovely country houses of brick or
stone set in spacious grounds, and of town houses which
managed to achieve a trim beauty in spite of their lack of
setting and their narrow fronts. And more and more the
century came to attach importance to its gardens, which
were granted, as a form of compensation, all the liberties

denied to its houses. It was in gardens, far oftener than in poetry or music, that the romantic impulses of the age found an outlet; and not without reason, for the impulse was as thin and whimsical as the form it took. The garden became the emblem of that eighteenth-century word and thing, the picturesque — and in a quite literal sense, for its aim was to look as much as possible like a picture. " All gardening," Pope had said, " is landscape painting." Every country gentleman, it was laid down, must have at the very least " one large room, a serpentine river and a wood "; and to be a person of distinction, he needed to see from his window something that, if he cared for classic charm, resembled a Claude; or, if there was anything wilder in his nature, a Salvator; or, if his was a truly morbid hunger, a Gothic scene. When the formal atmosphere of their houses seemed too confining, the eighteenth-century leisure class flung themselves out of doors to turn moody and romantical, to linger near grottoes or daydream by trees all purposely leafless and dead, sigh over a made-to-order ruin, cross a Chinese bridge, or indulge in a reverie near a waterfall. On occasion these landscapes served for show as well as reveries, when their owners gave brilliant fêtes-champêtres, thereby adding Watteau to their list of inspirations.

In painting, the age might suffer from the tyrannies of fashion, but it revolutionized the artist's opportunities, and it produced a great deal of beautiful art. During the first half of the century an English-born painter did not find it easy either to learn or to practise his trade. It was not merely that foreigners usurped most of the patronage, although that was ruinous in itself: even Hogarth kept going much more from selling cheap prints of his work than from the prices fetched by the originals. But unless a young painter could find his way to the Continent, or work — not always to the advantage of his art — under a successful painter in England, he could seldom get the proper training. As late

The Morning Walk (William Hallett and Wife)
by Thomas Gainsborough

COLLECTION OF BARON NATHANIEL MEYER VICTOR
ROTHSCHILD, TRING PARK

as 1747 there was but one art school in all London. Worse, most artists, despite how many fine pictures there were in England, could never catch sight of them. There were virtually no galleries; and there was not even the chance to get to the auction sales, since only the fashionably dressed were admitted. Worst of all, there were no exhibitions. It was extremely hard for a painter to get his pictures displayed: with luck, he managed to hang them in a shop or tavern; and he got no publicity in the newspapers unless he paid for it.

In their need — which reached up to almost the highest among them — the artists sought, with growing determination, for something that would improve their own position and raise the lowered prestige of art. By now there existed the Dilettanti Society, composed of cultivated young aristocrats who, while they might drink themselves into stupors toasting " Grecian taste and Roman spirit," did send promising painters abroad and provide them with commissions when they came home again. And the Dilettanti offered to help finance an academy which should train and patronize artists; but when it came to light that these amateurs wanted to help run it as well, the professionals balked. But they could find no better kind of backing elsewhere.

It was not, indeed, until 1760 that a group of painters, soon to organize as the Society of Artists, managed to hold a real exhibition. After that, all through the sixties, there was activity and progress, until in 1768, with the King's patronage, the Royal Academy was established. It became at once the official, perhaps the too arrogantly official, art society in England, with a membership that should never exceed forty. But whatever vices it displayed, its virtues at the outset were undeniable: besides staging notable exhibitions, it sent students abroad on scholarships and set up an excellent drawing-school at home.[2]

---

[2] In this school no student under twenty could draw from the female nude unless he was married; and no one — " the Royal Family excepted " — could visit the Academy while the female model was sitting.

By the time the Royal Academy was founded, the whole scene had changed, and England's greatest age of painting was in full swing. Reynolds had long since become the rage in London, and Gainsborough at Bath. The Ciprianis and Zoffanys might be popular, but foreign domination had ended: even the King favoured no one more exotic than an American, Benjamin West, and a Scotchman, Allan Ramsay. It had required genius to turn the tide, but the tide was turned at last. Taste, however, ran in much the same channels: it still derived from the ruling classes, and the ruling classes still preferred their own portraits to anything else. They might approve, now and then, a florid historical work or a heroic battle scene, but they had turned their backs on Richard Wilson, despite the beauty of his landscapes; they were scarcely friendlier to the landscapes of Gainsborough; they looked askance at the finer traditions of genre painting — indeed, the whole Dutch school was outlawed; and certainly no one since Hogarth had dared to paint his own servants. In terms of fashionable art the only thing that had come to rival portraiture was that mere extension of it, the conversation piece. In Hogarth's hands the conversation piece had shown signs of character, but with the Zoffanys it became a merely flattering version of family life and upper-class living.

The age had, indeed, captured an ideal and thrown away an opportunity. It had caught to perfection, in paint, a way of life, but life itself it had largely ignored. The aristocrats and their apes offered the patronage by which artists could live and flourish; and where they found their patronage, artists were forced to find their subject-matter also. In one sense this was all to the good, since the grace and colouring of Reynolds, or the lightness and delicacy of Gainsborough, were perfectly adapted to the patrician scene — were better adapted to it, perhaps, than they might have been to anything else. Reynolds and Gainsborough do not merely evoke an aristocratic ideal: they provide it. Gains-

borough's *The Morning Walk* might be chosen, along with,
let us say, *The Rape of the Lock* and the very finest Heppelwhite, to designate a supreme grace and refinement. The
tradition in which these men painted belongs, moreover, to
a high order of art as well as the highest order of society.
Even where it is tinctured with a desire to please, as in
Reynolds, or degenerates into rather empty charm, as in
Romney, it can retain a good deal more loveliness than we
are always prone to allow. But though we may grant, as
cardinal to it, that a way of life selects and excludes and
refines — for only so can it achieve perfection — the question remains as to how ultimately satisfying is the result,
as to how much that is richly personal and true is wanting,
regardless of whether it would be discordant or out of place
if it were there. And we must conclude that a very great deal
is wanting. Even Mr T. S. Eliot, who is not likely to under-
estimate the aristocratic outlook, has confessed that there
is somebody more important than the aristocrat, and that
is the individual. And, in the profoundest sense, the individual hardly exists in the art we are examining; and not
simply because of the men who sat for their portraits, but
equally because of the men who painted them. Gainsborough, the most independent as well as the finest of them,
could hardly bear to work with an unsympathetic sitter;
and after granting an artist the freedom to choose his material, and fully allowing for temperament, we still feel that
such a circumstance was a limitation and that, since it arose
so often, it implies a defective interest in humanity, in life.
Reynolds, we know, painted his own portrait almost a
hundred times; how often did he sketch a revealing street
scene or an exciting, but anonymous, face? The painters of
that era were fettered by the patronage of the great, and can
be excused for making a living in the only safe way possible;
but even after they were living in comfort, few of them did
anything to show that their values or even their interests at
all equalled their gifts. Romney, it is true, forswore portrait-

painting in weary disgust, but only to indulge a taste for the pretentious and lead that incredible life at Hayley's in Sussex.[3]

There are important distinctions to be made among these people, however, and the two most celebrated painters of the age will supply them. Sir Joshua Reynolds, with his ear-trumpet and his snuff, survives as an urbane and society-loving bachelor, the intimate of Johnson and Burke, and in every respect the most honoured and successful painter of his time. He seems a wise, obliging, kindly man — full of helpful advice, given to princely hospitality, forever providing friendly letters of introduction. But slowly one comes to feel that there is something suspicious about him, as one comes to feel it about Addison; and indeed the two men were in many ways alike. If Addison was the first, then Reynolds — so seemly, prudent and moral — was the second Victorian. He too was a sinuous social climber, never making the parvenu blunder of turning his back on Bohemia after obtaining the entrée in Mayfair, but shrewdly remembering, rather, that each would delight in meeting the other in Sir Joshua's drawing-room. He was altogether like Addison in being able to endure " no brother to the throne." He was ungenerous, if not downright unfair, to Romney and Wilson; and when he publicly toasted Gainsborough as " the greatest landscape painter of the day," it required someone else at the table to add audibly: " Yes, and the greatest portrait painter too." That he occupied the throne, that he was the Dr Johnson of the art world, there can be

---

[3] Where he became " Raphael " to the " Pindar " of his host and the " Sappho " of Anna Seward. Allan Cunningham has preserved the scene: " When the party assembled at breakfast the ordinary greetings were Sappho, Pindar, and Raphael; they asked for bread and butter in quotations, and ' still their speech was song.' They then separated for some hours. . . . When the hour appointed for taking the air came, the painter went softly to the door of the poetess, opened it gently, and, if he found her ' with looks all staring from Parnassian dreams,' he shut it and retreated. If, on the contrary, she was unemployed, he said, ' Come, Muse,' and she answered, ' Coming, Raphael! ' "

no doubt: he was the first president of the Royal Academy, holding office, which he finally resigned in a pet, for over two decades; he had " 184 sitters and one dog " in a single year; he went abroad, as Johnson never did, in an " immodest chariot " all painted and gilded; and at length a whole galaxy of dukes and marquesses bore his coffin to St Paul's.

You catch the hang of him best in his own words, as when he remarked of something Goldsmith had said: " What a fool he is thus to commit himself! " or in that remark to his pupil and biographer Northcote, that " lovers had acknowledged to him, after seeing his portraits of their mistresses, that the originals had appeared even still more lovely to them than before by their excellences being so distinctly portrayed." There is also the tale of his painting Mrs Siddons's portrait and signing his name on the fringe of her mantle; for, he told her, " I could not lose the honour this opportunity afforded me of going down to posterity on the hem of your garment."

The man who showed that kind of circumspection, and made that kind of boast, and paid that kind of compliment, would scarcely not seek, in his painting, to please; and the pleasure he gave was inordinate. We never find in Reynolds the servility of a fawning courtier; what we find is a sort of tact, an instinctive avoidance of the disagreeable, a form of artistic duplicity which can always be explained as " goodness of heart " or " seeing the bright side of things." How far this manœuvre was unconscious in Reynolds one cannot precisely say; an element of rationalization almost surely enters in, and it is well to remember somebody's observation that the greatest hypocrite is the man who does not know he is a hypocrite. But all the wonderful grace and charm that accompany the manœuvre cannot quite conceal it, and the body of Reynolds's work thus suffers from more than the limitation of its aristocratic subject-matter; [4] it is

---

[4] Reynolds's historical paintings, from their being artistic failures, can be ignored.

marred by its inoffensiveness and general want of character.

To turn from Reynolds to Gainsborough is in every way refreshing; is to encounter an even finer artist and an infinitely more attractive man. The great world did Gainsborough no real harm because he directly alchemized it into art; it was, in fact, of service to him as the fittest object of his own patrician sensibility. Left alone, no doubt he would have followed his bent for landscape-painting (grandiose historical compositions he always, with admirable self-knowledge, avoided); but in spite of present-day opinion, it is not easily demonstrated that Gainsborough's landscapes are so immensely superior to his portraits. The point, at any rate, is that Gainsborough saw through the great world and would have no truck with it outside business hours. " Damn gentlemen! " he exploded: " there is not such a set of enemies to a real artist in the world as they are, if not kept at a proper distance." And when *he* painted Mrs Siddons, there was no talk about going down to posterity on the hem of her garment: " Damn your nose, Madam," he cried out, " there's no end to it! " Damning one thing or another was a vital part of his nature; so were drinking too much wine and spending too much money and hurling insults at the Royal Academy. He was open and guileless, though possibly not easy to live with. But however he lived, no one ever died more charmingly, with those last whispered words to Reynolds: " We are all going to Heaven, and Vandyke is of the company." [5]

Thus, caring nothing for the great world in the flesh, Gainsborough, on canvas, fulfilled for it, by means of the artist's sensibility, that aspiration it was powerless to fulfil for itself. But if everything ugly is banished from Gains-

---

[5] The last words of a number of eighteenth-century figures are attractive. Henry Fox concluded wittily with: " If Mr Selwyn calls again, show him up; if I am alive I shall be delighted to see him, and if I am dead he would like to see me." (Selwyn enjoyed the sight of corpses almost as much as he did executions.) And Chesterfield, courteous to the end, expired with: " Give Dayrolles a chair."

borough's world, it is at any rate on grounds of temperament and not expediency. The world is no doubt small and
narrow and satin-lined, hovering somewhere outside reality; but the only final comment on it is one of thankfulness
and praise.

The age was almost out when Rowlandson emerged to
impale its foibles and pretensions and vulgarities, and at
last show life — through the lens of caricature — in outrageous and bestial forms, and when Blake, to whom Reynolds
and all his kind were anathema, began to proclaim those
visions which hardly admit of great ladies. Rowlandson,
carrying the comic spirit to its grimmest lengths, was to
blast the tame pretty world of the face-painters to splinters;
while with even greater daring, Blake simply denied that
any such world existed. At seven he had seen the prophet
Ezekiel standing in a field, and from that day on he needed
only his imagination to populate the universe. But we are
passing into another age as well as another country: an age
that Reynolds and Romney and the people who employed
them did not live to see and in any case could not possibly
have understood.

2

BETWEEN Vanbrugh, who wrote his last play in 1705, and
Goldsmith, who wrote his first in 1767, the English theatre
hardly saw the sun. More and more the shadow of morality
and the steamy mists of sentiment came between. Keeping
virtue "always in view," the egregious Colley Cibber reformed the stage at the cost of emasculating it; and emotion — which the theatre had lacked — soon became urgent
in it, and at length ubiquitous. There was nothing strange
about these developments: inside four or five decades England — by Restoration standards, if not by Victorian ones —

grew intolerably squeamish and genteel. The upper classes, who had once paraded their vices, came after a time to cloak them, and finally — having discovered the new vice of hypocrisy — to disown them altogether. Thus, to paraphrase an eighteenth-century commentator on the theatre, the less moral these people were in real life, the more they applauded morality on the stage. Meanwhile, having long shunned the theatre, the middle classes swarmed back into it, echoing with far deeper sincerity the moral demands of the great world. Innately genteel, the middle classes soon threw " vulgarity " as well as vice on the dustheap. Low manners were as severely condemned as low morals: it was not enough that stage characters should practise virtue; they had to do so in the drawing-room.

The genteel comedy which resulted was accordingly a high-flown travesty on human nature. Worse, it turned maudlin as well as preachy: " Comedy had grown, like Niobe, all tears." Wit vanished from the dialogue, and humour from the situations; what chiefly remained were windy moralizing, hollow virtuousness, simpering attitudes, and a perpetual weepsiness that expressed " soul " rather than suffering. During a period when the novel of sentiment came of age in Richardson and Sterne, the theatre acquired only the humourlessness of the one and the insincerity of the other. The English stage was launched on that career of impoverishment from which it has never recovered. In Elizabethan, Jacobean, and to some extent Restoration times, the drama mirrored man's approach to life, his feelings about it, his efforts to find meaning in it, his impassioned struggles against it. But from the moment the English novel was born, the English theatre has always lagged behind it, using fiction's ideas — and usually just their husks — at second hand, and never developing them with a comparable robustness or penetration.

But the eighteenth-century theatre was breaking new, if yet wholly arid, ground. For one thing comedy, which had once demanded wit and been written in prose, and tragedy, which had once supported rhetoric and been written in verse, were becoming inextricably fused in the fashionable plays of sentiment. Out of these plays emerged a new form, neither comedy nor tragedy, but domestic drama. As early as 1731 Lillo, with his famous *London Merchant,* carried a lower-class hero (in prose) to a tragic end. The age would not grant that the hero's social position was suitable to the stage, but it henceforth allowed that the woes of humanity need not rhyme, and it began to prefer characters with whose struggles it had something in common to the agonies of long-dead heroes and awesome kings. Drama, except for a diminishing amount of high tragedy, became a prose art.

What gave some lift to so largely moribund a theatre was the success of the pantomime and the ballad play. The pantomime — which still flourishes in England today — spun out a popular myth or fable in dumb-show, enriching it with a comic courtship of harlequin and columbine, special music, and elaborate scenery. The ballad play, bouncing to life in *The Beggar's Opera,* preserved something of the high spirits of the old comedy, introduced satire, and throve on music. It is significant that when, after fifty years, a new stage work — Sheridan's *The Duenna* — had a longer initial run than *The Beggar's Opera* had had, it too was a ballad play.

But the chief distinction of the fallow years is to be found in the players, not the plays. Of such purveyors and hacks as Kelly and Home, or even Colman and Foote, little survives except what is dutifully cited in the textbooks; but Kemble and Kitty Clive and Peg Woffington are still touched with glamour, and Garrick is drenched in it. It is difficult to assess their talents, not simply because we must rely on the word of spectators long dead, but also because standards of acting were in a state of transition, and some of the old and inferior standards still prevailed. We may be sure that many celebrated players of the age, as of ages yet to come, espoused a flatulent and high-busted manner. But much worse, many of them failed to stay in their parts and talked, during the most emotional and private scenes, directly at the audience. Almost all of them, furthermore, abused the star system to the point of exhibitionism; each sought self-glory; few worked in harness; and still fewer cared how inadequate was their support.

The coming of Garrick quickly renovated the scene. A sensation from his first entrance, he not only triumphed personally but ended by discrediting the old school. The veterans grasped the revolutionary nature of his acting at once: " If the young fellow is right," said the pomp-loving Quin, " then all the rest of us have been wrong." All the rest of them fiercely opposed the young fellow's methods, but the town applauded them, and

> *When doctrines meet with general approbation*
> *It is not heresy, but reformation.*

With Garrick, the old mouthing and strutting and declaiming were pretty well flung aside; and the old mechanical rules, such as the following, were gradually outlawed: " In *Astonishment* and *Surprise* arising from *Terror*, the *left leg* is drawn back to some distance from the other: under the same Affection of the Mind, but resulting from an *unhop'd for Meeting* with a beloved Object, the right leg is advanced to some distance before the left. *Impatience* and *Regret* . . . may be heightened by shuffling of the *Feet*."

Garrick, unlike most of his rivals, was versatile. He sought to be natural or, as we should put it, realistic. In time he appeared to overcome, what earlier was too palpable, a desire for applause and a self-conscious attitude at the close of a big speech. He tried to suppress his own personality, aiming at a careful characterization of the part he played, even in terms of costume; and that he succeeded, in his own day at least, is clear from the unfading epigram about Garrick and a competing actor:

A king — nay, every inch a king,
   Such Barry does appear.
But Garrick's quite a different thing,
   He's every inch King Lear.

Garrick is best remembered, of course, for his enthusiasm for Shakespeare; he produced more than twenty of the plays, and turned a growing vogue for Shakespeare's work into a fixed tradition. It would, to be sure, have been better had he remained content with producing Shakespeare and interpreting his roles. But he chose to follow theatrical custom and edit and rewrite him as well, though for this there was not the excuse there might once have been. By Garrick's time Shakespeare had been reintroduced to the public in a succession of new editions, had been resaluted as a poet, and as a dramatist enjoyed the homage of all cultivated people; there was no need to vulgarize him. Before Garrick ever appeared, the habit of truckling to the crowd had been noted and denounced: " For, as Shakespeare is already good enough for people of taste, he must be altered to the palates of those who have none." Garrick himself insisted it was his

    . . . *only plan*
To lose no drop of that immortal man,

yet he went courting him with a sieve. No doubt some of his cuts were in the interest of good theatre; beyond doubt some of his adaptations gave Shakespeare greater unity and conciseness than he contrived for himself. But too often Garrick committed outrage. Consider a *Hamlet* from which Osric and the gravediggers are removed, in which Laertes turns meek and Gertrude goes mad, and in which some lines originally assigned to Laertes are tacked on to Hamlet's wonderful farewell to life.

As manager of Drury Lane during thirty years, Garrick seems to have produced a host of bad plays and to have made many of them, besides Shakespeare's, worse by touching them up. He had great success with works like Kelly's *False Delicacy*, while refusing to consider Goldsmith's *Good-Natur'd Man*, which was written to put Kelly's sentimentalities to flight. Garrick — and in this he was scarcely unique as an actor — seems to have *preferred* third-rate plays, for " he was rather pleased to elevate, by his own theatrical powers, feeble diction and sentiment." But however dubious his services to the drama, he served his own profession well. He enforced teamwork among actors, and variation of pace; he grasped that good acting derives, not from blind surrender to emotion, but from careful study that creates the illusion of surrendering. At Drury Lane, when he could not teach actors to perform well through example, he cured them through mimicry. And he made acting socially more respectable; so much so that he himself was received among gentlemen and buried among kings. He was, to be sure, a man of the highest social gifts; Goldsmith put him, among wits, in the very first line, and his old schoolmaster Johnson called him " the first man in the world for sprightly conversation." And at his death Johnson paid him that tribute which, all things considered, is worth more, even, than being buried in the Abbey, speaking of that stroke " which has eclipsed the gaiety of nations, and impoverished the public stock of harmless pleasure."

But if Garrick advanced the position of the star, the run of actors were still despised. Far from being accepted in society, they were often pelted with oranges on the stage, and when they had given offence, were forced to get down on their knees, before a full house, and beg the audience's pardon. These were the audiences, moreover, that were eulogized in every prologue for their taste and understanding. But the ordinary actor was not much worse off at the hands of the audience than the ordinary playwright. Not only had the public the right, upheld by law, to hiss (as well as a less legal tendency to riot), but author-baiting had

Peg Woffington by William Hogarth

come to be a profession, and plays were cried down and killed off merely because playwrights had the "wrong" political convictions, or were personally disliked or professionally disparaged, or from sheer malice, or for no discernible reason at all. Even the presence of the King in the theatre was no guarantee of decorum.

At the other extreme, the art of puffing plays was just as much of a scandal. Newspapers could be bought, and were: Horace Walpole sniffed at the praise he read of Garrick on the ground that Garrick had written most of it himself. Puffers were also hired to talk up plays in coffee-houses, and it is clear that the press agent was infinitely more powerful than the drama critic. The only sound criticism appeared belatedly, in the monthly magazines.

On the physical side, the theatre slowly changed for the better. The bare, stereotyped sets, which could seldom express what they were meant to, gave way to something approaching a picture of real life on the stage. As late as 1750 — the reason being that all scene-shifting had to be made in full view of the audience — even an "elegant" drawing-room was characterized by a table and a few chairs. But around 1750 the old custom of keeping the curtain up throughout the play was discarded in favour of lowering it between the acts; and with the stage concealed, stage hands could more easily embellish it. A Drury Lane play of 1760 was enriched by a harpsichord and a bookcase!

Stage lighting, which had been miserable, also improved. After Garrick returned from the Continent in 1765, he tore down the chandeliers that hung in front of the stage, substituting lights in the wings. These allowed the scene to be dimmed or brightened, with a consequent gain in atmosphere; and by 1782 a playwright could happily indulge in the following stage directions: "In the first act, the sky clears by degrees, the morning vapor disperses, the sun rises, and at the end of the act is above the horizon."

Not much is to be said for costumes: they were ancient

[289

and modern, fancy and plain, brand-new and falling apart, all in the same production; and though a Henry VIII might dress for all the world like Royal Harry, Garrick's Romeo " might have stepped on the stage straight from Ranelagh." It is not that expensive costumes were never provided, but that they were provided haphazardly, and put to wrong use, as hand-me-downs, long after they had served their proper purpose.

The age survives, apart from its memories of Garrick, in Goldsmith and Sheridan. Their comedies, indeed, are the only ones that made any contribution to the English stage during the hundred and eighty-five years that separate *The Beaux' Stratagem* from *Lady Windermere's Fan*. It is for this reason, perhaps, that their names shine brighter than they otherwise might. Neither the lively good humour of the one nor the glittering artifice of the other constitutes a first-rate talent: of even the better of the two men it is hardly possible to say more than that he was skilful and dashing and witty. But it is important to remember, not only what Goldsmith and Sheridan represent in themselves, but what both of them sought to discredit. *The Good-Natur'd Man* and *She Stoops to Conquer* opened an attack on the vices of sentimental comedy which *The Rivals* and *The School for Scandal* successfully concluded; [6] while *The Critic* so hilariously hooted tragic balderdash off the boards that for years at Drury Lane the tragedy-makers could not get a hearing.

It is in Goldsmith, I think, that we have the truer refutation of sentimental comedy, for in *She Stoops to Conquer* he produced genuinely unsentimental comedy; whereas Sheridan, however superior in talent, for the most part simply produced satire. The one took the line of ridicule, but the other set an example. Sheridan was fully a man of the world, and the defects of his age lay pat to his hand; had they been different defects, they would have lain as patly,

---

[6] Although *The Rivals* still showed traces of a sentimental subplot.

for he was born to hold something — it did not much matter what — up to laughter. It is manners that interest him, and manners that he is brilliantly qualified to portray.

Except historically, Goldsmith's plays have not the slightest importance: they are merely diverting. They offer no great insight into character and no very great insight into manners. Tony Lumpkin is an excellent comic creation, and real in the sense that no lively booby was ever artificial; but he is not " interesting " in the sense that a Squire Western is, or a Mr Collins, or a M. Jourdain. *She Stoops to Conquer* is essentially a bright farce-comedy of situation, as *The Good-Natur'd Man* is largely a dullish one of intrigue; and Goldsmith, like any real humourist, has flavour. It was his merit to bring liveliness into the theatre, and to take waxen gentility out of it.

Goldsmith, attempting no criticism of humanity, freely resorted to such stock comic devices as mistaken and concealed identity; and Sheridan followed suit. In Sheridan, however, the practice constituted a real limitation, since the student of manners succumbed to the conniving playwright. It is impossible not to brand Sheridan as superficial, not to find his sense of the theatre winning out over his knowledge of the world. *The School for Scandal* has more motion and continuity than the Restoration comedy because it has more plot and less incident, more characters whose fortunes are at stake and fewer characters that express a point of view. In Congreve it would be enough to portray false virtue; in Sheridan false virtue must be craftily exposed, put into the dock, and condemned. Even in the realm of manners one feels a difference: Congreve reveals them, lightly, casually, for what they are; Sheridan scores them off.[7]

Sheridan, on the whole, only made fun of what was patently silly (a Lydia Languish, a Sir Fretful Plagiary) and

---

[7] It is perhaps worth noting that both Congreve and Sheridan quit the theatre when very young: Congreve at thirty, from pique; Sheridan at twenty-eight, from political ambitions.

[291

only inveighed against what was demonstrably safe (a Lady Sneerwell, a Joseph Surface). That, in any age, is enough to make a very gifted man into a very successful satirist, since in any age that is as much satire as the general public will either approve or pretend to understand. But it is hardly enough, however scintillating it may be as theatre, to constitute a serious criticism of life. The wittiest man of his age quite wisely wrote of the only class of society he knew or cared about; less wisely, he also wrote for it. His satire is impudent, but not treacherous, and not at all subversive. Given a congenial target, however, Sheridan never failed to hit the bull's-eye. His scandalmongers are scored off on the highest level — as artists in their line. And the sheer burlesque of *The Critic* is still at moments as funny at Beerbohm's *Savonarola Brown*.

For all his shortcomings Sheridan, I suppose, perpetuates an age. But by reason of his shortcomings he perpetuates it romantically — gives it glamour and an air of fancy dress in which, after the intrigues are unknotted and the shams exposed, happiness and virtue are reconciled. We, conscious of the satire, are apt to forget the sentiment. Yet it ought to be noted, for it detracts from the truthfulness of the picture, and further reveals how the best playwright of the century, for all his brilliance, was not in the least profound.

3

THE AGE was not profound in literature either, but it had less need to be. For it produced, thanks to Boswell and Gibbon, the most delightful book in the language, and the most imposing; it remains unrivalled for written prose or spoken eloquence; it provided much the finest of English letterwriters, and such novelists as Fielding, Richardson, Smollett, and Sterne. It provided too — rounding out the line of Ben Jonson, Dryden, and Pope — the last of the great dictators, whose voice still booms in his disciple's pages, and whose name is still the official one for his period.

The writers of the new age would not, like those of the old, be the companions of the great aristocrats, and would never rise by their pens to become ambassadors or secretaries of state. Writing had grown again to be a profession, with a certain loss of distinction and servility alike. Patronage was ending: after the Augustan age noblemen hobnobbed very little with writers, and used them, politically, much less; while writers themselves were finding publishers more satisfactory than patrons, and were helped by the knowledge that a large middle-class public had emerged which dwarfed the importance of the polite world. A vivid sentence of Carlyle's has created the legend that Johnson's crushing letter to Chesterfield ("*Is not a patron, my Lord, one who looks with unconcern on a man struggling for life in the water, and when he has reached the ground encumbers him with help?*") sounded the doom of patronage; but in reality it did no such thing. It is not so much — though it is worth remembering — that the letter was not made public until thirty-five years after it was written; it is rather that patronage had all but died out before Johnson solicited it. For the future, writers might continue to laud noble names in ceremonious dedications, but only for the prestige, no longer for the money, it would bring them. If they were still to be helped financially, it was from the King himself, by way of a pension.

Their business, for the most part, was with the publishers,[8] who, in spite of the bad name they have been given by history, were not notoriously worse in the age of Johnson than in any later age. Johnson himself spoke of his own

---

[8] Authors might also still publish by subscription: appealing in advance to the public (and too often spending the money before they were half started writing the book). Pope's *Homer* at the beginning of the century, and Cowper's at the end — together with Johnson's *Shakespeare* and many other books — were published this way; it was enough competition for the publishers to keep them from becoming despotic.

publisher as just and generous. The greatest hindrance, for authors, was that the royalty system had not yet been devised, so that most of their manuscripts were simply sold outright. Sometimes, however, publishers sent extra remuneration to authors whose books had caught on, for goodwill; and they often paid authors extra money for " corrected " editions. History abounds with tales of masterpieces sold for pittances, but barely notices such other masterpieces as were published at heavy loss. Hume's *Treatise of Human Nature* was to become perhaps the most celebrated philosophical work of the century, but there was no way for the publisher to know it would, and he actually lost five hundred pounds by publishing it. Sometimes the author himself was in fault: Johnson foolishly asked only two hundred guineas for undertaking *The Lives of the Poets;* he might have had six times as much, and in fact did get something more. If Goldsmith got only sixty guineas for *The Vicar of Wakefield* (which Johnson, as a matter of fact, considered a fair price for a book by an unknown author), Fielding got a thousand pounds for *Amelia,* and Smollett twice as much for his history of England.

All the same, authorship was full of the usual hazards, and no well-known writer after Pope did very well by it. Fielding, Smollett, and Goldsmith were all ill-paid hacks in their time — Smollett ran a literary factory — and all died badly off. But as professional writers these men were saved from obsequiousness and gained an experience of life and a sense of life's hardship never possessed by the gentlemen authors. And they were better served, on the whole, by the disdain of the Chesterfields [9] and Horace Walpoles than their predecessors were by the friendship of the Bolingbrokes and Halifaxes. They preserved a kind of independence, a kind of dignity: even Smollett's choleric resentments

---

[9] It was Chesterfield who said, perhaps without irony: " We, my lords, may thank Heaven that we have something better than our brains to depend upon."

are more bearable than, say, Richardson's exulting in the thought that he had climbed into the great world (when he hadn't). For the great world still beckoned. " I wrote not to be fed but to be famous," said the Reverend Laurence Sterne, who meant that he wanted the homage of high society. He got it, and it brought out all the worst in him. One turns with almost a sense of relief to Fielding supping off a dirty cloth " with a blind man, a whore and three Irishmen " — though research discloses that the blind man was his brother, and the " whore " probably his wife. One turns with genuine affection to Johnson setting forth to pay his visits on " clean-shirt day." Nor did it always turn out so badly. Johnson might never be taken up by the world of fashion — " Great lords and ladies," he remarked, " don't like to have their mouths stopped "; but Johnson came at last to look round the table of the Turk's Head at Reynolds and Goldsmith and Burke, at Garrick and Boswell, at Fox, Gibbon, and Sheridan, with some supernumerary peers thrown in for good measure. And after the degrading high-flown compliments of Augustan days, it is no bad thing to hear Johnson saying to Adam Smith at Edinburgh: " You lie "; and Smith replying: " You are a son of a bitch." " On such terms," wrote Scott a generation later, " did these two great moralists meet and part, and such was the classical dialogue between these two great teachers of morality."

The great new middle-class public was to dominate the age, docking its literature of the old thin-blooded cynicism and drenching it with morality and sentiment. The middle classes did not feel at home with elegant frivolity and callous jesting; they wanted to satisfy their emotions without outraging their conscience; and they liked nothing better than the spectacle of endangered virtue. Their idea of virtue might be essentially vulgar, as was almost every other of their ideas. They might take greater pleasure in weeping (for weeping's sake) than in laughing, and relish morality

[295

far more when it was tied to a plot than when it was preached from a pulpit. There was, at any rate, a sincere desire to be moved and edified. The "luxury of grief" which the new age came to dote on was nothing more, really, than a form of self-indulgence; but one that, if not known to earlier ages, would be sought as well by later ones. What is to be specially noted of eighteenth-century sentimentalism is how ravenously it was pounced upon. People's emotions had too long been starved; hence the quality of the sentiment concerned them very little.

The word cropped up with the thing; and both owed their vogue, if not their origin, to Richardson. The humdrum, prating milksop of a printer was well on in years when, as much by accident as design, he turned novelist. He had set about writing a series of model letters which not only should indicate the proper style for familiar correspondence, but should teach people "how to think and act justly and prudently" into the bargain. In them we encounter every form of mouldy morality:

> Lay together [an uncle advises his pleasure-loving nephew] the substance of the conversation that passes in a whole evening, with your frothy companions, after you are come from them; and reflect what solid truth, what useful lesson, worthy to be inculcated in your future life, that whole evening has afforded you; and consider, whether it is worth breaking through all rule and order for?

There is even a letter to fire at "a young Man too soon keeping a horse":

> . . . the expense of the horse is not the least thing to be considered: It will in time, very probably, lead you into a more dangerous one, that of bestowing too much of your time in the use of it. It will unhinge your mind, as I may say, from business, and give your servants opportunity to be remiss in your absence. And as a young man . . . you should lay up against a more advanced age, when the exercise a horse affords will seem more suitable.

Richardson was afterwards ashamed of this performance, though he can only have been exhilarated while working at it, and was in fact inspired to pass on from offering advice to recounting adventures: by Letter LXII a young lady is breathlessly informing her sister how she narrowly escaped the clutches of a " wicked Procuress." And by the time he reached Letter LXII, our expansive moralist had surely decided to attempt something much more ambitious than a series of model letters. That something was a novel, and in November 1740 appeared *Pamela; or Virtue Rewarded.* Written also in the form of letters, it at once became immensely successful, and opened an era.

Into this tale of a servant girl pursued by the fine gentleman who employs her, the printer who forswore " wine and flesh and fish " had flung all the bursting sentiment, lush pruriency, and detestable moralizing he could devise; not forgetting before the end to give Pamela, for a husband, the man she resisted as a seducer. It was a tale to delight multitudes, to edify thousands, to send the good people of Slough, who had heard it read aloud in the village smithy, off to ring church bells in honour of Pamela's marriage. We are far away now from Pope's shrill hatreds, though still within hailing distance of his hypocrisy. And if the story is tedious, its premise is immortal. Pamela has thoughts galore to titillate the reader's imagination, but her actions never forfeit his respect. Virtue is vindicated and prudence rewarded; and to make everything shipshape, the rake is reformed.

We do right to sneer at *Pamela,* for its values are hideous; and they are to prevail, unsweetened and undisguised, with their prudential and genteel demands foremost, in all the inferior literature of the age. Morality and sentiment hover round the idea of physical chastity like flies round a jam-pot. " Be good, sweet maid, and let who will be foolish " — that is about all one can extract from Richardson's bulging novel. But there is more to Richardson than that. His earnestness was unconquerable, his analysis of human feeling was minute, and he was to show in his next book that his practice could be better than his preaching.

Clarissa, which was to reverberate through all the literature of Europe,[10] simply wallowed in sentiment, and struck the chord for which the pent-up emotions of the age were waiting; for this was the story of a young lady of quality forced to run away from an intolerable family; pursued, tormented, and finally drugged and raped by a fashionable villain; and then courting death as the only honourable release from her misfortunes. To the pleadings of overwrought readers that he should save Clarissa (whose history was published in instalments) from being debauched, Richardson turned a deaf ear; which is often properly cited as evidence of his artistry, but less often as equal evidence of his moral fervour. Artistically *Clarissa* at its worst challenges *Elsie Dinsmore,* which means that it is as nauseating as it is silly; yet it has, by virtue of an intensity that withstands its enormous bulk, and of an insight that redeems all Richardson's extravagances, a sort of subterraneous grandeur. Clarissa's story is moving and even tragic, despite everything that her creator can do to make it seem foolish, highfalutin, and unreal. We have lost the acute sense of evil, as well as the sense of disproportion, that was able to lend a real nobility to Clarissa's resolution; we respond to it today, not because it any longer seems appropriate, but because it still seems so intense and indomitable. Therein lies Richardson's power, and it prompts us to ask at what point moral fervour becomes identical with art. As for eighteenth-century readers, we can feel pretty sure that it was the pathos in Clarissa's situation, not the tragedy, that appealed to

---

[10] Diderot, Rousseau, Goethe, and Balzac were all deeply impressed by the book, and Musset called it " *le premier roman du monde.*" All the same, we may echo a more modern judgment: " Probably, a person eager to enjoy Richardson's novels now would do well to take them as his only recreation for a long holiday in a remote place and pray for steady rain."

them; and that they gushed tears of hysterical pity far removed from the Aristotelian katharsis.

Clarissa, in any case, brings us back to the morality of the age, which Richardson, while seeking to flatter, helped to form. In Defoe's novels the moralizing seems hasty, almost irrelevant, for among his heroes and heroines we witness a struggle, completely soulless, for survival. With Richardson the soul begins to take part in the struggle, but it is a paradoxical kind of soul — a materialistic one. There is a search for rewards: in *Pamela* earthly, in *Clarissa* heavenly. For if what is permanently valuable about Clarissa is that she dies of a broken heart, with the courage not to pawn her values, what is much more reprehensible (and in Richardson's view just as important) is that she dies believing she will be all the more blessed in heaven for having had to suffer so horribly on earth.

It was Fielding who retorted upon Richardson, as it was Sterne who refined him. From being born into a higher class and from having consorted with a lower one, Fielding emerges with a roundedness of view and suppleness of movement quite lacking in his rival. Where the creator of Pamela sat demurely in his printing shop, and later gathered pious ladies about him to drink tea, Fielding had been rake and country gentleman, debtor and hack, and was to become a Bow Street magistrate who would see the faces and hear the stories of thieves and highwaymen and whores. Life was not to use him well, and he would die, in some distress, still young; but it would not embitter him, and it would equip him admirably for his trade. He, like Defoe, writes out of experience; and his own is wider.

Fielding's retort was direct and instantaneous: he parodied *Pamela* in *Shamela,* and he started to parody it again in *Joseph Andrews,* where Pamela's brother is depicted as a model of sexual virtue. The mere shift from a female to a male virgin is almost comic enough in itself to annihilate

[299

Richardson's thesis; but it was not enough to fill a real novel, or satisfy a real novelist, and *Joseph Andrews* soon turns into a lively picaresque tale of which the true hero is not Andrews but Parson Adams. Then, with *Tom Jones,* Fielding went far forward. *Tom Jones* might be called the first English novel which converts the picaresque into the panoramic. It records the life of all sorts and conditions of men; not the Partridges and Westerns and Lady Bellastons only, but innkeepers, gypsies, pettifoggers, beggars, and soldiers. We are in a wide world, which Richardson will never know, and we are seeing the world's hypocrisy and vanity, its false virtue and true desires, exposed with shrewdness and forthrightness and humour. It is lusty and animated, and it is the right answer to the sentimental homiletics of the Richardson school; but we may refrain from overpraising it. On the score of art, no sillier remark was ever made than Coleridge's, that *Tom Jones* has one of the three greatest plots in the world. On the score of art, too, the contrast between Tom and Blifil is the contrast — between the heart of gold and the pious fraud — that, watering down through Charles and Joseph Surface, has come to dominate all schoolboy literature. The truth is, also, that Fielding could furnish dialogue as wretchedly highfalutin as Richardson's, and could smudge his work — *Jonathan Wild,*[11] by its nature, is an exception — with as easy and catchpenny moralizing, and is lacking in all delicacy and depth. His view of the world rings true, not because it is profound, but because it is empirical. Fielding, with his deep distaste for hypocrisy, is one of those novelists much better able to detect lies than discover truth. Richardson is of exactly the opposite party: his whole universe is a lie, but he discovers truth notwithstanding. Under the debris of *Clarissa* lies something almost great; *Joseph Andrews* and *Tom Jones* are, in the final

---

[11] From which book one may indulge oneself to quote again that unforgettable sentence: " He in a few minutes ravished this fair creature, or at least would have ravished her, if she had not, by a timely compliance, prevented him."

sense, entertainments; in the latter the entertainment is prodigious, for the scene is all England faithfully reproduced;
but they are predicated of a first-rate experience, not a first-
rate mind.

One of Fielding's less successful habits (notwithstanding
the many critics who have praised it) was that of pushing
himself into the picture; for though a careful craftsman, he
lacked the finer artist's touch that can fuse self with story.
The ability to do this turned up in Sterne, who flooded the
novel with temperament and made it so personal that it is
nearer akin to Montaigne or Burton than to either earlier or
later fiction. What *Tristram Shandy* and *A Sentimental Journey* owe to their age, however, are their sentimental preoc-
cupations, their turn for whimsical feeling, and their purely
decorative touches of humanitarianism. This rejection of
sense for sensibility Sterne took from Richardson, but he
took nothing else. His tone is always as playful as Richardson's is earnest; and not convinced that goodness could get
by on its own merits, he sought for all he was worth to
make it charming.

Sterne's world, like Richardson's, is all a lie; but it is the
modest lie of escapism, the silky lie of art. It is an altogether
personal world with hardly a social context, a world of in-
laid pathos and comedy, of lovable crackpots and eccentric
philosophers, all unified by Sterne's own personality, and
all belonging to the printed page. The literary critic has
much to say of Sterne, but the social historian almost nothing. Essentially his faults are æsthetic, not moral, just as his
virtues are. Sterne the man was far from admirable; but one
really finds fault with the writer not because one would
decry his affectations but because one catches on to them;
not because he writes frivolously of sex but because he leers
at it; not because he lacks nobility but because he pretends
to have it. His great weakness is that of too patently soliciting the reader — a proof of shallowness no less than insincerity.

As art, at least in the narrower sense, Sterne's novels stand far higher than Richardson's and Fielding's, but his values are, like theirs, imperfect. The recoil of the age from the cynical " good sense " of the previous one, and the recrudescence of feeling and even at times of fellow-feeling, are valuable only up to a point. Emotions were too often squandered on false and unworthy objects, and in one way or another the greatest problems of life were left unexplored. On the spiritual side, Fielding is virtually blind to any struggle, while Richardson has only vulgar ideas about it, and Sterne only pretty ones. In terms of character, there is nowhere any grasp of richness and complexity, of the dilemma of the *homme moyen sensuel,* of the thinking individual in conflict with his age; there is no one with the tragic realizations of a Hamlet, or the romantic egoism of a Julien Sorel. There is, finally, no deep questioning of the social structure, and no real correlating of social causes with social consequences. Middle-class morality may be catching up with aristocratic vice, but vice, for the most part, means profligacy and godlessness, and even when it means greed or irresponsibility or corruption, the chastisement is personal rather than social. Of passionate, positive humanitarianism there is very little; of a true feeling for democracy there is almost nothing at all.[12]

On the contrary, Richardson was not simply priggish: he loved the genteel as only a petty snob can love it and a shoddy taste can stomach it. We have glanced at his notions of virtuousness; let us see how he mirrored perfection. His high-born paragon, Grandison, is first endowed with every grace and charm and advantage, so as hardly to know the meaning of temptation; and then left to maintain that people should know their station in life and that, all things considered, the poor had better not learn to read. The class system is, indeed, the actuating idea of all Richardson's novels; and

---

[12] This is not to indict the age for what it understandably did not have; it is only to make plain that it did not have it.

not simply accepted as a fact, nor even acquiesced in as a social law, but shamelessly pandered to as a triumph of the human intelligence.

Sterne, wrapped up in himself, was — if one takes the most cynical view — too anxious to seem like a good man to care very much about the rest of the world. Lacking both a noble nature and a rebellious mind, he put his extraordinary sensibilities to merely picturesque use. Uncle Toby's fly and the dead ass whom Yorick cried over are not to be condemned in themselves, but neither are they to be raised to the wrong level. The point is that Sterne's is not really a grown-up world, and that its childlike charm and delicate eccentricity represent a humanitarianism that has no real roots in life and can accordingly never bear leaves or fruit.

Smollett comes closer, and Fielding much closer, to the centre of things; they, at least, never ignored brambles for thistledown. But the irascible and intemperate Smollett, besides resorting to caricature, enjoyed filth and brutality too much for their own sake, and even at his best, in much his mellowest book, can only achieve the crude irony of: " Heark ye, Clinker, you are a most notorious offender — You stand convicted of sickness, hunger, wretchedness and want." Fielding, alone of his age, is in earnest about some of the right things. In him we encounter, as nowhere else among eighteenth-century novelists, a true sense of decency, and a conception of human goodness that has nothing to do with creeds or conventions. But though he is masterly in ferreting out shams, his actual delineation of true worth seems commonplace. Squire Allworthy has much virtue, but unfortunately not a spark of life; and though the muscular Parson Adams is an attractive figure, he is — like the Uncle Tobys and Dr Primroses he perhaps helped beget — one of those simple souls who vindicate human nature much more than they illumine it. Fielding is commonly called a Hogarth in prose, but though they are akin in many ways, the writer is less penetrating, less adult, than the artist. The one had doubtless seen as much of life as the other, but Hogarth, we feel, was not left merely undeceived; he was profoundly informed. Hogarth no more than Fielding can create " faces imbued with unalterable sentiment, and figures that stand out in the eternal silence of thought "; but he is more penetrating in his own sphere, he has a genius for emphasis which Fielding lacks, and on occasion a true, however grotesque, sense of the tragic. A rake's progress in Hogarth may be too much of a homily, but it is not, as in Fielding, the mere obstruction to a romance.

Fielding did not go deep enough. Tom Jones is traditionally praised as a " whole man," but he is actually a juvenile. It is one thing, perhaps, for him to bow to the sexual code which turns Sophia against him; it is quite another that he never questions the social and economic considerations which make him, from the outset, *non grata* with her father. (He never, for that matter, thinks twice about her father!) He is not a thinking man at all, and it is not simply the autobiographical element in him that makes us finally conclude that his creator is not a thinking man either. Fielding might champion Tom for what he was, but he still felt it necessary to reform him. Fielding could mark out all that was coarse, selfish, and incredibly narrow in Squire Western, but could never quite decide whether or not he was a merely comic figure. Fielding could expose the pretentious and highfalutin, but in doing so was as likely as not to condemn certain genuine aspirations as well. He was, indeed, Taine's " good buffalo ": a man with no knack and hence no use for the subtle or the complex — which is why his novels, aside from their fine portrayal of manners, are so thin; and a man who, though he might denounce injustice and corruption, never dreamt of questioning the conditions that produced them.[13] He too had not a rebellious mind, only a satiric nature; and as a good buffalo, a sturdy Eng-

---

[13] Some distinction needs to be made between Fielding the novelist and Fielding the practising magistrate.

eenth century, like any other age, had imagination of a kind, but it was for the most part fashionable or eccentric, and it never heaved itself into literature as the emotions finally did. (The imagination is not a middle-class necessity.) To indulge it, writers went back to yellowed books rather than out into life; it was an eighteenth-century-born poet, after all, who remarked that distance lends enchantment to the view. With their reactions to nature predefined for them, and their feeling that ordinary life was colourless and low, they were compelled to turn back to the "middle ages," which meant any period dark and wild, for inspiration. Even as it was, they were violating the best canons of taste: during most of the century the word *Gothick* was used as a slur.

Though isolated scholars were tugging at the roots of all the old literatures, from the Oriental to the Icelandic, actually few writers — and fewer readers — knew one kind of mediæval armour from another. They knew only a poetic instinct, which no amount of classical good sense could quite stifle, for something rich and strange; and if it was strange enough, it did not have to be noticeably rich. Thus, with precocious talent and a striking ability to live in the past, Chatterton fabricated his poems in the name of a man long dead; and for a while took in Horace Walpole, who, with idle cleverness, was himself fabricating a mediæval world in which everything clanked and shivered and groaned. Percy went back to the old ballads and some later poetry, bringing them together in the *Reliques;* while in Scotland Macpherson, on the flimsiest of foundations, "translated" Ossian. There was a response to all this. On the heels of Walpole's *Castle of Otranto* a whole school of Gothic romance sprang up, to chill people's spines until it was laughed out of existence by Jane Austen; and with the weird strains of Ossian, which the age thought of as "sublime," most of England and then much of Europe, even a Goethe and a Napoleon, were to become intoxicated.

Meantime the poets began to notice scenery that lay beyond their gardens, and to think in bolder images, and write in freer stanzas, and feel mild romantic passions, and have pensive and melancholy moods. But none of this really meant very much. Then Rousseau came, to disturb or impress or horrify them — but, whatever he did, to make himself felt. Young and Blair and Shenstone, Collins and Goldsmith and Gray having filed past and gone to their graves, suddenly Cowper appeared to disparage artifice and town life with rustic scenes and religious thoughts; Crabbe appeared, to paint what he saw instead of what he should pretend to see; Burns appeared, to be pungent while remaining lyrical, to reclaim the bacchanalian spirit, and sound the note of democracy; Blake appeared, to trample down every hedge to the imagination with a mystic's and a prophet's power. But by then Dr Johnson was dead, and the age to which he gave his name was over.

CHAPTER VI

THE BULLY AND THE FOP

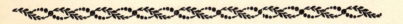

Dr Johnson

EVERY WRITER MAY with propriety assume some few things
of his readers: he may assume, for example, that they have
read Boswell's *Life of Johnson*. He may not, therefore, de-
scend to bringing in the brown " cloaths " and the wig, the
scraped lemon peels, the dishes of tea, the falling upon
food, the sarcasms about Scotland, or even the letters to
Chesterfield and Macpherson or the *Dictionary* definitions;
though he may perhaps, if the occasion really warrants it,
bring in the " No, Sir," or the " Sir, you *may* wonder." But
let us not be fools enough to suppose that the picturesque
side of Johnson can be paraphrased.

After Boswell, what remains for an outsider is to assess
Johnson's quality as a man and his relation to his age. One
begins by agreeing that he was a complete and obstinate
Tory. He detested what he called " the fury of innovation ";
he stood for those things that tradition sanctifies and reason subverts. In religion he was a sincere and humane
bigot who enjoyed theology because he enjoyed dialectics:
he had no trace of that rational scepticism which we associate with a Hume or a Voltaire. In politics he was a sincere
and humane reactionary: he loved the Stuarts, he denounced
the American rebels, he defended inequality; and all in all

[309

he probably talked a good deal for effect. In literature he
never got past the age of Pope, if indeed he ever got past
the age of Augustus. In philosophy he talked the learned
gibberish of the mediæval schoolmen. His economics were
nonsense. He knew as much about art as Tom Jones, and
about music as Squire Western.¹ He had (as have many
Tories) a gouty independence of mind: it was rugged and
dauntless and ursine, and it made of Johnson a superb personality. But the broad base of common sense he is credited
with having remains, I think, to be questioned.² The man
had lived in the world, he had been poor and miserable, he
had seen a great deal of human greed, hypocrisy, and pre-
tension. From that point of view, he was not to be imposed
upon by any *O altitudo!* of verbiage or gesture; but of common sense rooted in reasonable perceptions he had, I think,
less than we imagine.

It is very wonderful that Johnson, throughout fifty years,
should have gone on making comments that were invariably pointed, but seldom to the point. Taken as a whole,
surely they are the most dazzling irrelevancies ever uttered.
As we know from Boswell, Johnson would defend (or attack) any position, simply from a desire to be impressive or
cantankerous. " ' Why, Sir, as to the good or evil of card-
playing — ' ' Now, (said Garrick) he is thinking which side
he shall take.' " But it was not this capricious taking of sides
that produced most of the nonsense; it was something else:

---

¹ " Opera," said Johnson, " is an unpleasant and irrational form of
entertainment." " The value of a statue," said Johnson, " is owing to its
difficulty. You would not value the finest head cut upon a carrot." And
when Nollekens made a bust of him, Johnson was annoyed that he had
not shown him wearing a wig: " a man," he remarked, " ought not to look
as if he had taken physic."
But even in these fields his wit could triumph over his unresponsiveness,
as when he remarked of a violinist's performance: " Difficult do you call
it, Sir? I wish it were impossible."
² Johnson shows common sense most often where what is called for
is an imaginative approach.

Johnson treated any topic as though it must be defined for eternity. It was his habit to pass absolute judgments on questions that were largely relative.

Where taste enters in, it is worse. Strachey, commenting affectionately on the *Lives of the Poets,* says — in his own heightened way: " Johnson's æsthetic judgments are almost invariably subtle, or solid, or bold; they have always some good quality to recommend them — except one: they are never right." It takes a kind of magnificent ingenuity to be so neatly and plausibly and untiringly wrong. Few men are brilliant enough to be wrong in just that way. In no one else as in Johnson is the divorce so striking between the born man of letters and the critic and artist. He had learning, skill, wit, imagination, language, assurance, manner. But to comprehend an author was not easy for him. He cried down Gray; everyone knows his verdict on *Lycidas;* he thought *Tristram Shandy* already dead and buried; he disapproved of a tragic ending for *Lear.* " He was the last great English critic who treated poets, not as great men to be understood, but as schoolboys to be corrected." He is best in his generalizations. When he turned out to be right, as about Ossian, it was for the wrong reasons.

Much of his writing no longer detains us. His often brilliant *Lives of the Poets* are far better than anything else, as they are far better written, reasoned, and suited to Johnson's abilities. There are some extremely fine lines among the poems, and some letters. *Rasselas* is a bore, and one might do penance by reading the *Ramblers.* The style, at its best, has astounding force, and is less wearisome for antithesis than Hervey's or Bolingbroke's. The wit survives, occasionally in the writings, overwhelmingly in the talk. One would no more dispute the conversational powers of Johnson dead than one would have disputed them of Johnson living. When we have said all we can against his conversation, as that it is overbearing, irrelevant, even — in a way — fraudulent, we return to idolize it. No other recorded conversation even approaches it; no other Englishman so " raised a life of talk to the level of a life of action."

For his talk, as for almost everything else, Johnson's debt to Boswell is enormous; except for his satellite, he would today not be much more than a name [3] and we should marvel that he arose to dominate an age. Yet Boswell has preserved a worthy man. The bigotry, and the bullying, and the boorishness [4] often shake but never quite unseat us. The man's convictions are frequently frightful, and the amount of intellectual error and false morality he propagated are not easily condoned. But he *had* convictions, and they shaped themselves into principles, and by those principles, undeviatingly, he lived. It was a sublime triumph of character that such an animal confined his gluttony to food and repartee. He gave up drink by power of will, and abstained from lechery from principle; he was a good son, a good husband, a good friend; and he was a great friend in need. He was neither a prig nor a hypocrite nor a liar. He endured much and enjoyed hugely. Only the youngest of cynics will sneer at Johnson's virtues, for though they are commonplace, they are not common; and in literary men they are very uncommon indeed. His morality may have been absurd, but his ethics were admirable. He was not, in one sense, great, for he had no values to match his principles; but of him, certainly, one may use such old-fashioned words as *large* and *noble*. And at times one overtakes him in scenes as delightful as that where Boswell, hearing that an old woman in the Hebrides is afraid that he and Johnson want to bed her, suggests it is the Doctor who has alarmed her virtue.

" No, sir," said he. " She'll say, ' There came a wicked young fellow, a wild young dog, who I believe would have ravished

---

[3] This is often disputed, but to me it seems indisputable.

[4] Johnson could be brusque at his own expense no less than at that of others, as when he was told that a certain Mr Pot had called *Irene* " the finest tragedy of modern times." Johnson replied: " If Pot says so, Pot lies."

me had there not been with him a grave old gentleman who repressed him. But when he gets out of the sight of his tutor, I'll warrant you he'll spare no woman he meets, young or old.' "No," said I, "she'll say, 'There was a terrible ruffian who would have forced me had it not been for a gentle, mild-looking youth, who, I take it, is an angel.'"

Johnson and Boswell, in staging this scene, doubtless remembered Falstaff and Prince Hal; but it is almost as good as Falstaff and Prince Hal.

As to Johnson's relation to his age, it is enough to say that he lagged fifty years behind it. All around him new thoughts, new feelings, new impressions were springing to life. He did not feel them, hence he could not understand what they meant. No man had more stimulating — or, from his own point of view, more frightening — contemporaries: Hume, Voltaire, Tom Paine, Rousseau. No man ever viewed his contemporaries with greater complacency. He had a vast influence over the mass of readers, those who like himself were far behind their day. He kept the old ship afloat: the versification of Pope, the popularity of books of sermons, the Latin and the epitaphs and the pompous dedications. Withal, from his hatred of cant and love of the world, and from his ability to rise above the melancholy that beat against his heart, he had a zestful and bracing effect. No wonder we are told that his death "kept the public mind in agitation beyond all previous example." "He has made a chasm," Boswell quotes someone as saying, at the very end of the *Life*. That is a statement which, without having known Johnson in the flesh, anyone who has known him in the pages of his disciple must willingly believe.

Horace Walpole

THERE have been Horace Walpoles in every age; most of their names are now confined to footnotes. One of them, we shall be told, invented the velvet smoking-jacket or the Ascot tie; another took a fancy to an obscure pastry shop and turned it into one of the great restaurants of Europe; a third had the taste to rediscover a lapidary of the *cinque-cento;* a fourth collected snuffboxes; a fifth coined epigrams. We shall never know much else about such men: they were the fops, the worldlings, the dilettantes of their time and, being what they were, could not long outlast it.

But Horace Walpole is certain of his place in letters; it will not even do to condescend to him. We may dismiss the fopperies and the posturings, and claim to see through the finished worldling who, in the pursuit of pleasure, remained content with toys. We may turn from a study of his personality, crying it down as vain, feline, and self-centred; we may ask whether there was ever such a pastiche of the false and the fanciful as Strawberry Hill; we may reprobate the man who abused Mme du Deffand's devotion; we may even decide that, notwithstanding all he was and had, Walpole never really lived — never felt genuine emotions, never knew real pain or happiness. The tone of his life is all artifice, the plan all facile symmetry. He is as neatly framed and as carefully hung as a picture. Yet his personality had the good luck to be right for illustrating an age, and his gifts were such that they will lastingly commemorate it.

The perfect exemplar of the eighteenth-century idea is, no doubt, Lord Chesterfield; he is like a statue erected to the times. Chesterfield clearly represents — and wanted to represent — the aspirations of his age and class. But Chesterfield, at bottom, is not so much of the eighteenth century as he is of the aristocracy and the polite tradition: one can imagine him just as ably defending the forms of Charles II's reign or James I's. On the other hand Walpole, the Chinese-Chippendale aristocrat, the picturesque and whimsical trifler, was pure eighteenth-century; a man so much at home in his period that he could afford to take liberties with it. Had he been born a century earlier he would have found the times crude and they would have found him unmanly; had he been born a century later he would have found the times vulgar and they would have found him absurd. But in his own age of ritualized and domesticated culture, when all the right people talked one language and the wrong people only technically existed, a certain measure of elegant dissent was almost the proof of how indisputably one belonged; at any rate it was safe for a Horace Walpole to dissent — it was more than safe, it was fashionable. The point, in any case, about Walpole's baroque dreams and genteel nightmares is that they are the gestures, not of a rebellious man, but of a privileged one; in their shallowness they tell us how little, not how much, he was at variance with his times.

Walpole's personality is not, to be sure, the explanation of his survival; simply on that score he too would long ago have become only a footnote in the history-books. What Walpole further happens to be is the greatest social historian of his age and the most constantly diverting letter-writer in English literature. Besides Walpole's exhaustive chronicle, Swift in his *Journal to Stella,* Boswell in his *Life of Johnson,* Chesterfield in his *Letters to His Son,* Fanny Burney in her novels and *Diary,* Pope in his verses, perhaps even Hogarth in his painting, are only auxiliary historians of the social scene. Walpole has, besides the broadest scope and the longest span, a truly incomparable feeling for detail; and in the letters, where so much of the social history is recorded, he reveals an instinct for tone, a quality of style that may claim to designate the artist.

Walpole grew up at Eton and Cambridge as the son of the Prime Minister of Great Britain. He set forth on the grand tour certain of the entrée in the best Parisian and Florentine drawing-rooms; he returned to England assured of an income, a seat in Parliament, a place in society. He was launched into a world that his temperament craved at pre-

cisely the moment when that world was approaching full
flower. Patrician London, which at the beginning of the
century still showed barbarous traces, and which long before the end was to become Corinthian in its glitter, acquired, during the 1740s and '50s, a true tone. Into this setting the young Horace Walpole, whom politics would never
agitate, whom women would never arouse, on whom life
itself would never crudely impinge, exactly fitted. He was
to live narrowly, for his make-up was neither lusty nor can-
did, but in that narrow way — the way of the perfectly
placed and perfectly poised observer — he was to live abun-
dantly. As time passed, he would occupy himself more ec-
centrically, though always with an air: he would set up his
version of the Gothic in pastoral Twickenham, and print
books and write them; he would acquire a rather gamy taste
for ageing great ladies with their fund of ancient scandal;
he would make a conquest of a blind old woman, the most
brilliant and bored of her time, and be discreetly conquered
in turn by two young girls. It is a life deficient not only in
drama but also in serious interests. It is the life of a dilet-
tante, guided by that quality which characterizes the dilet-
tante: a curiosity about odd and exceptional and bravura
things. Walpole had, which is of the first importance in a
social historian, an intensely concrete mind: the philosophic
or long-range meaning of an event might elude or never occur to him; but the bagatelle, the eloquent detail, would
never elude, would always occur to him. Today the detail
Walpole clutched at sometimes reveals more than the towering event he misjudged.

In Walpole's career the man of fashion (who must have
appealed to his contemporaries as a man of wit) is quickly
indicated. " Comes the Duke of Richmond," writes Walpole
at forty-seven, " and hurries me down to Whitehall to dinner — then the Duchess of Grafton sends for me to loo in
Upper Grosvenor-street — before I can get thither, I am
begged to step to Kensington, to give Mrs Anne Pitt my

opinion about a bow-window — after the loo, I am to march back to Whitehall to supper — and after that, am to walk with Miss Pelham on the terrace till two in the morning, because it is moonlight and her chair is not come." Or there is Lady Caroline Petersham's celebrated party at Vauxhall, where the guests "minced seven chickens in a china dish, which Lady Caroline stewed over a lamp with three pats of butter and a flagon of water "; or a ridotto at Vauxhall, or the grand circuit of Ranelagh, or an account of Almack's, or a ball at Lord Stanley's, or whist with the "Archbishopess of Canterbury" and Mr Gibbon. So runs the record for upwards of fifty years. This part of Walpole's life, though admirably reproduced, has no character; he himself must have enjoyed it most for the sense of being in society, not to speak of the opportunity to write about it. Sooner or later the worldling turns away, and his most characteristic self comes out amid the curiosities of Strawberry Hill. He doted on his Gothic abortion, with its piecrust battlements, its manufactured gloom, and its complete misrepresentation of the past. The gingerbread castle became in turn an object of wonder for others, which princes and foreigners visited that they might say they had seen it. Walpole himself was careful not to take it too seriously: "I did not mean," he said, "to make my house so Gothic as to exclude conveniences and modern refinements in luxury." [5] It was all quaint and genteelly anachronistic, so as to be at the worst a *succès de fiasco*. And it did contribute something to the later revival of true Gothic; Walpole has his place in the history of architecture by reason of a travesty upon it. *The Castle of Otranto*, his Gothic romance, has more merit because, though its horrors are stale and mechanical, it is written in eighteenth-century, not thirteenth-century, prose. *Otranto* likewise has a certain importance, for from it proceeds the whole stream

---

[5] Whether it was roomy enough is another matter. When old Lady Townshend saw it, she cried out: "Lord God! Jesus! What a house! It is just such a house as a parson's where the children lie at the foot of the bed."

[317

of mediævalism which culminates in Scott. Walpole's own mediævalism, though shallow in feeling, was genuine in impulse: it drained off the romantic and highfalutin elements in a cool and cynical nature, it satisfied the demands of a not quite morbid but never quite healthy imagination. Actually, of course, Walpole knew very little about the past; we need only recall how easily he was fooled by Chatterton.

But if he had no educated sensibilities for the pageant of other days, the pageant of his own released the artist in him. On the lowest level, he breathes life into the social and political routine of his time, catching the voices and gestures of its personages, from the fools to the most finished actors among them. He has his own cynical sarcasm and wit: "Well!" he writes at the outbreak of the American Revolution, "we had better have gone on robbing the Indies; it was a more lucrative trade." And the next year: "The army, that was to overrun the Atlantic continent, is not half set out yet; but it will be time enough to go into winter quarters." But it is wrong to suppose that it is only at chatter and persiflage that Walpole excels; there is solid fare, too, relating to big events; and when the occasion arrives, there are the great descriptive pieces, such as the funeral of George II and the trial and beheading of the Jacobite lords. These, it should be said, are anything but florid: in them Walpole's passion for the eloquent detail provides insight into character, and stunning dramatic effects:

When they [the Jacobite lords] were brought from the Tower in separate coaches, there was some dispute in which the axe must go — old Balmerino cried, "Come, come, put it with me." At the bar, he plays with his fingers upon the axe, while he talks to the gentleman-gaoler; and one day somebody coming up to listen, he took the blade and held it like a fan between their faces.

Or again, in describing Balmerino's beheading:

Then came old Balmerino, treading with the air of a general. As soon as he mounted the scaffold, he read the inscription on his coffin, as he did again afterwards: he then surveyed the spectators . . . and pulling out his spectacles, read a treasonable speech. . . . He said, if he had not taken the sacrament the day before, he would have knocked down Williamson, the lieutenant of the Tower, for his ill usage of him. . . . Then he lay down; but being told he was on the wrong side, vaulted round, and immediately gave the sign by tossing up his arm, as if he were giving the signal for battle.

Despite a lifetime spent in artistic pursuits, as a critic Walpole nowhere had first-rate taste. His romantic sense, for all it fed on Gothic or Ossian, stopped at the lurid or the grandiose; his classical sense, satisfied by a Gray or Pope, responded to neatness rather than order. He found the greatest Italian art in the productions of Guido Reni and Salvator Rosa; Michelangelo was "much too fond of muscles." Hogarth had "slender merit." Chaucer was best in the modern version of Dryden. *Tristram Shandy* represented "the dregs of nonsense." Obviously, Walpole could not abide Dr Johnson; less obviously, he thought ill of Boswell's life of him.[6] It is plain that the sniffing aristocrat, for all his efforts to seem singular, never got above his age.

The man himself has been much despised and perhaps a little unfairly maligned. Macaulay, who crystallized opinion about Walpole as about so many others, hit on many of his weaknesses, but could never have had a proper sympathy with his temperament. Yet Macaulay can scarcely be blamed for exposing the fop, the trifler, the poseur, the skin-deep liberal, the lip-service Whig; Macaulay is not even extreme in saying that all big things seemed little to Walpole, and all little things big. The truth is that because the times fitted him and lent a sheltering dignity to his frivolities, they pro-

---

[6] And Boswell's *Tour of the Hebrides* he called "absurd . . . the story of a mountebank and his zany."

foundly marred him. His vain, velvety, catlike nature basked in the sunlight of an age when aristocrats dared not work hard at serious things, when gentlemen scorned being thought of as writers, when warmth was no necessary part of friendship, and virtue was a word in the mouth of those who discredited it. "Virtue knows to a farthing what it has lost by not having been vice," wrote Walpole with prevailing cynicism. It would be foolish to look for exalted emotions in such a man. It is not that he was evil or insensitive; it is rather that he had been schooled to selfishness and harried into a fear of ridicule. To seem ridiculous was the worst of fates: the horror of it underlies his snide and despotic relations with Mme du Deffand. She, old and bored and desperately searching for someone to love and believe in, pinned all her devotion, with embarrassing intensity, on Walpole. He liked and admired her; but, knowing that their letters might be opened by the French postal authorities, he was haunted by the thought that the passionate avowals of a blind old lady might make a fool of him. Accordingly, he decreed that she might write to him only in a moderate tone about impersonal things. She, who had no choice but to accept his terms and constantly violate them, must have found them the supreme humiliation of her life. Often, with the anger of the wretched, she upbraids and lashes out at him. He — for his part often sorely tried — remains glacially unyielding.

When the French Revolution came, the man who so long had styled himself a republican saluted Burke's *Reflexions* as "sublime" and "profound." Things were breaking up, Walpole himself was old, and there was little left but to go on writing letters in that wonderful eighteenth-century style, on to the end, to the muted valedictory: "I shall be quite content with a sprig of rosemary thrown after me, when the parson of the parish commits my dust to dust." This is no human voice speaking; it is merely the voice, subdued, evocative, attenuated, of an age and a tradition.

READING LIST

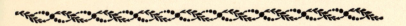

[*popular-priced editions*]

Everyman's Library.	[*E. P. Dutton & Company*]
Modern Library.	[*Modern Library*]
Modern Student's Library.	[*Charles Scribner's Sons*]
World's Classics.	[*Oxford University Press*]

ADDISON, JOSEPH, AND STEELE, RICHARD:
Selections. Modern Student's Library.
The Spectator. Everyman's (4 vols.).

BOSWELL, JAMES:
Life of Samuel Johnson. Everyman's (2 vols.). Modern Library Giants. Modern Student's Library.

BURNEY, FANNY:
Diary. Everyman's.

CHESTERFIELD, LORD:
Letters to His Son. Everyman's. World's Classics.

COWPER, WILLIAM:
Selected Letters. Everyman's. World's Classics.
Poems. Everyman's.

DEFOE, DANIEL:
Captain Singleton. Everyman's. World's Classics.
Journals of the Plague Year. Everyman's.
Moll Flanders. Everyman's. Modern Library.
Robinson Crusoe. Everyman's. World's Classics.

FIELDING, HENRY:
Amelia. Everyman's (2 vols.).
Joseph Andrews. Everyman's. Modern Library. Modern Student's Library.

[321

Tom Jones. Everyman's (2 vols.). Modern Library.
Jonathan Wild and *A Voyage to Lisbon.* Everyman's.

GAY, JOHN:
Poetical Works (including *The Beggar's Opera*). Oxford
University Press.

GIBBON, EDWARD:
Autobiography. Everyman's.
The Decline and Fall of the Roman Empire. Everyman's
(6 vols.). Modern Library Giants (2 vols.).

GOLDSMITH, OLIVER:
Poems and Plays. Everyman's.
The Vicar of Wakefield. Everyman's.

GRAY, THOMAS:
Poems and Letters. Everyman's.

JOHNSON, SAMUEL:
Lives of the Poets. Everyman's (2 vols.). World's Classics
(2 vols.).
Selected Letters. World's Classics.

MONTAGU, LADY MARY WORTLEY:
Letters. Everyman's.

POPE, ALEXANDER:
Poems, Epistles, and Satires. Everyman's.

PRIOR, MATTHEW:
Poems on Several Occasions. Cambridge English Classics
(New York: The Macmillan Company).

RICHARDSON, SAMUEL:
Clarissa Harlowe. Everyman's (4 vols.).
Pamela. Everyman's (2 vols.).

SHERIDAN, RICHARD BRINSLEY:
Plays. Everyman's. World's Classics.

SMOLLETT, TOBIAS:
Humphrey Clinker. World's Classics.
Peregrine Pickle. Everyman's.
Roderick Random. Everyman's. World's Classics.

STERNE, LAURENCE:
A Sentimental Journey. Everyman's.
Tristram Shandy. Everyman's.

SWIFT, JONATHAN:
  Gulliver's Travels. Everyman's. World's Classics.
  Gulliver's Travels, A Tale of a Tub, and *The Battle of the Books*. Modern Library.
  Journal to Stella. Everyman's.
  Selections. Modern Student's Library.
  A Tale of a Tub, The Battle of the Books, etc. Everyman's.

WALPOLE, HORACE:
  Selected Letters. Everyman's.

INDEX

[*Birth and death dates of important figures will be found after their names.*]

[i

[v

PRINTER'S NOTE

The text of this book is set in Caledonia, a Linotype face designed by W. A. Dwiggins. Caledonia belongs to the family of printing types called " modern face " by printers — a term used to mark the change in style of type-letters that occurred about 1800. Caledonia is in the general neighborhood of Scotch Modern in design, but is more freely drawn than that letter.

    The book was composed, printed, and bound by The Plimpton Press, Norwood, Massachusetts.

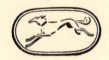